Response to Disaster

Fact Versus Fiction and Its Perpetuation

The Sociology of Disaster

Third Edition

Henry W. Fischer, III

University Press of America,® Inc.
Lanham · Boulder · New York · Toronto · Plymouth, UK

Library of Congress Control Number: 2008930725
ISBN-13: 978-0-7618-4117-3 (paperback : alk. paper)
ISBN-10: 0-7618-4117-2 (paperback : alk. paper)
eISBN-13: 978-0-7618-4227-9
eISBN-10: 0-7618-4227-6

THIS BOOK IS DEDICATED
TO ALL OF THOSE WHO ARE THE REASONS WHY

Donna M. Fischer,
Betsy A. Fischer & Jennifer L. Fischer;
E.L. Quarantelli, Russell R. Dynes, Dennis E. Wenger; &
All My Students: Past, Present, Future

Contents

Foreword

One of the major conclusions reached by the earliest social science disaster researchers in the United States in the 1950s, was that human beings at the height of disasters did not behave in commonly expected ways. That is, they generally did not flee in panic, engage in looting behavior, and were not shocked into passive psychological resignation in the face of the extreme stress of a disaster. This absence of widespread irrational, antisocial and dysfunctional behavior came to be known as the *disaster mythology* or the disaster myths believed by citizens generally as well as emergency management and community officials.

For nearly four decades now, this basic notion about disaster behavior has been passed down somewhat uncritically in the literature. The early researchers of course had arrived at their basic conclusion on the basis of their observations and field studies. However, for the most part, the early research was somewhat unsystematic and uneven in its coverage of most topics or questions. Thus, the continuing belief among disaster researchers about disaster myths rests on an empirical base that is not as strong as would be desirable.

Professor Fischer has made the study of the disaster mythology one of his major research interests. He has tried, especially in chapter two of this volume, to further systematically and empirically document the existence of the mythology.

Probably even more important, Professor Fischer has also attempted to document the sources and consequences of the disaster myths. While earlier researchers had mostly implied without any study of the hypothesis, that the mass media were a major source for the mythology, he has attacked the problem directly. His third chapter is a report of an empirical examination of the links between media portrayal of disaster myths and the existence of the mythology. In chapter four, he looks at some of the consequences from the preoccupation with the media on the part of local emergency managers.

Overall what we have in this volume is work by a third generation disaster researcher in the United States building upon and enlarging the studies of first and second generation researchers in the area. Scientific fields can only advance through such systematic accumulations of knowledge. As such, the studies of Professor Fischer are examples of the kinds of semi-replicative and cumulative studies that should be more widely undertaken.

                              E. L. Quarantelli
                              Disaster Research Center
                              University of Delaware

Preface

In recent years disasters have struck with increasing regularity and ferocity. The Federal Emergency Management Agency (FEMA), as well as state and local emergency organizations, has been heavily criticized for what has been portrayed as their inadequate response to disaster events. If each of us were to gain a better understanding of the behavioral and organizational problems commonly encountered during a disaster, we may facilitate more effective mitigation, planning, and disaster response activity in our own communities and in the nation. Perhaps our expectations are inappropriate, perhaps our perceptions are inaccurate.

The work you are about to read was written with three audiences in mind: (1) undergraduate and graduate students with an interest in the problems our society encounters when a disaster strikes, (2) my colleagues in the disaster research community, and (3) those who are charged with the responsibility of responding to disaster, i.e., local, state, and national emergency response personnel. Of course, potential victims (includes every citizen) would benefit from a better understanding of the problems encountered in responding to and planning for a disaster. And, media personnel and decision makers at all levels of government would serve their publics better if they had an accurate understanding of disaster response problems.

The research findings and generalizations shared in this text are primarily applicable to the United States and Canada. Most of the observations and conclusions probably hold for most of the rest of the world as well, especially the developed countries. We still do not have solid data for developing countries, however.

The research reported herein is an attempt to further develop both the disaster response research literature and to share what was learned with the appropriate publics. It is hoped that the writing style will facilitate both.

Acknowledgments

Any author owes a debt of gratitude to more individuals and institutions than the writer normally can recall or acknowledge. Hence, to those I overlook, I want to thank you first and apologize. I must thank Millersville University of Pennsylvania, the institution I currently work for, as without their support, this work would not have been possible. I want to thank my colleagues for their support of my activities.

My graduate school experience included working at the Disaster Research Center, the University of Delaware, where my interest in disaster research was born. Thanks to E.L. Quarantelli, Russell R. Dynes, and Dennis E. Wenger, I have been guided, directed, and nurtured in my quest to contribute to the field.

I am also grateful for the support of several other disaster research colleagues: Denis Mileti, Thomas E. Drabek, Joseph Scanlon, Joanne Nigg, Kathleen Tierney, David Neal and Brenda Phillips, Bob Stallings, Ron Perry and Lori Peek. A special thank you is necessary to all those emergency response personnel and media personnel who responded to my questionnaires, agreed to interviews and allowed me to observe their work. A special thank you goes to the Natural Hazards Research and Applications Information Center of the University of Colorado for three quick-response grants which supported research reflected herein. I also appreciate the support I received from the Millersville University Professional Development and Faculty Grants Committees who awarded several grants for work reflected in this volume. I wish to thank Research Planning, Inc., Falls Church, Virginia (especially Corey Gruber and Kyle Olsen) for their involving me in the Domestic Terrorism Program pursuant to their contract with the U.S. Department of Defense. And, I want to thank the National Science Foundation (NSF) for their grant support that funded work on mass fatalities management after both the South Asian Tsunami and Hurricane Katrina.

I special thank you is necessary for my daughter, Jennifer, who helped her father with the photo editing and general software challenges encountered regularly by this author. And, I warm thank you to both the Sociology/Anthropology Department secretary, Barb Dills, and to the CDRE secretary, Jill Stahl, for their continued assistance and never ending patience.

I thank the editors of the *International Journal of Mass Emergencies and Disasters*, the *International Journal of Disaster Management* and the *Interna-*

tional Journal of Disaster Prevention and Management for their allowing me to include work in this volume which was reflected in articles I wrote for their publications. Thank you to the University Press of America for publishing the 1st, 2nd, and now the 3rd edition of this book.

I offer a warm thank you in appreciation to my family: my wife Donna and my daughters Betsy and Jennifer who were supportive of my efforts even when it cost them my physical and mental presence, my parents Mary and Henry Fischer who socialized me to pursue and enjoy learning, as well as my parents-in-law Betty and Donald McCabe who have always nurtured my quest.

Chapter 1

What is a Disaster?

INTRODUCTION

Late one afternoon in early September 2006 a *Today Show* staffer called me in my office for background on the emerging disaster in New Orleans following Hurricane Katrina. We discussed the situation at the Superdome and the Convention Center. I advised against framing the story around the alleged murder, looting, and panic suggesting that it is too early to know what is factual and such behaviors are often reported, but frequently turn out to be false. Despite this advice, Matt Lauer led the show the next morning with "despite all the problems the victims of Katrina have already suffered they are being preyed upon by looters and worse . . . don't people have any morals" (paraphrased)? While the aftermath of Katrina did include some looting, the ensuing days confirmed that much of the reported behavioral misdeeds never occurred. I telephoned the *Today Show* staffer and suggested they do a follow-up piece correcting the earlier broadcast's impression of mass deviance. I was thanked, but my advice was once again ignored. Why was I ignored on both occasions? What do we believe as a society about disaster response and why do we believe it? Why do we perpetually fail to adequately prepare? Why do emergency organizations appear to not rise to the occasion? What role does the mass media play in the entire process? Why do we never seem to really master the "lessons learned" that are published after every major disaster since the 1906 San Francisco earthquake?

The average American believes that panic, disaster shock and looting are part of the normal behavioral response to disasters. They expect the Governor to call out the National Guard to prevent looting. They expect would-be victims to flee in panic during an evacuation. Emergency management personnel around the country plan on these things happening. Their written disaster plans indicate what they will do to avert panic, shock and looting.

The above would appear prudent and reasonable, but is it? How do we know? We know citizens support the spending of millions of dollars each year to prepare for disasters. Emergency management personnel spend their working lives planning to respond to major emergencies and disasters. Reporters converge to disaster sites to report on what they believe is occurring. Are their perceptions of reality correct? Do victims and emergency organizations really respond the way we all think they do? What is reality? Does common sense govern our sense of reality? What does research into the behavioral and organizational response to disaster tell us? Does it support our beliefs? Is what we read in the newspapers and news magazines accurate? Is what we view on television news representative of reality? To what extent does this reality vary by the magnitude of the disaster?

On the other hand, do communities often prepare for imaginary problems and ignore those that are likely to occur? Do the media help to perpetuate this problem through their own misunderstanding of how people and organizations respond before, during and after a disaster? Perhaps the misconceptions and ill-preparation begin with the confusion over what differentiates an every day emergency from a major emergency or a disaster.

What constitutes a disaster? Most Americans believe they know. All segments of society, however, have continued difficulty clearly differentiating a disaster from a major emergency. Many in the lay public, political leaders, reporters, and even emergency personnel are often confused. Two studies (Fischer, 1989; Fischer and Trowbridge, 1992; Fischer, et al, 2006) found local emergency management agency (LEMA) directors listing both emergencies of various degrees of severity, along with FEMA declared disasters as examples of *disasters* they had responded to during their tenure as LEMA directors. There is an important difference between emergencies and disasters. The public and emergency management personnel often believe that the problems they are likely to encounter after a disaster will be very similar to those which occur in an emergency (Fischer, et al, 2006). They may, in fact, be adequately prepared to deal with an emergency, but be greatly mistaken if they believe the demands placed upon them during a disaster will be little more than an extension of that required during an emergency. The result is likely to be not only overwhelming but catastrophic.

DEFINITION

Researchers continue to seek clarity in just what constitutes a disaster (for example see Perry & Quarantelli, 2005). Differentiating between everyday emergencies, major emergencies, "regular" disasters, and catastrophic disasters is extremely important (Fischer, et al, 2006) and elusive (Perry & Quarantelli, 2005). Charles Fritz, a pioneer of disaster research, defined disasters (1961:655) as:

> actual or threatened accidental or uncontrollable events that are concentrated in time and space, in which a *society*, or a relatively *self-sufficient subdivision* of a society undergoes severe danger, and incurs such losses to its members and physical appurtenances that the *social structure is disrupted and the fulfillment of all*

or some of the essential functions of the society, or its subdivision, is prevented [emphasis added].

The above definition is consistent with current national policy which is supportive of the local community organization taking the primary responsibility for developing a comprehensive, multi-hazard approach to emergency management, i.e., a coordinated response at the local level in conjunction with state and federal authorities (Drabek, 1986:7; McLoughlin, 1985; Perry, 1982).

Fritz's definition suggests that the normal daily routines must be severely disrupted for a large segment of the community before an incident can be considered a disaster. For major segments of the community, going to work would seem impossible or, at least, very inappropriate. Shopping trips for birthday gifts and cooking dinner for the neighborhood picnic are unthinkable. Search and rescue efforts become the primary concern. Clearing the debris, restoring essential services, and so forth, become the normative focus, rather than the everyday "normal time" concerns. In other words, it is not the physical damage or personal injuries that are operative in defining an event as a disaster (in fact, the event may be free of injuries and physical destruction), it is the disruption of adherence to daily behavioral norms that renders the event a disaster.

Even when an event is clearly a disaster and normal time activity is severely disrupted on a large scale, one must ponder the degree to which the response patterns may vary by the disaster's size and scope. For example, the tornado that impacted the Silver Spur Mobile Home Park in April 1991 (Fischer, Schaeffer, and Trowbridge, 1992) devastated the homes of some 1,000 individuals. This event was devastating for Andover since a fifth of the community had experienced a disastrous impact which severely disrupted normal time activity. However, this event cannot compare to the experience of Homestead, Florida, in August 1992, when Hurricane Andrew devastated an area of approximately 100 square miles. And, Hurricane Katrina's 2005 Gulf Coast (USA) impact dwarfs both the Andover and Andrew events. The needs of the community vary by the scale and scope or magnitude of the disruption. The challenges vary and, therefore, the necessary resources, planning and mitigation activities must be adjusted accordingly. A disaster scale (for example see Fischer, 2003) needs to be used to assess the efficacy of the research literature in order to determine the circumstances under which the research findings vary with disaster magnitude. We may find looting is a rare occurrence unless a catastrophic disaster impacts a population that experiences normal time deprivation. More research is needed to continue to assess the extent to which the variation in size and scope of a disaster results in varied needs, responses, and planning—the Katrina experience reinforces this argument.

A DISASTER SCALE

If we consider the events faced by both the victims and responders to Hurricane Katrina, we find at least one very clear message. That message, in conjunction with the on-going discussion in the research literature (Perry & Quarantelli, 2005) on what constitutes a disaster, is that it is time to consider the extent to which everything we think we know about the behavioral and organizational response to disaster may vary by the severity, i.e., scale and scope, of the disaster as it disrupts the everyday normal time activities of human beings (Fritz, 1961). In the current discussion, the argument is advanced that the knowledge base in the researcher literature should be examined and compared to a disaster scale going forward. A testing of the research literature findings should then be initiated pursuant to assessing the extent to which previous findings articulated in the second assessment (Mileti, 1999), for example, may vary according to the scale and scope of a disaster. It is argued, therefore, that the research community needs a viable disaster scale in order to initiate the aforementioned. While the disaster scale previously advanced (Fischer, 2003) may or may not be the final version adopted, it serves as a model or illustration to help develop the argument and its potential synthesis.

Such a scale, when cross-referenced with the research findings of the past 50 or more years, will serve to instruct researchers and practitioners as to when, for example, looting is more, versus, less likely to occur. Such applied outcomes will assist in better preparing to mitigate challenges most likely to occur depending upon the level of disaster encountered.

Disruption and Social Structure Adjustment

The proposed disaster scale is based upon the degree of social disruption resulting from a possible or actual precipitating event. The greater the degree of disruption (in terms of scale, scope and time), the more the social structure is impacted (i.e., the greater the extent of temporary or permanent social change in response to the perceived needs by a critical mass). For example, after impact, going to work, holding a birthday party, going for a hike in the park—all of these would be viewed as undoable for those within or near the disrupted area. By definition, these routine activities would be viewed as unacceptable, perhaps immoral. Other norms and roles would emerge, replacing the routine with the "more appropriate" behavior, e.g., search and rescue, feeding survivors.

A disaster scale, therefore, should assess the degree or extent to which this everyday social activity is disrupted resulting in temporary or permanent changes in the social structure within a community, primarily, as well as for the larger society, by extension. As has been articulated with great clarity by others (Quarantelli, 1998), it would not be appropriate to measure disaster disruption in terms of death, injury, and damage—that would be neither sociological, nor would it provide a consistent standard (numbers of dead and injured do not function as a reliable indicator of social structure disruption). The proposed scale will link the scale and scope of disruption (tied to an actual or potential precipitating event or disaster agent) within a community(s), and by extension a society, with the scale and scope of social structure adjustment within a community(s) and society. Figure 1.1 provides a linear view of the process, but not the scope and scale.

FIGURE 1.1   LINEAR VIEW OF DISRUPTION AND ADJUSTMENT

Social Structure: The Status-quo*	Precipitating Event: The Big Bang**	Disruption: The Big Mess**	Adjusted Social Structure: Collective Response*

*Focus of the Sociology of Disaster **The Actual Disaster Event

Scale, Scope and Time

Three issues impact on the extent of social structure disruption. These three issues are scale, scope, and time or duration. The first two actually impact on the third within the community and, by extension, the society.

Scale

How severe is the destruction and distress? Are most community homes missing a few roofing tiles or are most community homes no longer in existence? The greater the scale of destruction, or actually disruption, the greater the collective distress is likely to be and the greater the collective response (temporary or permanent social change). A disaster scale must take into account these differences.

Scope

How widespread is the disruption within the community? Is a significant portion of the community experiencing disruption to the extent that adherence to routine social structure is impossible for those individuals? Are most community members still able to continue their routine without perceiving or being perceived as acting immorally for doing so? Is the disruption so widespread that the entire community has replaced the routine with the moral imperative? Are numerous communities so affected? A disaster scale must take into account these differences.

Time or Duration

The greater the scope and scale of disruption, the more likely the time for recovery will be extended. Both community and societal social structures are likely to continue in a state of disruption as scope and scale increase. A disaster scale must take into account this issue.

Figure 1.2 provides a two-dimensional view of the intersection of disruption and adjustment with scale, scope, and duration.

FIGURE 1.2   TWO-DIMENSIONAL GENERIC CONSTRUCT***

	DISRUPTION*	ADJUSTMENT**
SCALE	Degree of Disruption	Degree of Adjustment
SCOPE	How Widespread Is Disruption	How Widespread the Adjustment Is
TIME	Duration of Disruption	Duration of the Adjustment

*Precipitated by the Disaster Agent   **Focus of the Sociology of Disaster
***Actual or Potential Disruption & Adjustment

Emergencies, Disasters, Catastrophe and Annihilation

Emergencies

Historically, disaster sociologists have identified two types of emergencies—neither of which were considered disasters (for example, see Fischer 1998). Everyday emergencies have been those which local authorities, e.g., a police or fire department, are trained to confront on a regular basis. Examples would include a building fire and an "everyday" traffic accident. Severe emergencies, on the other hand, would be those requiring response by several fire houses or companies. It has, perhaps, been a mistake to artificially draw a line between emergencies and disasters. Both experience disruption, it is the degree of disruption that varies. And, both experience social structure adjustment, again it is the degree that varies in terms of scale, scope and time.

Disasters

Historically, disasters have been viewed as conceptually different from emergencies. While it is true that disastrous precipitating events result (with the Fritz definition in mind) in disruption beyond the everyday and may overwhelm local authorities, it is, however, scale, scope and time that are the key issues. Both disasters and emergencies experience disruption and adjustment. It is the degree of disruption and adjustment that varies.

Catastrophe and Annihilation

Historically, it is difficult to discern what constitutes a disaster from a catastrophe. It seems a catastrophe is an extreme disaster. What is constant is that there is disruption and adjustment; again, what varies is the scale, scope and recovery time. Annihilation occurs when a society is so severely and completely disrupted that it cannot continue to exist as a separate societal entity. It ceases to exist.

It would be prudent, and logically consistent, to view emergencies, disasters, catastrophe and annihilation as all variations (in terms of scale, scope and duration) along a continuum. This is the approach the proposed disaster scale employs.

Disaster Scale Categories

Why might this be a useful tool? Disaster researchers and practitioners would both benefit from the availability of a uniformly accepted disaster scale. Such a scale should enable researchers to differentiate between degrees of disasters. A disaster scale would be a tool which would aid researchers in delineating the applicability and limitations of their findings. The findings amassed in the disaster research literature may apply to any disaster regardless of its severity. On the other hand, it very well may be that some findings may vary by disaster severity. It would also serve as a generator of research questions, as not all responses are equal. Practitioners would also benefit from such a tool. It could assist them in alerting their communities to the likelihood of an oncoming category 3 (less severe), category 5 or category 8 (very severe) disaster—thereby assisting in communicating appropriate preparatory and response actions. Such a tool would also assist government decision makers in their mitigation, preparation, and response efforts in much the same way the Richter scale provides a construct for envisioning the severity of an earthquake's impact. Working with the generic construct, a ten category disaster scale is proposed. It is based upon the degree of disruption and adjustment a community(s)/society experiences when we consider scale, scope and duration or time. A detailed description of each disaster category is provided below along with a summarized version in Figure 1.3.

FIGURE 1.3:	SCALE CATEGORIES—Focus on Disruption & Adjustment
Disaster Category 1 (DC1)	Everyday Emergencies (EE)
Disaster Category 2 (DC2)	Severe Emergencies (SE)
Disaster Category 3 (DC3)	Partial Small Town (PST)
Disaster Category 4 (DC4)	Massive Small Town (MST)
Disaster Category 5 (DC5)	Partial Small City (PSC)
Disaster Category 6 (DC6)	Massive Small City (MSC)
Disaster Category 7 (DC7)	Partial Large City (PLC)
Disaster Category 8 (DC8)	Massive Large City (MLC)
Disaster Category 9 (DC9)	Catastrophe—Many Populated Areas (C)
Disaster Category 10 (DC10)	Annihilation—Entire Society (A)

Disaster Category 1: Everyday Emergency (EE)

The everyday emergency or the first disaster category (DC1) includes those events the first responders, e.g., police and fire, encounter on virtually a daily basis. Their training enables them to usually respond by applying the norms and roles that enables them to address the temporary situation. For example, a burning house results in the fire department extinguishing the fire and the local police directing traffic as well as assisting with any necessary evacuation. The precipitating event is defined by victims and responders as large in terms of scale for those impacted, but small in scope (in this case, one house is directly affected while perhaps several more are potentially threatened). Normal time activities are severely disrupted for those living in the house and will remain disrupted for some duration of time. After the fire is extinguished, the responders return to their normal routine as does the rest of the affected neighborhood. The key issue for disaster category 1 is: while scale may be large (or even small in other examples) and while duration may be lengthy for those impacted, scope is extremely limited. Both the disruption and the social-structural adjustment is very limited in the impact to the community (unit of analysis) and, by extension, the society. DC-1 is reserved for those everyday emergencies that occur in any community whether it is a township, borough, small city, medium or large metropolitan area. The focus is on the limited adjustment occurring with respect to social change. A large city or a small town experiencing the same kind of limited scope (and potentially scale and time as well) is able to respond to an everyday emergency that, by definition, impacts on only a narrow part of the population necessitating a limited community adjustment. Alternately, a large city may experience a minor disruption (loss of an average of three roof shingles) for many people (200 homes for example). In this instance the scope would be broader, yet both scale and duration would be very limited—resulting in very limited adjustment. The homeowner's insurance companies would be the primary responders.

DC1 is applied when social structure adjustments are necessitated in response to an actual or potential disruption that is either minor in scale, scope, and duration; or major in scale and duration, but minor in scope; or larger in scope for part of the larger community (partial), but minor in scale and duration.

Disaster Category 2: Severe Emergency (SE)

The second disaster category (DC2) is operable when responders and victims are confronted with actual or potential disruption, and the resulting adjustment, that is more extensive than "everyday" emergencies. For example, an actual or forecast major snowstorm may result in widespread (scope: "massive") disruption of normal activity and adjustments such as school closings, alternative child care arrangement implementation, and perhaps even the use of the National Guard for transporting medical emergency personnel. The scale (destruction and/or distress) would be minor and the adjustment time period would usually be rather short in duration (the snow melts or is at least moved to facilitate the return to normal activity). Alternately, a fire that consumes a neighborhood or a factory would be major in terms of scale and time of disruption and adjustment, but would partially affect the community (limited scope).

DC2 is applied when social structure adjustments are necessitated in response to an actual or potential disruption that is either major or massive in scope, but minor in scale and duration or is localized in scope, but massive in scale and duration.

Disaster Category 3: Partial Disruption & Adjustment in a Town, Township or Rural Area (PST)

The third disaster category (DC3) is reserved for small populated areas (town, township, rural area) that experience actual or potential disruptions and their necessitated adjustments which go beyond everyday or even severe emergencies in that the community is so impacted that continued adherence to the normal routine is inconceivable on the part of a significant portion of the community's members (experience the adjustment)—not only victims and official responders. Both the destruction and/or distress (scale) are severe enough that the resulting adjustment is severe enough to interfere with the normal routine for a significant portion (partial) of the community. An example would be the crash of an airplane in or very near a small town. A significant portion of the community may not only be totally or partially destroyed, but the distress experienced throughout the town would result in the total disruption of the normal routine for a large portion of the community population.

DC3 is applied when the social structure adjustments are necessitated in response to an actual or potential disruption that is major or massive in scale and duration for a significant portion of a community that is a town, township or populated rural area.

Disaster Category 4: Massive Disruption & Adjustment in a Town, Township or Rural Area (MST)

The fourth disaster category (DC4) is designated for small populated areas (town, township, rural area) that experience actual or potential disruptions and their necessitated adjustments beyond the everyday or even severe emergencies in that the community is so impacted that continued adherence to the normal routine is inconceivable on the part of virtually the entire community's members (all experience the adjustment). An example of this category would be a brush or forest fire that threatens to, or actually does, destroy virtually the entire community. Evacuations, fire fighting, and so forth involve everyone in some level of adjustment. Scale, duration, and scope all combine on a major level to massively impact a town, township or populated rural area.

DC4 is applied when the social structure adjustments are necessitated in response to an actual or potential disruption that is major or massive in scale and duration for virtually the entire community that is a town, township or populated rural area.

Why the differentiation between partial and massive? To be more than an emergency, the disruption must be significant enough to render the continuation of normal time activities moot. Most garden variety disasters impact part of the community significantly enough to disrupt normal time activities for a significant portion of the community. However, if the disruption resulting from threatened or actual disaster impact is massive, the normal time activity disruption would be more significant, the necessitated response more all-encompassing and, by definition, a larger event in sociological terms.

Disaster Category 5: Partial Disruption & Adjustment in a Small or Medium City (PSC)

The fifth disaster category (DC5) signifies actual or potential disruption and the resulting adjustment to a small or medium city. In this event, continued adherence to the normal routine is inconceivable on the part of a significant portion of the community's members. Both the destruction and/or distress are severe enough that the resulting adjustment is severe enough to interfere with the normal routine for a significant portion of the community. An example would be an airline crash in a small or medium sized city. A significant portion of the community may be severely damaged or destroyed. Most importantly, the distress would be experienced so broadly in the community that a significant portion would be unable to continue the normal routine. They would instead engage in search and rescue activities, and so forth.

DC5 is applied when the social structure adjustments are necessitated in response to an actual or potential disruption that is major or massive in scale and duration for a significant portion of a community that is a small or medium city.

Disaster Category 6: Massive Disruption & Adjustment in a Small or Medium City (MSC)

The sixth disaster category (DC6) is designed for populated areas that comprise a small or medium sized city. The actual or potential disruptions and necessitated adjustments render normal routines impossible for virtually the entire community. An example would be conflagration that consumes most of the city, an earthquake that severely impacts most of the city, as well as a biological terrorism event that impacts and threatens the entire city.

DC6 is applied when the social structure adjustments are necessitated in response to an actual or potential disruption that is major or massive in scale and duration for virtually the entire community the size of a small or medium city.

Why the differentiation between population size? The larger the affected population, the greater the disruption, adjustment, and response will be. Sociologically speaking, the disaster is of greater magnitude or scale.

Disaster Category 7: Partial Disruption & Adjustment in a Large City (PLC)

The seventh disaster category (DC7) signifies actual or potential disruption and the resulting adjustment to a large city. In a DC-7 event, continued adherence to the normal routine is inconceivable on the part of a significant portion of the community's members. Both the destruction and/or distress are severe enough that the resulting adjustment is experienced by a significant portion of the city. An example would be the airline crash that occurred in New York City in late September 2001. A major portion of a NYC borough was severely damaged and/or destroyed. A significant portion of the community was not capable of continuing in their normal routine.

DC7 is applied when the social structure adjustments are necessitated in response to an actual or potential disruption that is major or massive in scale and duration for a significant portion of a community that is a large city.

Disaster Category 8: Massive Disruption & Adjustment in a Large City (MLC)

Disaster category eight (DC8) signifies actual or potential disruption and the resulting adjustment to a large city. In a DC8 event, the disruption and adjustments are experienced by virtually the entire community. An example would be a severe earthquake in San Francisco resulting in such disruption that the adjustments would be implemented by virtually everyone in the city.

DC8 is applied when the social structure adjustments are necessitated in response to an actual or potential disruption that is major or massive in scale and duration for virtually the entire community the size of a large city.

Disaster Category 9: Catastrophic and/or Simultaneous Massive Disruption & Adjustment in Several Communities (C)

The ninth disaster category (DC9) signifies actual or potential disruption and the resulting adjustment in more than one community essentially simultaneously. This circumstance may be referred to as a catastrophe. The scale and duration as well as the scope are such that adherence to the normal routine is not possible throughout most of more than one community. One example would be the terrorist attack of September 11, 2001 which simultaneously involved the World Trade Center towers (NYC), the Pentagon (Washington, D.C.) and the airline crash outside of Pittsburgh, Pennsylvania. Another example would be the impact of Hurricane Katrina on the Gulf Coast in 2005—from the Alabama to the Texas borders. Many communities, i.e., small towns, small cities, to the large city of New Orleans, were massively impacted simultaneously. In these examples, not only was the normal activity disrupted throughout the impacted cities, but the larger society also experienced severe adjustments.

DC9 is applied when the social structure adjustments are necessitated in response to an actual or potential disruption that is major or massive in scale, duration and scope across several population centers simultaneously—impacting dramatically on the larger society as well.

Disaster Category 10: Simultaneous Massive Disruption & Adjustment of a Society (A)

Disaster category ten (DC10) is reserved for the circumstance where actual or potential disruption and the resulting adjustment is so severe in terms of scale, duration, and scope that the society experiences annihilation—it is unlikely to continue to exist as a separate society. An example would be that which might result from a nuclear, biological and/or chemical (NBC) terrorist attack constituting delivery of weapons of mass destruction (WMD) to enough population centers that the societal disruption and adjustment constitutes annihilation.

DC10 is applied when the social structure adjustments are necessitated in response to an actual or potential disruption that is major or massive in scale, duration and scope across enough population centers to render a society annihilated.

In summary, the application of scale, scope, and (time) duration to disruption and adjustment provide us with a conceptual, sociological construct that differentiates between ten different disaster categories. This scale will facilitate testing of the prior findings and the generation of research questions. It will also assist practitioners in discerning between the types of mitigation, planning and response that may be appropriate based upon disaster category.

The Efficacy of the Disaster Scale

In this disaster scale we find that emergencies experience a limitation of at least one of the three criteria—scale, scope and/or duration, while disasters (six different categories) all experience actual or potential major disruption and adjustments in all three elements (scale, scope, duration). There are two issues involved in determining whether a precipitating event results in disaster category three, four . . . or eight: the size of the population impacted and the portion of the community's population impacted. It is reasoned that the greater the size of the impacted population, the greater the degree to which adjustments are experienced in terms of scope within the larger society (e.g., Hurricane Katrina in 2005, NYC on September 11, 2001 versus the Andover, Kansas tornado in 1991). And, hence, the greater the adjustment experienced indirectly throughout the larger society itself. Similarly, whether a given community is partially or wholly disrupted, is used to differentiate between disaster categories within the variable of community population size.

FREQUENCY OF DISASTER EVENTS

The potential for victimization grows steadily in the United States every year. As the population of the United States continues to increase, the number of potential victims continues to grow. Exacerbating the problem is the fact that more and more people are building homes or vacationing in disaster prone areas, e.g., the barrier islands off the southeastern U.S. coast.

A quick search of the Internet will yield a perhaps shocking revelation of just how frequently disasters occur. Floods, hurricanes, tornadoes, earthquakes, tsunamis, major transportation accidents, oil spills and other hazmat incidents suggests the world experiences a plethora of disaster events. Barely a day goes by that I do not hear of another major event somewhere on this planet. And, I am not even including common or major emergencies. We begin to realize that disasters are not that uncommon, perhaps they should be viewed as a normal life experience.

Change is constant and the same is true when it comes to potential disaster agents. New disaster agents continue to emerge. The September 11th, 2001 terrorist attack on the USA (Fischer, 2003) as well as the threat of nuclear, biological and chemical terrorism (Fischer, 1998) exemplify newer challenges. The potential for an internet collapse which could cripple a large segment of a society (Quarantelli, 1997) adds to the array of catastrophic future possibilities.

With so many disaster agents and the frequency events regularly occurring we can anticipate a continually increasing tax and insurance burden. There is irony in the fact that disaster researchers experience an ever-increasing opportunity to conduct applied research. Their research effort is ultimately aimed at helping to mitigate these burdens.

TYPES OF DISASTERS

Acts of God? Acts of Humans?

Disaster researchers divide disaster agents into two categories: technological and natural. Technological agents are often said to cause "(hu)man-made disasters." Most, if not all, disasters have a human origin, however. Mobile homes, for example, are far more easily destroyed in hurricanes, tornadoes, and floods than more substantially built homes. The manufacture, sales, and use of mobile homes literally increases the degree of destruction attributed to "acts of God." Their risk is further elevated by the tendency to locate mobile homes on less desirable, less expensive building sites. Have you ever noticed how many mobile homes are located on flood plains? The resulting destruction, injury and death can be attributed to man's inhumanity to man. How many times do we open a newspaper or turn on the evening news to find that, once again, those who can least afford the loss are the victims? How many times do we find neighborhoods of mobile homes sustaining the most damage in the community? Some people must wonder if hurricanes, tornadoes and flood waters are magnetically attracted to such structures. They are acts of man far more than they are acts of God. We humans know better, but in the quest for profit we ignore the risk to our fellow humans. The conflict theorist has an easy task explaining "who benefits" in the competition for the limited wealth, power, and prestige in this situation.

Civil disturbances, e.g., the 1992 Los Angeles riots, are also often mistakenly thought to be a third disaster category, in addition to natural and technological disasters. Their origin, the behavioral response to them, and the required organizational response are all quite different from what constitutes a technological or natural disaster. Riots are, therefore, historically not addressed within the context of "disaster research." To the extent that many in U.S. society continue to view them in this context has led some researchers to include this form of collective behavior in the discussion out of need to clarify the difference between the precipitating events leading to riots versus natural or technological disasters. Terrorism has a foot in both camps when viewed from a collective behavior perspective (see Miller, 1989; Curtis & Aguirre, 1993; McAdam & Snow, 1997).

Natural versus Technological Disasters

The United States experiences major emergencies or federally declared disasters every year. Unfortunately, there is never a shortage of such events for researchers to study. There are traditionally six types of natural disaster agents which may impact a community. These include earthquakes, floods, hurricanes, tornadoes, volcanoes and tsunamis. The Loma Prieta earthquake (1989), the Roanoke floods (1986), the Texas floods (1990), Hurricane Elena (1985), Hurricane Gilbert (1988), Hurricane Hugo (1989), Hurricane Andrew (1992), the Andover tornado (1991), the 1993 mid-western floods, the 1994 North Ridge earthquake in California, Hurricane Katrina (2005) all serve as just a few of the examples of natural disasters in the United States within a 15 year period. Droughts and famines are also increasingly viewed as two additional natural disaster agents (Drabek, 1997; Mileti, 1999). The effects of the latter two are all too often exacerbated by human conflict situations, e.g., civil wars. Hence, disaster researchers have traditionally avoided studying the behavioral and organizational response challenges to these two types of disasters believing that conflict situations may result in significantly different outcomes. This author argues that we should continue to determine the extent to which the disaster research literature is applicable to other disastrous settings such as drought and famine.

Industrialized societies increasingly experience technological emergencies and disasters. The list of disaster agents traditionally includes accidents involving hazardous materials (both fixed site and transportation), nuclear power plant accidents, mass transportation accidents (airplane and rail) and conflagrations. For example, the worst commercial nuclear accident in the United States occurred at the Three Mile Island reactor March 28, 1979 as equipment failures and human mistakes led to a loss of coolant and partial core meltdown. The most serious nuclear accident to have occurred anywhere was the April 1986 meltdown at the Chernobyl plant. It was located approximately 60 miles from Kiev in the Soviet Union. The Chernobyl area was devastated and several European nations were exposed to elevated levels of radiation. The March 24, 1989 grounding of the Exxon Valdez resulted in the spewing of over ten million gallons of crude oil into Prince William Sound in Alaska. Iraq's deliberate spilling of 130 million gallons during the 1991 Persian Gulf War was a major HazMat incident. A major fire at the New York City Social Club claimed 87 lives on March 25, 1990. Major transportation accidents occur with sufficient frequency to fill several pages in any almanac.

New forms of technological disaster agents are unfortunately emerging on what may be the *not too distant* horizon. The world's increasing dependence upon computer systems and the Internet point to a new future danger which may have catastrophic consequences for an entire society(s) or large segments thereof (Quarantelli, 1997). A computer virus, massive power failure, or other form of computer breakdown may result in a disastrous outcome. Another type of virus, one from a biological weapon (as well as from nuclear or chemical weapons) may be employed by terrorists seeking revenge or attempting to influence policy decisions. If anthrax, for example, were deployed by aerosol upon a major metropolitan area, it is quite possible that hundreds of thousands, perhaps millions would die within days (Fischer, 1998). The terrorist attach on the United States on September 11th 2001 serves to illustrate the challenges societies face going forward.

Disasters are separated into two categories not only because they differ in agent origination, but because from the outset the focus of the organizational response and the orientation of the reconstruction period differs significantly between the two. Natural disasters are typically responded to via what Quarantelli (1984) characterizes as the *command post perspective* where the local emergency management coordinator often seeks to integrate the organizational response to the disaster by primarily involving public agencies such as the police and fire departments as well as the Red Cross and Salvation Army. The response to a technological disaster is more likely to be multi-faceted with the local emergency manager attempting to coordinate the activities of police and fire personnel, while there is usually another command post attempting to manage the response of the private agency involved, e.g., the company or airport. For example, in December 1987, a Pittsburgh area company suffered the collapse of an oil storage facility resulting in the pollution of the Ohio River. The company sought to respond to the incident prior to, and separately from, any work done by the emergency management personnel of Allegheny County, Pennsylvania. The event may quickly become nationalized in the case of the "9.11" terrorist attack. Under these circumstances it quickly becomes a police and military action.

DISASTER TIME PERIODS

For research purposes we divide a disaster into five time periods. These include the pre-impact period, the impact period, the immediate post-impact period, the recovery period, and the long-term reconstruction period. Each disaster period contains different elements of behavioral and organizational response. The *pre-impact period* is one in which preparation *should* occur (during normal time on the part of both emergency organizations, e.g., hazard assessments, education, training, planning and mitigation; and, ideally, among the citizenry, e.g., education, disaster kits purchasing or creation, family evacuation planning). During the actual pre-impact days and hours if the need to prepare is clearly communicated to potential victims in such a fashion as to provide them with sufficient warning time, then misery, death and injury should be dramatically reduced. Some disaster agents, e.g., hurricanes, often provide sufficient time to prepare for impact because of the slow development of the storm. The National Hurricane Center in Florida monitors the development of the storm and tracks it, alerting citizens as the need arises. Thus alerted, potential victims can prepare their possessions for impact and evacuate to a safer location if one is available. Unfortunately, not everyone who is alerted chooses to leave. Many have been injured or killed as a result of not evacuating during the impact period.

And, all too often officials are slow to suggest or order an evacuation. Hurricane Katrina (New Orleans in particular) serves as a dramatic illustration.

The *impact period* is often the shortest, yet most dangerous, part of the disaster. The hurricane blows through; the tornado touches down and is gone; the plane crash is virtually instantaneous, and the earthquake shakes for seconds. While floods and nuclear accidents may, of course, have extended impact periods, most disasters move very quickly from pre-impact to post-impact.

During the *immediate post-impact* period the survivors must confront their new reality. After some disasters, many survivors will find that they have lost nothing of value while others will have suffered devastating losses, human and/or material. Search and rescue activities begin, debris clearance is initiated, and lost essential services (such as electricity and telephone) are restored. Emergency organizations respond and attempt to coordinate the community response to the disaster. State and federal agencies, when applicable, initiate their support. The local media initiates coverage providing helpful information to the community while national media venues begin continual coverage about the event.

During the *recovery period* debris clearance is usually completed, essential services are completely restored, insurance claims are filed, preliminary reconstruction plans are designed, and a sense of normalcy begins to return to the community. Normal time expectations, e.g., norms and role behaviors, once again begin to give direction to daily life.

Finally, the *reconstruction period* begins which may, depending upon the scope of the disaster, extend for years. A tornado struck the central business district of Covington, Kentucky in the spring of 1986. A disaster research team from the Disaster Research Center was on-site within 48 hours of impact. When the team leader returned a year later he discovered some damaged industrial property had not yet been repaired and a church steeple was still under reconstruction--and this event was more a major emergency than an actual disaster. This author visited Charleston, South Carolina during the summer of 1990 which was ten months after Hurricane Hugo had impacted the area. Debris was still being burned, many buildings had only undergone temporary repair, and the mental health units were still on-site. It was readily apparent that reconstruction would take many years to complete. Completion of reconstruction after Hurricane Andrew continued for many years and Katrina reconstruction in New Orleans may take decades. In some cases, segments of the community may never be rebuilt, depending upon the political will and financial resources.

FOUR PHASES OF EMERGENCY MANAGEMENT

Emergency managers have the primary responsibility for leading the community (state or national) preparation for any possible future disaster that may impact their population. For purposes of anticipating, educating, and preparing for such, the process is currently viewed as broken down into four phases: *planning, response, recovery,* and *mitigation.* Each is briefly examined.

Planning for a disaster begins with conducting a hazards assessment. What hazards are likely to impact a community? The emergency manager is in a key position to educate and lead the community leaders and businesses to conduct hazards assessments. In addition to identifying the hazards, steps can then be taken to mitigate their occurrence. For example, if a business is storing a toxic chemical in barrels on a flood plain, it would be prudent, upon discovery, to relocate those chemicals to a less vulnerable location. Planning also includes the creation of written disaster plans, for the community and for each entity within it (businesses, schools, families for that matter). The written disaster plan needs to be practiced, tested, revamped when it does not seem to work, and updated regularly. Those implementing the plan need training and practice on a regular basis.

The *response* phase of a disaster requires emergency organizations to serve the community (local, state, and federal organizations as needed) they have been hired to serve. The level of preparedness becomes readily apparent during this phase. During the response to Hurricane Katrina, as reported to our field research team, many first responders *thought* they were prepared for the event, however, "we knew early on that this was far beyond our ability to respond—we then knew we were not prepared for anything beyond a lower level disaster" (Fischer, et al, 2006). A proper response would include emergency operating center (EOC) coordination of the information flow during the response and emergency organization response to needs of the community (such as evacuation, debris clearance, restoration of services, medical assistance, and so forth).

The *recovery* phase, depending on the magnitude of the event, may be relatively short or go on for years, even a decade or more. Rebuilding characterizes the recovery phase. Using Hurricane Katrina and the Gulf Coast as our example, rebuilding the cities and communities between Biloxi, Mississippi, and New Orleans will take a very long time. The challenge includes rebuilding roads, housing, businesses, and so forth before the population can reconstitute. After a community is declared a Presidential Disaster Area, it is a long, slow process to move from application for aid, to receipt, use and return to normalcy.

The *mitigation* phase is be characterized as a brief window of opportunity (for example, see Mileti, 1999) after a disaster impacts a community. A disaster certainly has a way of riveting one's attention to the need for implementing measures to make it less likely for the community to be re-impacted in the future. For a relatively brief period of time after a disaster mitigation is possible more than any other time. Miss this opportunity and planning, response, and recovery will revisit all too soon. It was widely known in the Gulf Coast region as well as throughout the USA that a category four or five hurricane would indeed impact New Orleans and the region. Never the less, Fischer, et al, (2006) found responders saying "we thought we were well prepared for up to a category three, at least, and we thought the feds would be able to bail us out if necessary—but they never came." What did they mean? They believed the state and federal governments would be in a position to respond in their support, especially after all the preparation the USA had embarked upon since September 11th, 2001. Prior mitigation efforts along the Gulf Coast did not rise to the occasion of August-September, 2005 during and after Hurricane Katrina. Variations of this story are all too frequent. In the first place, too many think it will never happen to them, or on their watch, and even when it does, too often believe it will then never happen again.

The future professional emergency management agencies at all levels will, hopefully, engage in *effective* planning, response, recovery and mitigation activities. Perhaps some day not too far over the rainbow we will have emergency management throughout the USA and beyond that is worthy of the name.

SOCIOLOGICAL THEORY

How is it that we understand human interaction? How do we know what we know about life during normal time or during time of a disaster? The sociological perspective provides us with insight into behavior and social organization. Without a basic understanding of the various sociological paradigms, we could not objectively interpret behavior, interaction or social organization. We would be limited to the perspective taught to us as a result of our individual socialization process. What you are about to read, learn is collectively referred to, by your author, as "the Social-Structural Model" or SSM.

Basic Sociological Concepts

How is it that we know what we think we know? How is it that we come to behave according to what we know how we are supposed to act in any situation (be it normal time or disaster time)? We turn to the "Sociological Perspective" and the use of what we call the "basic sociology concepts" to begin to answer the above questions. The following should serve as lenses through which to view our familiar world. It will discuss the basic building blocks of social structure, i.e., norms, values, roles and statuses. It will also outline how this social structure is acquired, learned, socialized or internalized—resulting in providing us with our view of reality and how we are to behave in it. Deliberate and non-deliberate socialization will be described, including an explanation of the looking-glass self process, the role of significant others, the use of sanctions, and the role of self-esteem in controlling are behavior and formulating our view of reality.

Group Animal

The basic sociological insight is that we humans are group animals. Our survival, our identity, sense of self and purpose, is tied to the group. Each of us is born into a group we call "family." We become members of play groups, work groups, neighborhoods, a community and the society. We are totally dependent upon the group. Without the help of a parent (or someone who plays the role of parent) we would not survive long after birth. Someone feeds us, nurtures us, and teaches us how to fend for ourselves so that we can become "independent" in the future—but we are always tied to group life. It is from the groups to which we belong that we learn what is expected of us, how to get along in order to survive in our environment. We learn the norms, values, roles and statuses of the group from the other members of the group.

Norms

Every group, whether it be as large as an entire society or as small as a two-person group, has rules that every member is expected to follow. The group believes that by following these rules the needs of the group and its individual members will be satisfied. We call these group rules norms. If you are behaving normally, you are following the rules or the group norms. Norms are defined as the rules expected of all members of the group by virtue of the fact that they are members of the group. For example, we are all expected to come to class dressed in clothing. The type of clothing may vary greatly, by gender, age, socio-economic status or personal taste, but everyone will normally be wearing something.

Actually there are two basic types of norms as some rules are considered to be more important than others. We have folkways, i.e., he common ways of the folk or people, which are the common everyday rules which, when followed, render us polite people. We try not to pick our nose in public or pass gas in class! While we may occasionally pick our nose or pass gas, we all act like this never happens . . . and especially try to refrain from doing so "in public." We do not want to be thought of as a pig. We do not want to break the folkways; we want to fit in.

Mores are the norms that are considered more important to preserving our very existence, not just politeness. To kill someone we are angry with is considered a violation of a more. People cannot just go around killing another as this would be a vital threat to our individual and collective survival.

Values

Every group believes that certain goals are worthy of group effort, to achieve these goals may even be deemed worthy of risking one's life. Americans believe that democracy is worth fighting to preserve, even going to ward to "protect our way of life," i.e., democracy. We value democracy. We also value education, freedom of speech, and the free enterprise system. A group's values result in the development of group norms. The norms are believed to help attain or preserve that which is valued. Because we value education, we raise money (pay taxes) to provide children with education (taxation a norm). We willingly, some more than others, give our money to educate not only our own children, but also those of others in the belief that an educated populace is a benefit to all of us.

Status

Every group has various positions. The heterosexual family has the positions of husband, wife, mother, parent, child, brother, sister, grandparent. The football team has the positions of quarterback, halfback, full back, and various linemen. When we assume a particular position within a group we begin to behave as we believe we are supposed to, i.e., we assume the role.

Role

Every position has a corresponding set of roles, behaviors expected of one who holds a particular position within the group. A professor is expected to prepare for class, sometimes lecture, give tests, grade papers and hold office hours. The student is expected to attend class, participate, take notes, learn the material and prepare for the exam.

Culture or Social Structure

When we join a group we immediately begin learning the social structure that the group adheres to and expects its members to follow. We learn the norms, values, statuses and roles. When we seek to be a good member of the group, we are seeking to exhibit the right values, follow the rules and proper roles germane to our position in the group. What we are learning and exhibiting is the group culture. Culture is defined as the way of lie, i.e., social structure (norms, values, statuses, roles), of the group. It is this culture that instructs us, governs our behavior, and gives us a sense of security in that we know what to expect of others, what their behavior means, and how to act ourselves. We feel good about ourselves when we think we are behaving "properly," according to the group expectations.

The Social Construction of Reality & Symbolic Interaction

Deliberate & Non-Deliberate Socialization

How do we learn this culture or social structure? We become socialized into the group. We learn the culture in essentially two ways. We experience both deliberate and non-deliberate socialization throughout our lives. When Dad tried to teach his son, John, how to eat peas with a fork instead of his fingers, little John was experiencing deliberate socialization. Most of our learning does not take place as a result of a planned, deliberate attempt to instruct us into the culture of the group, however. Most group members live their lives, practice the norms and roles, and others observe and emulate them. For example, non-deliberate socialization occurs when Dad swears after hitting his finger with the hammer. After observing Dad's response on a regular basis, little John is increasingly likely to adopt Dad's approach when John feels pain. In other words, John may also begin damning his finger, and so forth.

We both know Dad did not intend to say to John, "okay, whenever you feel pain start having a temper tantrum with a foul mouth." Dad would actually be quite disturbed with little John's behavior, even though he taught it to him!

Looking-Glass Self

How do we determine if we are behaving according to the group culture? We develop a looking-glass self. The looking-glass self is defined as our perception of the perception that others have of us. We in essence look into the eyes of those people who are important to us (in our groups), e.g., spouse, lover, boss, friend, to determine how they feel about us. We use them as a mirror. We try to determine if they believe we are a good person, i.e., following the norms and roles. Our sense of who we are is dependent upon our perception of the perception others have of us. We continually use others to judge ourselves. We would have no other way of knowing. Again, we are group animals, dependent upon group members to teach us the culture and to let us know if we are getting it right.

There is plenty of room for misinterpretation though. We could perceive that they think we are a poor friend, when in fact they may be feeling the opposite. Conversely, we might mistakenly believe we are just fine, when they are thinking we are behaving like a jerk.

Significant Others

Who are the important others we use as a mirror? We use the significant others in our lives. For example, it is often a parent, spouse, child, peers, colleagues who serve in this capacity. While we may care if a stranger thinks we are good looking, their opinion is not nearly as important to us as a close loved one—significant other.

Socialization Agents

While our significant others are usually socialization agents for us, non-significant others may also serve in this capacity. Family members, friends, peers, colleagues may all be significant to us in our group memberships and serve as initial socialization agents (deliberately and non-deliberately teaching us the group norms, values, statuses and roles). Others who are distant to us may also play a part in our socialization. The Media would serve as one example. When we watch a movie we may then emulate a character. When we watch the evening television news or read the morning newspaper we may learn information or a point of view as a result. The textbooks we read in the educational system (as well as handouts—smile!) may have a similar socialization influence. At least professors hope they do! The socialization process is ongoing throughout life; it is not limited to the first several years of life.

Sanctions

Our significant others use sanctions to let us know if we are performing appropriately. When we use them as looking-glasses we see them using an array of possible responses aimed at influencing us to continue or discontinue our behavior. These are called sanctions and they include three pairs: position and negative sanctions, physical and psychological sanctions, as well as formal and informal sanctions. When Dad gives John a pat on the back for mastering the use of the fork to eat his peas, Dad is giving John a positive sanction. At the same time, this positive sanction is also a psychological sanction as it is designed to make him feel (emotion) good about himself. If Dad said, "stop eating like a baby, only infants eat with their finger," a negative psychological sanction would be employed. When I tell a student he or she did a good job in class today, I am being informal as well as positive and psychological. At commencement, graduating with honors is positive, psychological and formal. Spanking is negative, physical and informal.

Self-Esteem

Just as each of us must have oxygen to breath, food to eat, water to drink in order to be sustained, we human animals also require a minimal level of self-esteem. The person who feels no self-worth is in danger of committing suicide. Suicide is often an attempt to kill the pain as a result of feeling worthless. The suicide kills the pain and also physically kills him or her self.

We seek to practice the culture of the group (follow the group structure) in order to enhance our self-esteem. The greater the individual perceives his performance (as we perceive it to be through the eyes of our significant others) to be, the greater the chance that he will feel high self-esteem (at least in the short term). If we perceive a continual array of such experiences, our sense of self-esteem in all likelihood will remain rather high over time. The converse, however, is also true.

To summarize, we are socialized to follow the group culture or social structure of every group to which we belong during our lives. The social structure controls our behavior, we are trained to follow it and are motivated to do so by the quest for self-esteem need satisfaction. The group is the source of this nurturing required by the human animal for survival.

Differential Association Theory

Edwin Sutherland observed that all behavior is learned, both that which is labeled non-deviant as well as that which is labeled deviant. We learn attitudes and behaviors from significant others in the groups to which we belong. If we learn non-deviant behavior, we are considered non-deviant; if we learn to exhibit deviant behavior, we are seen to be a deviant by those who have the power to do the labeling (if our behavior is known). We are socialized, deliberately and non-deliberately, through the looking-glass self process discussed previously.

Differential Opportunity Theory

Cloward and Ohlin observed that not all individuals have the same "opportunity" to learn the same type of behavior, albeit considered to be deviant or non-deviant. For example, our social class position (lower class versus upper class) may predispose the lower class youth to attitudes and behaviors quite different from what the upper class youth may come to embrace and exhibit through two very different socialization experiences. We are not exposed to the same social environment whether it is one labeled deviant or non-deviant.

Role Theory

Andersen observed the instrumental impact that socialized gender roles plays in our behavior. Gender roles have often been labeled as the natural order by elites. Used as a division of labor, gender roles have traditionally been viewed as functional to meeting our basic survival needs. However, post-industrial societies have increasingly viewed traditional gender roles as perhaps dysfunctional to human need satisfaction. Behavior proscribed on the basis of gender can lead to some very problematic outcomes. For example, when females are socialized to be pleasing and passive, they are often more vulnerable to abuse. When males are socialized to define their gender-based participation in war as glory and heroism, they are unwittingly taught to be victims in a type of holocaust.

Self Attitudes Theory

Howard B. Kaplan argues that each human animal has self-esteem needs. Just as we need air, water, food, and rest to survive, we also must maintain at least a minimal level of positive sense of self through the looking-glass self process. We are, again, tied to the group. If we perceive that our esteem needs are being met through affiliation with the groups to which we presently belong, we are likely to continue our affiliation with them and feel some level of satisfaction. If, on the other hand, we believe that our self-esteem needs are not being met, then we, at some point, we leave these groups or at least seek alternative groups in the hope of finding acceptance. For example, if we are constantly verbally abused and feel no worth in the eyes of present significant others we eventually select a mode of adaptation, one of which may be to seek acceptance and identity maintenance in another group.

The kid who comes from a so-called good family, yet one which does not satisfy his need for self-esteem, may cast about for an alternative source. If, by chance, he joins a football team and finds acceptance, his need is not only met but he is also seen as a non-deviant. If he happens to begin differentially associating with a gang, e.g., someone befriends him and brings him into the gang, the new group's culture may include role behaviors which the dominant culture, and his family, consider deviant. If his self-esteem deficiency is great enough, he may be willing to do anything for acceptance into the new group.

Structural-Functional Theory

From the perspective of structural-functionalism, the family as a social institution exists as a social structure to provide for the needs of the individual family member, the family as a group, and the society. This paradigm seeks to answer the question "what purpose or function does the norm, value, role, or status serve in meeting needs. Our individual needs must be satisfied, as least to some minimal level, if we are to literally survive. The family group needs must also be met, to some minimal level, or the group will cease to survive which would make it more difficult for each individual member's needs to be met--threatening their survival as well. And, the society cannot survive if the health it's individual groups and members is undermined. A quest of this theoretical paradigm may be said to identify those functions served by group social structure pursuant to finding those which best function to meet our needs and, hence, foster survival.

Conflict Theory

Within any group, each individual is continually on the quest to satisfy his or her basic and acquired needs. For example, we may seek the power, wealth, and prestige we believe we require to satisfy our own needs and those of our families. While we are in competition with one another, we are in a state of conflict as there is limited power, wealth, and prestige [1] available within any group (society, community, family). Some, but not all or even most, will be able to attain the elite group position(s), or have these positions bestowed upon them in some way. Examples of some of these positions might include the U.S. Presidency, the company CEO, or head of household as well as socio-economic positioning within the society, gender position, and age position. Those who hold the elite position(s) at any given time, have the power to label what is and what is not acceptable or deviant behavior. By "acceptable" we mean what is acceptable as the means to attain what they have attained in life or what is acceptable in their eyes in any context. Elites, within the society, within the community, on the job, or within the family, have the power to label who and what is appropriate, i.e., the power to do the labeling and make it stick. Through this process we say that conflict theory helps to explain how the elite within a group create deviance. It is created when the elites label acceptable versus unacceptable behavior, persons, and groups. Those through accident of birth or by the luck of being socialized "appropriately," are labeled non-deviant and perhaps ascend the ladder toward the elite positions within the group. The others conflict with the elites and are labeled deviant.

Feminist Theory

Feminist theory may be viewed as an application of conflict theory in that it focuses on providing an understanding of how the patriarchy in western cultures has resulted in privilege for males, certain groups of males in particular, and the domination of women. Many females have been socialized to believe in a false ideology. As a result they adhere to norms and roles that are dysfunctional to their own need satisfaction. It is increasingly coming to be understood that males also suffer from dysfunctional aspects of their gender roles as well. The effective meeting of the needs of all has been seen as being adversely affected by the norms and roles created and enforced by a patriarchy that has traditionally been part of the cultural heritage of western European cultures.

Labeling Theory

Sociologist Howard Becker argues that no act is inherently deviant. Behavior, characteristics, individuals, and groups are labeled as deviant or non-deviant by those who have the power to do so. The labeling comes primarily from the elites (conflict theory), but others participate in the labeling as well. As we become socialized into the group values, norms, roles and statuses, we tend to adopt the view, or ideology, of the elites when it comes to defining who or what is acceptable or unacceptable. Our definition of a social problem being that which is so labeled by those who have the power to do the labeling and make it stick is obviously labeling theory.

Post-Modern Theory

Modernists believe that social change leads to progress, the forward movement to-ward a more utopian social structure to benefit all, i.e., meet the needs of everyone. From a modernist perspective, the movement from hunting and gathering societies to horticultural, agricultural, industrial, and now informational social organization is to be viewed as progress as evidenced by the improved standard of living (where we view ourselves as developing and others as undeveloped nations). The socialization that has accompanied modernization has been the view that the social institutions of the developed nations are, by definition, superior (the result of progress). The fact that this kind of progress has been made testifies to the self-evidence of this notion of association of progress with the accompanying forms of social organization (economic, family, education, religious, political). Hence, the modern view is to hold that all would benefit from adopting the singular successful form of social organization, i.e., the social structure of the advanced nations should be the singular form socialized into all peoples within and without of societies such as the United States.

Conflict theory, especially feminist theory, calls the above into question by noting that the social structure of the advanced nations is not 100% functional—that there are inherent socially structured dysfunctions that result. Hence, Post-Modernists argue that diversity is a better model than the singular superiority of the social institutions of the advanced nations. For example, the social structures of the United States are the amalgamation of many cultures over hundreds of years (a na-

tion of immigrants) . . . hence, diversity has resulted in the social structures associated with certain successes in the western world (however, there are also dysfunctions which are part of the current social structures in the U.S.). Hence, diversity is
the most functional model for providing any hope of real "progress" for the future,
i.e., removing the remaining dysfunctions that are socially structured into the culture.

HOW DO WE COME TO KNOW WHAT WE KNOW ABOUT DISASTERS?

Socialization agents and significant others teach us the group view of what constitutes a disaster, what to expect in one, how to prepare for one, who prepares, and
what the outcome will be. Our families, neighbors, friends, colleagues, public officials, and the mass media all contribute to this socialization process. During the
course of this semester, we will examine what these socialization agents teach us
about disaster culture. We will also consider what deliberate socialization we may
now seek to take in direct response to the disaster culture as it currently exists. We
will also examine the impact of competing constituencies in the process of allocat-
ing mitigation and response resources.

INTEGRATION WITH THEORY

For years disaster researchers have noted the paucity of theory in the disaster literature. Some have sought to redress this problem. Dynes and Quarantelli have been
central in leading the way and urging others to follow. David McEntire more recently has embraced the task in his body of work. There is, of course, the issue of
theory of emergency management versus emergency management theory. Both are
important, yet distinctly different. McEntire (2004) addresses this very nicely. The
reader should reference his work for a detailed examination.

The objective at hand, however, is to apply the enumerated sociological theory
to a few examples which should demonstrate their utility in explaining certain processes reported in this volume. The student is urged to ground his or her work in theory going forward. The following illustrates are offered as merely a started point.

An Example of a Structural-Functionalist Approach

What function does the National Guard serve when activated during a disaster? Ostensibly they serve the function of restoring and maintaining order. They also serve
the function of enabling residents to perceive that their possessions are safe as a
result of the Guard's presence. These residents may the feel more comfortable
evacuating. Without this functional use the of the National Guard, the death and
injury count may be larger in many disasters as residents are more inclined to remain in their homes to protect their property against possible looting.

What function does disaster planning serve for the community? It seems obvious. A community formulates plans for responding to a disaster in order to protect itself. It wants to reduce the potential deaths, injuries, and damage. It wants to be prepared to evacuate the population when necessary. Is there another function? When evacuation plans are unveiled in some American cities, the efficacy of the plans is often criticized. It is very difficult to move large urban populations in a timely manner. Even if an effective evacuation were possible, where do we send these large populations? Should we move the seven million residents of New York City to another urban area like Philadelphia or a rural area like Lancaster County, Pennsylvania? How would they get there and where would they stay? More than one emergency manager has privately acknowledged the problems with planning for large scale evacuations. Disaster planning and evacuation planning in particular, sometimes serve the function of providing the public with the *illusion* of preparedness. Local decision-makers, e.g., the mayor, must contend with a plethora of budgetary needs. They are more likely to fund requests to deal with community needs demanding their response daily, e.g., more police officers for crime control, than requests to support disaster mitigation and planning. After all, a disaster may never impact their community.

In some instances it could be argued that disasters themselves function to stimulate sectors of the local economy during the recovery stage. Insurance money provides an economic stimulus as rebuilding begins, e.g., replacing roofs or entire homes. While some individuals may never economically recover, others may experience some advantages. Restored community buildings may be in better condition after rebuilding than they had been before the disaster. It could be argued that a community does not want to be totally successful in mitigating all disasters. The function or dysfunction depending on one's perspective, of flood insurance could be examined at great length from a structural-functionalist perspective. We already know that the availability of flood insurance, as humane as it may be, appears to contribute to the continual building of homes and resorts in areas where they really should not be built. Some structures are almost guaranteed to be destroyed, and not just once. Rebuilding on the same location continues the cycle. Zoning which permits such building may be functional to the builder who profits from the construction project, but it is dysfunctional to the community and larger society.

An Example of a Conflict Approach

The construction company specializing in condominiums, for example, is in competition for limited resources with other sectors of the economy. Building on a flood plain or barrier island enhances profit for the builder, but potentially decreases profit for the insurance company and increases the cost of insurance for those who pay the premiums. In many communities, those who inhabit homes on a flood plain are often members of the lower socioeconomic strata. This deliberate targeting of the poor or near poor as likely flood victims is immoral. It places profit above people.

As mentioned above, the budgetary needs of any community conflict with one another. A community could hire ten more police officers in an attempt to increase deterrence by increasing the certainty of catching and prosecuting offenders. Or, the same community could build a flood wall in an attempt to mitigate future flood damage to the city's central business district. In a high crime area which is infrequently flooded the choice is probably obvious. Building the flood wall would appear to be dysfunctional to meeting the community's needs-- until a major flood impacts the community, then blame assignation begins.

Conflict theory may help explain the decisions politicians and city managers make in regard to many other issues. For example, the previously noted need to better educate the public on disaster mitigation, planning and response, would require additional revenues . . . from the taxpayer. In an era of "no new taxes" politicians find it difficult to improve services. In the competition for limited wealth, power, and prestige, the apparent more pressing need, or politically necessary allocation, will likely win the battle of the budget. Those charged with the responsibility of planning to respond and to mitigate, need to acquire good political skills enabling them to garner a more equitable allocation during the funding cycle. After a major hurricane impacts another community it may be a good time to demonstrate the need for additional mitigation activities locally before the story fades from the news and the decay curve takes effect.

An Example of a Symbolic Interactionist Approach

This volume described the process by which the public comes to believe in the disaster mythology. This process is actually an example of non-deliberate socialization. The mass media serves as a socialization agent when it portrays the disaster mythology. The public believes the news being presenting and *learns* that people are deviant during a disaster. Reality is that which is perceived. Change the perception of the reporters and the mythology will cease to be portrayed as reality.

The reporters are also socialized to believe in the mythology. Education is perhaps the key to embarking on a re-socialization program which will alter the perceptions the reporters use as their frame of reference to reconstruct the reality portrayed in their print or broadcast news stories. Disaster researchers have an obligation to the communities and society they serve to lead the educational process which needs to reach the public generally, and specially the emergency managers and reporters who play such an important role in the process of public perception of and response to major emergencies and disasters. The Natural Hazards Center of the University of Colorado has led the way through its annual workshop commingling researchers with national, state, and local emergency managers, but we must all do better.

Chapter 2

Who Does Disaster Research?

INTRODUCTION

Academic researchers, often located at research centers, are at the focal point of data gathering, publishing, mentoring, consulting, and teaching the findings from the field. In this chapter a brief history of disaster research is followed by brief descriptions of several academic research centers, a primer of many who comprise a who's who of the discipline, and the journals in which they publish. The author can only hope those who by mere chance have not been included, will forgive him.

A Brief History of Disaster Research

Samuel Prince completed the first study of human and organizational response to disaster in his 1920 Columbia University doctoral dissertation. Prince's case study carefully described the organizational response to a massive explosion that occurred on December 6, 1917. At 9:06 in the morning a French munitions ship, the *Mont Blanc,* collided with a Belgian ship in the Halifax, Nova Scotia, harbor. The *Mont Blanc* was carrying explosives (TNT) and caught fire after the collision. Soon the fire caused a massive explosion that destroyed the ship, created a tsunami in the harbor area and destroyed much of the town of Halifax. Prince, an Anglican Priest, was onsite and immediately began helping the survivors. Afterwards he compiled notes on the event and generated a long list of tentative hypotheses on organizational response to disasters. While many of his hypotheses were eventually found to be inaccurate, his work was the first social science case study of a disaster event. Today we trace the origin of the field of disaster research to Prince's work. Joseph Scanlon, professor emeriti, Carleton University, has compiled a great deal of information on the Halifax disaster and Samuel Prince. Scanlon would be an excellent resource for obtaining more information on both.

It was not until 1949, however, that a sustained research effort received funding to support on-going disaster research. Fritz and Marks (1954:27) and Killian (1954) conducted research which sought to catalog behavioral response to disaster. During the 1950s members of the National Opinion Research Center (NORC) research staff investigated various topics concerned with human response to disaster. After reviewing the findings of the emerging field of disaster research, Fritz (1961) wrote a chapter for a "social problems" text, edited by Merton and Nisbet, in which he suggested that disasters were a special type of social problem.

Barton (1969) reviewed the literature generated during these early decades of disaster research and produced a lengthy, impressive volume which carefully outlined several interrelated networks of hypotheses. His work was more a codification of hypotheses than an inventory of findings. It directed field work for years thereafter.

The Disaster Research Center (DRC) was established at the Ohio State University in 1963 by E.L. (Henry) Quarantelli and Russell Dynes. The founders focused on organizational response and carried on the quick response tradition initiated by earlier NORC field teams. From this work, they developed several analytic typologies to explain organizational response. Quarantelli and Dynes have been the two key leaders in the field for decades, have published many articles and books, have mentored many disaster researchers, and are recognized internationally for their work. Students of disaster research become very familiar with the works of both Dynes and Quarantelli.

In 1972, Thomas Drabek, Dennis Mileti and James Haas, began to develop an inventory of research findings. Ron Perry, University of Arizona, and Robert Stallings, University of Southern California, are both well known in the field for their work. In 1986, Drabek published a major work comprising an inventory of research into codified levels of disaster response. This work guides the field work of many contemporary disaster researchers. In 1999, Mileti was the editor of the second reassessment of the research literature published since the first assessment.

The DRC moved to the University of Delaware in 1985. The original founders were joined by Dennis Wenger who served as field research director before becoming center director. Wenger has since founded the Hazards Reduction & Recovery Center at Texas A&M University and he has served at the National Science Foundation. Joanne Nigg and Kathleen Tierney served as DRC co-directors. Tierney became sole director before becoming director of the Natural Hazards Center, University of Colorado-Boulder after Mileti retired. While Quarantelli and Dynes had retired at the University of Delaware, they continue to conduct their work at the center. Havidan Rodriguez followed Tierney as DRC director. The DRC core faculty then included Ben Aguirre (previously at Texas A&M University), Tricia Wachtendorf as well as Joanne Nigg, Henry Quarantelli and Russell Dynes, the latter two continuing as professor emeriti. The DRC has expanded the number of issues it examines. The DRC continues to be known for its ever expanding publications series.

At the University of Colorado, Gilbert F. White created the Natural Hazards Research and Applications Information Center which provides an important forum for interdisciplinary studies. The center sponsors quick response studies and hosts an annual workshop for the dissemination of new disaster response knowledge between researchers and practitioners. It also coordinates a national computer network of disaster research findings. In 1993, Mileti became the new director, replacing White, who re-entered "retirement." Mary Fran Myers joined Mileti as co-director. Tierney then followed Mileti and Myers as center director.

Disaster research activity has emerged at various other universities. Gary Kreps made a major contribution by developing a theoretical model while working at the College of William and Mary. Joe Scanlon has widely published on the media's work in disasters while working at Carleton University in Canada. Duane Gill has been recognized for his work on the Alaskan oil spill. Charles Faupel, Auburn University, has made major contributions to the literature on various disaster response issues. Fred Bates was actively engaged in a disaster research agenda as director of the International Laboratory of Socio-Political Ecology at the University of Georgia. Shirely Laska, University of New Orleans, is known for her studies of evacuation behavior. John Pine is very active at Louisiana State University.

Walter Peacock was formerly at Florida International University before moving to Texas A&M University after Wenger founded the Hazards Reduction & Recovery Center (HRRC). The HRRC grew to include Michael Lindell and Carla Prater.

David Neal directed the Institute of Emergency Administration and Planning at the University of North Texas, then the Emergency Management Institute at Jacksonville State University, and is creating the Center for the Study of Disasters & Extreme Events at Oklahoma State University in conjunction with Brenda Phillips. Phillips conducted research into various organizational response issues (particular focus on the impact of gender on disaster response) at the Texas Women's University before continuing in work at Jacksonville State University, and then Oklahoma State University. Both Neal and Phillips created and taught the first totally online program in the area of emergency management at Jacksonville. They created a master's degree program in public administration with a specialty in emergency management.

Henry (Hank) Fischer, your author, created and served as the first director of the Center for Disaster Research & Education at Millersville University of Pennsylvania. He also served as program coordinator for the minor in environmental hazards and emergency management as well as program coordinator for the first totally online master's degree in emergency management as a multi-disciplinary program. Fischer's primary research focus has been the behavioral, organizational, and media response to disasters.

The first PhD program in emergency management was established at North Dakota State University by Arthur Oyola-Yemaiel and Jennifer Wilson, who were followed by Carol Cwiak and others.

In this ever expanding field, there are many bright faculty researchers making an impact on the field. They include, but are not limited to, Gary Webb, Oklahoma

State University, Tricia Wachtendorf, University of Delaware/DRC, Lori Peek, Colorado State University, Joseph Trainor, University of Delaware/DRC, and many more . . . I would mention my other former students at the University of Delaware and Oklahoma State University (since I am extremely proud of Bill Donner, Lauren Barsky, Lynn Letukas—all currently graduate research assistants at the University of Delaware/DRC, Shireen Hyrapiet, Robert Whitaker—both currently graduate research assistants at Oklahoma State University) but to do so would make me look self serving. These few examples are illustrative of the ever growing list of contemporary disaster researchers.

The examples of disaster researchers are primarily drawn from the USA—my apologies to my many colleagues from Europe, Australian, India, China and beyond. I also apologize to the many others laboring in the discipline and coming up through graduate schools, for not including you, the above serve as examples from the growing field.

The next several pages include information of a few leading disaster research centers, as well as their web site addresses so that you can readily access them in order to identify their current personnel, research projects, education programs, publications, and so forth. You would benefit from becoming very familiar with the work of these, and other, centers of research and education. Keeping up to date on advances within the field is the responsibility of every student of disaster research and emergency management going forward.

Several U.S. Centers of Disaster Research

Disaster Research Center (DRC)
University of Delaware
http://www.udel.edu/DRC/

The DRC is the first social science research center in the world devoted to the study of disasters. It was established at Ohio State University in 1963 and moved to the University of Delaware in 1985. It conducts field and survey research on group, organizational and community preparation for, response to, and recovery from natural and technological disasters and other community-wide crises. DRC researchers have carried out systematic studies on a broad range of disaster types, including hurricanes, floods, earthquakes, tornadoes, hazardous chemical incidents, and plane crashes. The DRC has also done research on civil disturbances and riots, including the 1992 Los Angeles unrest.

The staff has conducted nearly 600 field studies since the Center's inception, traveling to communities throughout the United States and to a number of foreign countries, including Mexico, Canada, Japan, Italy, and Turkey. Faculty members from the University's Department of Sociology and Criminal Justice direct the DRC projects.

Professor Havidán Rodríguez is Director. Core Faculty: Benigno E. Aguirre, Joanne Nigg and Tricia Wachtendorf. Russell R. Dynes and E. L. Quarantelli are the founding directors and Emeritus Professors. The DRC staff includes postdoctoral fellows, graduate students, as well as undergraduates and research support personnel. [With permission, the above was drawn from the DRC web site.]

Natural Hazards Center
University of Colorado-Boulder
http://www.colorado.edu/hazards/

The mission of the Natural Hazards Center at the University of Colorado at Boulder is to advance and communicate knowledge on hazards mitigation and disaster preparedness, response, and recovery. Using an all-hazards and interdisciplinary framework, the Center fosters information sharing and integration of activities among researchers, practitioners, and policy makers from around the world; supports and conducts research; and provides educational opportunities for the next generation of hazards scholars and professionals. [With permission, the above was drawn from the NHC web site.]

Hazard Reduction & Recovery Center
Texas A&M University
http://archone.tamu.edu/hrrc/

The Hazard Reduction & Recovery Center (HRRC) was established at Texas A&M University in 1988 by Dennis E. Wenger. The center engages in research on hazard mitigation, disaster preparedness, response, and recovery. The staff of the HRRC is interdisciplinary in nature and includes the expertise of architects, engineers, geographers, psychologists, and sociologists. The HRRC is dedicated to providing access to hazards information for homeowners, professionals, business investors, and the academic community. [With permission, the above was drawn from the HRRC web site.]

Center for Disaster Research & Education (CDRE)
Millersville University of Pennsylvania
http://www.millersville.edu/~CDRE/

The CDRE is currently comprised of 15 faculty members and several student research assistants. It conducts research into various issues related to disasters and terrorism. The Center's work includes, but is not limited to, investigation of behavioral and organizational issues related to mitigation, planning, and response to disasters and terrorism. The Center also develops educational and training opportunities directed toward public policy makers, emergency personnel, the mass media, and average citizens. The Center has previously completed work for the Federal Emergency Management Agency (Higher Education Project), Research Planning, Inc., the Pennsylvania Emergency Management Agency, and various academic research centers. Contract and grant support currently come from FEMA and the National Science Foundation (NSF). The CDRE publishes the official newsletter of the International Research Committee on Disasters (RC 39, International Sociological Association). *UnScheduled Events* is published three times a year (January, May, September). The Center also publishes the *Contemporary Disaster Review*: An International Journal (CDR) three times a year: February, June, October. The CDR is the official online journal of reviews (books, websites, distance learning, CD-ROM materials) of the International Research Committee on Disasters. The Center also hosts (online) the *International Journal of Mass Emergencies and Disasters* (IJMED), the official journal of the International Research Committee on Disasters. The Center engages in research and educational activities aimed at serving the Commonwealth of Pennsylvania, the region, the nation and beyond. The Center also manages the undergraduate minor in environmental hazards and emergency management (EHEM) and teaches the totally online Master of Science in Emergency Management program drawing from faculty from across the University who are CDRE Faculty Associates. [With permission, the above was drawn from the CDRE web site.]

WHO'S *WHO* IN DISASTER RESEARCH?

Apologies to all who are not listed here, but should be! We tried! As you know, dear reader, humans make mistakes. As soon as this edition goes to press, I will no doubt realize I have overlooked someone and wonder how that was possible. Never the less, stuff happens in life and I am not immune. So next time . . . in the meantime here a brief description of many of those in the discipline.

BENIGNO E. AGUIRRE is a Professor in the Department of Sociology and Criminal Justice at the University of Delaware and a core faculty member of the Disaster Research Center. He obtained his Ph.D. in Sociology at Ohio State University. He is past president of the International Research Committee of Disaster. He has served in committees of the National Science Foundation and has received NSF funding. Aguirre has published in the areas of disasters, ethnic and minority populations, and collective behavior and social change. Some of his recent publications include: "The Sociology of Collective Behavior," in Clifton D. Bryant and Dennis L. Peck, editors, The Handbook of 21st Century Sociology, 2005, Berkeley: Sage; with Russell R. Dynes, James Kendra, Rory Connell, "Institutional Resilience and Disaster Planning for New Hazards: Insights from Hospitals," Journal of Homeland Security and Emergency Management, 2005, 2; "Emergency Evacuations, Panic, and Social Psychology." Psychiatry, 2005, 68 (2): 121-129' with Gabriel Santos, "A Critical Review of Emergency Evacuation Simulation Models," Pp. 27-52 in Richard D. Peacock and Erica D. Kuligowski, editors, Workshop on Building Occupant Movement During Fire Emergencies, June10-11th, 2004; International Journal of Mass Emergencies and Disasters, 2004, 22, 2, 103-115; "Los Desastres en Latinoamérica: Vulnerabilidad y Resistencia." Revista Mexicana de Sociologia, 2004, 66, 3, 485-510.

WILLIAM ANDERSON holds a PhD from the Ohio State University. After serving on the faculty at Arizona State University, he accepted an appointment with the National Science Foundation. Bill is known by all researchers in this discipline as one of those who works with the NSF to support research and disseminate new knowledge.

ALLEN H. BARTON is a pioneer and was a professor at Columbia University. He authored a seminal work entitled Communities in Disaster.

SUSAN CUTTER is a Carolina Distinguished Professor of Geography at the University of South Carolina. She is also the Director of the Hazards Research Lab, a research and training center that integrates geographical information processing techniques with hazards analysis and management. She is the co-founding editor of an interdisciplinary journal, Environmental Hazards, published by Elsevier. She has been working in the risk and hazards fields for more than twenty-five years and is a nationally recognized scholar in this field. She has authored or edited eight books and more than 50 peer-reviewed articles. Her most recent book, American Hazardscapes, for the Joseph Henry Press/National Academy of Sciences, chronicles the increasing hazard vulnerability to natural disaster events in the United States during the last thirty years. In 1999, Dr. Cutter was elected as a Fellow of the American Association for the Advancement of Science (AAAS), a testimonial to her research accomplishments in the field. Her stature within the discipline of geography was recognized by her election as President of the Association of American Geographers in 1999-2000.

RUSSELL R. DYNES is a founding Director, of the Disaster Research Center (DRC) at the Ohio State University. He earned a B.A. and M.A. at the University of Tennessee and his PhD from the Ohio State University. Dr. Dynes has served as chair of the Department of Sociology at the Ohio State University and the University of Delaware. From 1977-82, he was Executive Officer, American Sociological Association in Washington, DC. From 1976-79, he chaired the Committee on International Disaster Assistance, National Academy of Sciences/National Research Council and in 1979, he served as head of the Task Force on Emergency Preparedness and Response for the President's Commission on the Accident at Three Mile Island. From 1986-90, he served as President, International Research Committee on Disasters (RC39), International Sociological Association. He has been a Fulbright lecturer in Egypt, India and Thailand. He has also been a Visiting Professor at University College, Cardiff. Dr. Dynes is the author or editor of ten books, including Organized Behavior in Disaster, Sociology of Disaster and Disasters, Collective Behavior and Social Organization and well over 100 articles, many on disaster related topics. He is not only prolific, but is a pre-eminent, internationally recognized authority in the discipline.

ELAINE ENARSON is an American disaster sociologist currently teaching full-time in the Applied Disaster and Emergency Studies Department of Brandon University in Manitoba, Canada. The author of Woods-Working Women: Sexual Integration in the U.S. Forest Service (1984) and co-editor of the international reader The Gendered Terrain of Disaster: Through Women's Eyes (1998), her research and publications have addressed social vulnerability issues with particular emphasis on women and gender. Among these are studies of the impacts of hurricane Andrew on women, response and preparedness in US and Canadian domestic violence agencies, women's paid and paid work in the Red River Valley flood, gender patterns in flood evacuation, women's human rights in disasters, and the impacts of drought and earthquake on rural women in Gujarat, India. Other publications have focused on gender and employment, international perspectives, strategies for addressing high-risk social groups in local emergency management. Before relocating to Canada, Elaine was lead course developer of a FEMA course on social vulnerability, project manager of a grassroots risk assessment project with women in the Caribbean and director of the on-line Gender and Disaster Sourcebook initiative. She has co-convened numerous workshops on gender and disaster risk reduction and consults with UN agencies on gender and disaster risk reduction. Ijn 2006, Elaine was the recipient of the Mary Fran Myers Gender and Disaster Award. Currently, she is researching the health of farm families affected by BSE ("mad cow" disease), co-editing a second international reader in the field, working on the ISDR's new gender mainstreaming project, developing new courses for Brandon University's students of disaster—and learning to survive the cold on Canada's wonderful prairies.

HENRY W. FISCHER, Professor of Sociology, Director of the Center for Disaster Research & Education (CDRE), Editor of UnScheduled Events, Editor of International Journal of Contemporary Disaster Review, Web Host for the International Journal of Mass Emergencies & Disasters, Program Coordinator for both the Master of Science in Emergency Management (a totally online degree program) as well as the Multi-Disciplinary Minor in Environmental Hazards & Emergency Management. His research specialty is behavioral and organizational response to disasters and terrorism. NSF grants supported work in south Asia after the 2004 tsunami and the U.S. Gulf coast after Hurricane Katrina. His body of work includes the presentation of more than three dozen papers at professional conferences around the world, the publication of more than two dozen scholarly journal articles, three books, two monographs, various consulting projects, e.g., Research Planning, Inc. (for the U.S. Department of Defense), TOPOFF2. He has appeared on CNN, MS-NBC, and radio programs in the U.S. and Canada. His PhD in Sociology was earned at the University of Delaware; he is a member of the American Sociological Association, the International Sociological Association, and the International Research Committee on Disasters.

GREG GUIBERT serves as Project Manager at the Natural Hazards Center, University of Colorado, Boulder. He has a master's of urban and environmental planning from the University of Virginia and a bachelor of arts in geography from Vassar College. His research interests are the impacts of climate change, urban/wildland interface, international hazards planning, sustainable community design and development, environmental quality and conflict, and the intersection of science and public policy.

JOHN HARRALD is the Director of The George Washington University Institute for Crisis, Disaster, and Risk Management (www.gwu.edu/~icdrm) and a Professor of Engineering Management and Systems Engineering in the GWU School of Engineering and Applied Science. He is the Executive Editor of the Journal of Homeland Security and Emergency Management (www.bepress.org/jhsem), and is a member of the National Academy of Sciences, National Research Council's Disaster Roundtable Advisory Committee and a member of the National Research Council's Computer Science and Technology Board's Committee on the use of Information Technology for Crisis and Disaster Management. He is the immediate Past President of The International Emergency Management Society (TIEMS). Dr. Harrald has been actively engaged in the fields of emergency and crisis management and maritime safety and port security and as a researcher in his academic career and as a practitioner during his 22 year career as a U.S. Coast Guard officer, retiring in the grade of Captain. Dr. Harrald received his B.S. in Engineering from the U.S. Coast Guard Academy, a MALS from Wesleyan University, a M.S. from the Massachusetts Institute of Technology where he was an Alfred P. Sloan Fellow, and an MBA and Ph.D. from Rensselaer Polytechnic Institute.

JAMES KENDRA holds a PhD from Rutgers University, he completed post-doctoral work at the University of Delaware's Disaster Research Center where he participated in post-September 11, 2001 research into the response to the terrorist attack on NYC. He is currently on the faculty of North Texas University. His research is supported by NSF funding.

MICHAEL K. LINDELL received his PhD from the University of Colorado (1975); he has over 30 years of experience in the field of disaster research and emergency management. His research focus has been on the processes through which individuals and organizations respond to natural and technological hazards. He has provided technical assistance to government agencies, industry groups, and private corporations in development of emergency plans and procedures. His NSF funded research has included work on response to the Mt. St. Helens eruption, risk perception for the U.S. Department of Energy (national surveys), and real time hurricane evacuation issues. He has an extension list of publications and presentations. Professor Lindell is the current editor of the International Journal of Mass Emergencies and Disasters.

DAVID A. MCENTIRE earned his PhD at the University of Denver. Dr. McEntire is an Associate Professor in the Emergency Administration and Planning Program in the Department of Public Administration at the University of North Texas. He teaches emergency management courses in both the undergraduate and graduate programs. His academic interests include emergency management theory, international disasters, community preparedness, response coordination, and vulnerability reduction. He has received several Quick Response Grants (funded by the National Science Foundation through the Natural Hazards Center at the University of Colorado) which allowed him to conduct research on disasters in Peru, the Dominican Republic, Texas, New York and California. Dr. McEntire is the author of Disaster Response and Recovery (Wiley) and the editor of Disciplines, Disasters and Emergency Management (FEMA). His research has also been published in Public Administration Review, the Australian Journal of Emergency Management, Disasters, the International Journal of Mass Emergencies and Disasters, Journal of Emergency Management, Journal of the Environment and Sustainable Development, Sustainable Communities Review, International Journal of Emergency Management, Towson Journal of International Affairs, Journal of the American Society of Professional Emergency Planners, and the Journal of International and Public Affairs. His articles in Disaster Prevention and Management have received Highly Commended and Outstanding Paper Awards. Dr. McEntire is a former Coordinator of the EADP program. Prior to coming to the University of North Texas in 1999, he attended the Graduate School of International Studies at the University of Denver. While pursuing his degree, he worked for the International and Emergency Services Departments at the American Red Cross.

DENNIS S. MILETI is recently-retired professor and chair of the department of sociology and director emeritus of the Natural Hazards Center. He is author of over 100 publications most of which focus on the societal aspects of mitigation, preparedness, response, and recovery for hazards and disasters. His book Disasters by Design, published in 1999, involved over 130 experts to assess knowledge, research, and policy needs for hazards in the U.S. He has served on a variety of advisory boards, and has co-founder and Co-Editor-in-Chief of the Natural Hazards Review, an interdisciplinary all-hazards journal devoted to bringing together the natural and social sciences, engineering, and the policy communities.

MARY FRAN MYERS was the co-director of the Natural Hazards Center from 1988 through her retirement in 2003. She was focused on maintaining the Center's global reputation as a driving intellectual force in the hazards field. Mary Fran's lifework helped bring about a fundamental change in national and international perspectives regarding hazards and fostered new, far-sighted, creative, and sustainable ways of dealing with extreme environmental events. One of Mary Fran's primary concerns was ensuring that participants from all sectors of the hazards community be represented at the Annual Hazards Research and Applications Workshop. She was par-

ticularly concerned that many who can greatly benefit from and contribute to workshop activities are among the least likely to be able to afford to attend.

DAVID M. NEAL holds a PhD from the Ohio State University, is currently on the faculty of the Oklahoma State University, and serves as Director of the Center for the Study of Disasters and Extreme Events. He has published widely, written numerous scholarly papers and presented his work throughout the world. He research has been supported by various agencies and organizations, including the National Science Foundation.

JOANNE M. NIGG is a Professor of Sociology and the former Director of the Disaster Research Center at the University of Delaware. Since 1975, she has been involved in research on the societal response to natural, technological, and environmental hazards and disasters. Currently, she is a core faculty member of the Disaster Research Center. Dr. Nigg has been a Principal or Co-Principal Investigator on over 20 research projects, totaling over $3.2 million, covering subjects such as: hazard/threat/risk awareness and behavioral response by individuals and organizations; attributions of responsibility for disaster outcomes; factors related to the development of governmental hazard reduction policies and actions; evaluations of hazard and risk reduction programs; risk perceptions and policy preferences among the public and key decision-makers; and disaster recovery of households, businesses and communities. Dr. Nigg also headed a multidisciplinary team that conducted a Congressionally-required public risk assessment for the proposed high level nuclear waste repository at Yucca Mountain in Nevada. She was also a member of the Research Committee (which set the cross-disciplinary research agendas) for the NSF funded Multidisciplinary Center for Earthquake Engineering Research. She is the author, co-author or editor of seven books and over 100 articles, book chapters, reports and papers on individual, organizational, and governmental response to, preparation for, mitigation of, and recovery from natural and technological threats and disasters.

WALTER GILLIS PEACOCK is Director of the Hazards Reduction and Recovery Center and Professor in the Department of Landscape Architecture and Urban Planning and in the Sustainable Coastal Margins Program at Texas A & M University (TAMU). Dr. Peacock holds a Ph.D. in Sociology from the University of Georgia. Prior to joining TAMU, he was a faculty member at Florida International University, in Miami, where he, among other positions, served as Chair of the Department of Sociology and Anthropology and as the co-Director of the Laboratory for Social and Behavioral Research at the International Hurricane Center at Florida International University (FIU). He also was a founding faculty member of the International Hurricane Center at FIU and served for three years as its Director of Research. His research focuses on natural hazards and human systems response to hazards and disaster with an emphasis on social vulnerability, evacuation, and the socio-political ecology of long-term recovery and mitigation. Over the last two years he has been involved in a NOAA sanctioned group, the Hurricane Forecast Social and Economic Working Group, tasked with developing a social science research agenda on hurricane forecast and warning and he was invited to speak to the National Science Foundation's National Science Board on hurricane research needs. His published work has appeared in a variety of journals including American Sociological Review, Natural Hazards Review, the International Journal of Mass Emergencies and Disasters, and Landscape and Urban Planning. He has published two books and his latest, coauthored with Betty Hearn Morrow and Hugh Gladwin, in entitled, Hurricane Andrew: Ethnicity, Gender and the Sociology of Disaster.

LORI PEEK is an assistant professor of sociology at Colorado State University. Lori has authored several articles in the areas of environmental risk, social vulnerability, and disasters. She also served for three years as the assistant co-editor of the Natural Hazards Review Journal. In addition to her interests in environmental sociology and the sociology of disasters, she specializes in the areas of religion, gender, race and ethnicity, social psychology, and ethnographic methods. Lori received her Ph.D. in 2005 from the University of Colorado at Boulder. Her dissertation research focused on the experiences of second-generation Muslim Americans following the events of September 11, 2001. Lori currently works with the Natural Hazards Center to coordinate the Mary Fran Myers Award and the Mary Fran Myers Scholarship.

RON PERRY obtained his PhD from the University of Washington. His research interests include emergency organizations and natural disasters, e.g., citizen response to evacuation warnings. He has been a member of the faculty of the School of Public Affairs at Arizona State University since 1983. His work has been supported by NSF funding, he has served on various commissions examining national issues such as evacuation response to Three Mile Island, he has served as the International Journal of Mass Emergencies and Disasters (1998-2003), and is currently serving as the President of the ISA's International Research Committee on Disasters. He has authored or co-authored 20 books and more than 200 scholarly papers.

BRENDA D. PHILLIPS, Ph.D. is a Senior Researcher with the Center for the Study of Disasters and Extreme Events and is a Full Professor in the Fire and Emergency Management Program, Department of Political Science, at Oklahoma State University where she teaches courses in emergency management, social vulnerability and community relations. Her work on vulnerable populations has been funded multiple times by the National Science Foundation, U.S. Geological Survey and others. Dr. Phillips has given invited presentations to the U.S. National Weather Service, the U.S. National Academies of Science, the New Zealand Ministries of Civil Defence and of Health, and the Australian Emergency Management Institute among others. Her work has been published in numerous scholarly journals, refereed proceedings and books and has been posted on the FEMA Higher Education web site.

JOHN PINE is a faculty member of the Department of Geography and Anthropology at the Louisiana State Univeristy (LUS) where is the head of the LSU Disaster Science and Management academic programs. He has conducted research on various topics in the discipline, is widely published and frequently presents his work at professional conferences.

CARLA PRATER is a Lecturer in the Department of Landscape Architecture and Urban Planning at Texas A&M University. She also serves as Executive Associate Director of the Hazard Reduction & Recovery Center at Texas A&M University where she has worked since 1990. She teaches courses including Organizational and Community Response to Disasters, Analyzing Risk and Hazard Policy, Hazard Mitigation and Disaster Recovery, Introduction to Emergency Management, and Applied Planning. Her research focuses on environmental politics and policy and natural hazards and disasters. Publications include "Risk area accuracy and hurricane evacuation expectations of coastal residents," Environment & Behavior, 2005; "Risk Area Accuracy and Evacuation from Hurricane Bret," Natural Hazards Review, 2004; "Assessing Community Impacts of Natural Disasters," Natural Hazards Review, 2003; "The Politics of Emergency Response and Recovery: Preliminary Observations on Taiwan's 921 Earthquake," Australian Journal of Emergency management, 2002; "Risk Area Residents' Perceptions and Adoption of Seismic Hazard Adjustments," Journal of Applied Social Psychology, 2002;" The Politics of Hazard Mitigation," Natural Hazards Review, 2000. Dr. Prater has a Ph.D. in Political Science from Texas A&M University, 1999; an M.S. in Urban and Regional Planning from Texas A&M University, 1993; as well as a B.A. in Foreign Languages, from Pepperdine University, 1975.

E.L. (HENRY) QUARANTELLI is a founding Director of the Disaster Research Center (DRC) at the Ohio State University in 1963. A native of New York City (b1924), he was Phi Beta Kappa in 1950 and completed his PhD in Sociology (1959) at the University of Chicago. Quarantelli received the AKD Graduate Teaching Award in both 1967 and 1971. He served as both Professor of Sociology and Director of the DRC at the Ohio State University 1963-1984; he continued in both roles at the University of Delaware when the DRC relocated, 1985-1990. He was a Research Professor at the DRC 1990-1998 and Professor Emeritus since 1999. He was the first President of the International Sociological Association's International Research Committee on Disasters, 1982-1986; founder and first editor of the *International Journal of Mass Emergencies and Disasters*, 1983-1987; and received the Charles E. Fritz Career Achievement Award in 1995. He holds numerous memberships in many domestic and foreign disaster-related committees (e.g., Board on Natural Disasters of the National Academy of Sciences and on Scientific Advisory Committee, World Institute for Disaster Risk Management).

He undertook the first systematic disaster field studies in 1949 as part of the National Opinion Research Center (NORC) team at University of Chicago that initiated social science research on disasters. And, he has been the Principal investigator on over 40 research projects mostly from National Science Foundation and the Federal Emergency Management Agency. Others from National Institute of Mental Health, the Air Force Office of Scientific Research, the Health Resources Administration, the Social Science Research Council, the Law Enforcement Assistance Administration, the NHK (Japan) Foundation, NATO, and the Advanced Research Projects Agency.

Quarantelli is the author or editor of 29 books and monographs as well as author of 94 chapters in books, 110 articles and 129+ other publications mostly on disaster topics. He has also been an international consultant, e.g., World Bank, World Health Organization, Greece, Italy, Mexico, Taiwan, Russia, Great Britain and the Netherlands.

He is not only prolific, but is a pre-eminent, internationally recognized authority in the discipline.

HAVIDÁN RODRÍGUEZ is the University of Delaware's Vice Provost of Academic Affairs and the former Director of the Disaster Research Center (DRC). He joined the University of Delaware in 2003 as Director of the DRC and Professor in the Department of Sociology and Criminal Justice. He obtained his Ph.D. in Sociology at the University of Wisconsin. He has vast administrative experience serving as Director of the Center for Applied Social Research (CISA), Associate Dean of Research, Acting Dean of Academic Affairs at the University of Puerto Rico-Mayagüez (UPRM), and Director of the Minority Affairs Program for the American Sociological Association (ASA). Dr. Rodríguez has been a visiting professor at the University of Michigan's Population Fellow's Program (2001-2003) and was selected as the Frey Foundation Distinguished Visiting Professor, at the University of North Carolina-Chapel Hill (Spring, 2002). He also served as the Chair of the Latino/a Sociology Section of the ASA (2003-2004). Currently, he serves as a member of the following committees of the National Research Council of The National Academies: Disaster Roundtables, Committee on Assessing Vulnerabilities Related to the Nation's Chemical Infrastructure, and the Committee on Using Demographic Data and Tools More Effectively to Assist Populations at Risk of Facing Disasters. Dr. Rodríguez has also served on a number of review panels for the National Science Foundation (NSF) and other funding agencies. Dr. Rodríguez has published in the areas of disasters, diversity in higher education, and Latinas/os in the United States. He is the co-editor (along with E. Quarantelli and R. Dynes) of the forthcoming (2006) Handbook of Disaster Research. Some of his recent publications include: Reflections on the United Nations World Conference on Disaster Reduction: How Can We Develop Disaster Resilient Communities (2005); A Long Walk to Freedom and Democracy: Human Rights, Globalization, and Social Injustice (2004); Disasters, Vulnerability, and Society: An International and Multi-Disciplinary Approach (2004 – Invited Editor with Wachtendorf); The Role of Science, Technology, and the Media in the Communication of Risk and Warnings (2004); Disaster Research in the Social Sciences: Lessons Learned, Challenges, and Future Trajectories (2004

– with Wachtendorf and Russell); Communicating Risk and Warnings: An Integrated and Interdisciplinary Research Approach (2004 with Diaz and Aguirre); and Promoting Diversity and Excellence in Higher Education Through Department Change (2002 – with Levine, Howery, and Latoni).

CLAIRE RUBIN, of *Claire Rubin Associates*, teaches at the George Washington University, and is associate editor of the *Journal of Homeland Security and Emergency Management*. She is the author of numerous publications and is widely known for her work in the discipline—an internationally recognized researcher.

JOSEPH SCANLON was on the faculty of Carleton University, Canada. His primary research focus has been media response to disasters, although he has studied a great variety of research topics. He has published numerous scholarly papers and made numerous scholarly presentations throughout the world. He is also past president of the International Research Committee on Disasters (International Sociological Association, Research Committee 39).

ROBERT A. STALLINGS received his PhD in Sociology in 1971 from the Ohio State University. As a graduate student he was a Research Associate at the Disaster Research Center. He served as chair of the Department of Sociology at the University of Evansville (Indiana), 1971-1975. He was on the faculty of the University of Southern California's School of Public Administration (1975-1998) and School of Policy, Planning, and Development (1998-2004) with a joint appointment in the Department of Sociology. He was a member of the Emergency Preparedness and Response Task Force of the President's Commission on the Accident at Three Mile Island. Stallings is the author of several books and book chapters as well as numerous journal articles. During 2002-2006 he served as president of the International Research Committee on Disasters (International Sociological Association, Research Committee 39). He served as editor of the *International Journal of Mass Emergencies and Disasters* (1996-2002).

DEBORAH THOMAS holds a PhD in Geography from the University of South Carolina. She is currently on the faculty of the University of Colorado, Denver.

KATHLEEN J. TIERNEY is Professor in the Department of Sociology and the Institute of Behavioral Sciences and Director of the Natural Hazards Center at the University of Colorado at Boulder. Funded by the National Science Foundation and by a consortium of federal agencies, the Natural Hazards Center has served since 1976 as the main U. S. clearinghouse for information on the societal dimensions of hazards, disasters, and risk. She is a also co-director of the National Consortium for the Study of Terrorism and Responses to Terrorism (START), a DHS academic Center of Excellence that was established in 2005. Tierney is responsible for coordinating the activities of the START working group on the societal dimensions of terrorism, which focus on such topics as risk perception and communication; household, organizational, and community terrorism preparedness within the U. S.; and behavioral and psychosocial consequences of extreme events. Prior to her move to Colorado in 2003, she was Professor of Sociology and Director of the Disaster Research Center at the University of Delaware.

With over twenty-five years of experience conducting research on social and behavioral responses to extreme events, she has studied the social dimensions of many major disasters, including the Loma Prieta, Northridge, and Kobe earthquakes; Hurricanes Hugo and Andrew; the 1993 Midwest floods, and the September 11 terrorist attack on the World Trade Center; and other large-scale natural and technological disaster events. Her current and recent research includes studies on risk communication, business preparedness and the business impacts of disasters, the use of information technologies in disaster response, and the structure of homeland security preparedness networks in U. S. cities.

Tierney is the author of dozens of publications, including articles in The International Journal of Mass Emergencies and Disasters, The Journal of Contingencies and Crisis Management, Sociological Spectrum, Sociological Forum, Research in Social Problems and Public Policy, Pre-hospital and Disaster Medicine, and the Natural Hazards Review. Her publications also include Disasters, Collective Behavior, and Social Organization (1994), co-edited with Russell Dynes, and Facing the Unexpected: Disaster Preparedness and Response in the United States (2001), co-authored with Michael K. Lindell and Ronald W. Perry. She is currently collaborating with Prof. William Waugh on the second edition of the International City and County Management Association's volume on Emergency Management: Principles and Practice for Local Government. Her publications on Hurricane Katrina include a book chapter in the edited volume On Risk and Disaster: Lessons from Hurricane Katrina (2005) and an article that appeared in the March, 2006 special Katrina issue of the Annals of the American Academy of Political and Social Science. Tierney's other new publications include chapters in the Handbook of Disaster Research, focusing on businesses and disasters and on the ways in which post-September 11th policies have affected emergency management in the U. S.

Tierney is a member of the National Construction Safety Team Advisory Committee, which oversaw the National Institute of Standards and Technology's investigation of the World Trade Center disaster. She also served on the National Academy of Sciences/National Research Council Committee on Disaster Research in the Social Sciences.

JOSEPH E. TRAINOR is a professional Staff Researcher at DRC and a Doctoral Candidate in the Department of Sociology and Criminal Justice at the University of Delaware. He has been involved in number of funded research projects focused on issues related to the social and organizational aspects of disasters and emergency management. He was the principal analyst in a network study of multi-organizational coordination after the September 11th World Trade Center attacks and was the lead graduate researcher on a project to examine the organizational and institutional development and operation of ESF#9/USAR in the United States. He also has extensive field research experience as part of a reconnaissance team that traveled to India and Sri Lanka immediately following the December, 2004 Indian Ocean tsunami and was the Lead researcher for DRC's reconnaissance effort to examine the social aspects of Hurricane Katrina. Trainor's foci include: the impact of organizational design on disaster response (including NIMS); issues relate to multi-organizational vertical and horizontal coordination; the integration of research and practice; and the general socio-behavioral response to disasters.

TRICIA WACHTENDORF is an assistant professor of Sociology at the University of Delaware and a core faculty member at the Disaster Research Center - the world's oldest research center devoted to the social science aspects of disasters. Her research over the past decade has focused on such topics as transnational disaster coordination, community based approaches to disaster mitigation and partnership building, and multi-organizational responses to natural and terrorist-induced disasters. In 2001, Dr. Wachtendorf led DRC's two month quick-response research at key operation facilities in New York City following the World Trade Center disaster and subsequently conducted interviews with key decision makers involved with the response effort. Her publications from this study have focused on creativity, improvisation, convergence, and resilience. She also authored *Improvising 9/11: Organizational Improvisation Following the Attacks on the World Trade Center* in which she examines the extent to which preplanning facilitated the response and the extent to which the response demanded organizational creativity, adaptation, and reproductive improvisation strategies to cope with emergent needs.

In addition to research activities surrounding the September 11th, 2001 attack, Wachtendorf has been involved in numerous other projects. She played an instrumental role in DRC's assessment of a FEMA supported community mitigation initiative (known as Project Impact). This study included interviews and focus groups with state and local government officials, private sector representatives, non-governmental organization leaders, and community participants from across the United States. She has studied some of the successes and challenges of this American mitigation program to generate changes in the way communities plan, organize around, and participate in mitigation measures. While at DRC, she has also worked on projects examining the risk perception and willingness to pay for loss-reduction measures in California as well as the long term disaster impacts on business districts in California and Florida.

Tricia Wachtendorf is particularly interested in transnational emergencies and cross-cultural disaster research. In 1997, she conducted a two year study of the cross-border interaction that took place between Canada and the United States during the Red River Flood and authored a report for the International Joint Commission based on this work.

WILLIAM WAUGH is on the faculty of the Andrew Young School of Policy Studies, the Department of Public Administration and Urban Studies, at Georgia State University. He is editor of the *Journal of Emergency Management*. He has published numerous scholarly papers.

GARY WEBB holds a PhD in Sociology from the University of Delaware and is currently on the faculty of the Department of Sociology at Oklahoma State University. He has published numerous scholarly papers and is the Secretary-Treasurer of the ISA's International Research Committee on Disasters.

DENNIS E. WENGER is interested in the areas of sociology, natural and technological disaster research, hazards mitigation, urban ecology, collective behavior and mass communication, and disaster and emergency planning.

Dr. Wenger has written or co-authored several books and articles including Hurricane Bret Post-storm Assessment: A Review of the Utilization of Hurricane Evacuation Studies and Information Dissemination, Texas: Texas A&M University Hazard Reduction & Recovery Center, 2000; Respuestas Individuales e Institucionales Ante ed Sismo de 1985 en la Ciudad de Mexico, Mexico: Cenapred, 1994; "A Test of the Emergent Norm Theory of Collective Behavior," Sociological Forum, 1998; "The Social Organization of Search and Rescue: Evidence from the Guadalajara Gasoline Explosion," International Journal of Mass Emergencies and Disasters, 1995.

Wenger received his BS, MA and PhD from the Ohio State University.

GILBERT WHITE was the Gustavson Distinguished Professor Emeritus of Geography at the University of Colorado from 1980 until his death in 2006. Prior to that, from 1970 to 1978, he was Professor of Geography and the Director of the Institute of Behavioral Science at the university. He was also the founder and Director of the university's Natural Hazards Research and Applications Information Center from 1976 to 1984 and again from 1992 to 1994. He received his undergraduate and graduate degrees from the University of Chicago, and his doctoral dissertation, Human Adjustment to Floods, has been called the most influential ever written by an American geographer. "Floods are 'acts of God,'" he wrote, "but flood losses are largely acts of man." Gilbert subsequently served from 1934 to 1940 in the New Deal administration of Franklin D. Roosevelt as the secretary to the Mississippi Valley Committee, National Resources Committee, and National Resources Planning Board. From 1940 to 1942 he worked in the Bureau of the Budget, Executive Office of the President. He published numerous papers, books and made countless presentations during his distinguished career.

SEVERAL KEY JOURNALS IN DISASTER RESEARCH

International Journal of Mass Emergencies & Disasters
www.ijmed.org
Editor: Michael K. Lindell
Web Host: Henry W. Fischer
The journal (IJMED) is published by the International Sociological Association (ISA), a non-profit association for scientific purposes in the field of sociology and social sciences. As the official journal of RC39, the publication focuses on the social and behavioral aspects of relatively sudden collective stress situations typically referred to as disasters or mass emergencies. For the first time, this journal is being offered to those outside the sociological community in the hopes of greater educational and professional understanding of disasters.

International Journal Disaster Prevention & Management: Disaster Prevention and Management
The journal sets out to advance the available knowledge in the fields of disaster prevention and management and to act as an integrative agent for extant methodologies and activities relating to disaster emergency and crisis management. Publishing high quality, refereed papers, the journal supports the exchange of ideas, experience and practice between academics, practitioners and policy-makers.

Journal of Contingencies and Crisis Management
Editor: Ira Helsloot
The journal is an invaluable source of information on all aspects of contingency planning, scenario analysis and crisis management in both corporate and public sectors. It focuses on the opportunities and threats facing organizations and presents analysis and case studies of crisis prevention, crisis planning, recovery and turnaround management. With contributions from world-wide sources including corporations, governmental agencies, think tanks and influential academics, this publication provides a vital platform for the exchange of strategic and operational experience, information and knowledge.

Journal of Homeland Security and Emergency Management
Executive Editor: John R. Harrald
Managing Editor: Claire B. Rubin
The journal publishes original, innovative, and timely articles describing research or practice in the fields of homeland security and emergency management. JHSEM publishes not only peer-reviewed articles, but also news and communiqués from researchers and practitioners, and book/media reviews.

Content comes from a broad array of authors representing many professions, including emergency management, engineering, political science and policy, decision science, and health and medicine, as well as from emergency management and homeland security practitioners. The journal seeks to provide new information and understanding of emergency management (EM) in the homeland security (HS) environment, and to foster a community of persons who share these interests.

Journal of Emergency Management

Editor-in-Chief: William L. Waugh

The journal explores the topics of emergency management, disaster response, case studies, terrorism, emergency wireless messaging, flood relief, infrastructure protection. It is a professional, bi-monthly journal with a simple but urgent goal: to better equip all those responsible for emergency preparedness and response to deal effectively with everything from acts of terror, fires, floods, and weather emergencies to gas explosions and catastrophic accidents on land, in the air, or at sea.

Chapter 3

Behavioral Response to Disaster

THE PUBLIC PERCEPTION OF HOW PEOPLE BEHAVE IN A DISASTER

The Disaster Mythology

Would you be afraid to arrive on the scene immediately after a disaster has struck an area? What is your image of the behavioral response of the survivors and those who come to their aid? Most people in the United States believe in what disaster researchers have described as a *disaster mythology* (Quarantelli & Dynes, 1972; Quarantelli & Dynes, 1970; Wenger, et al, 1975). Most of us assume that *individuals* cease to act in a predictable, orderly fashion, i.e., that the norms which govern our behavior collapse into Durkheim's anomie. They are expected to flee in panic, suffer from psychological dependency and disaster shock. It is often believed that evacuation of these people must not be called too soon for fear of causing massive flight behavior. It is believed that shelters overflow beyond capacity with organizers unable to deal with the mob mentality. Both survivors and those converging to the scene are believed to be driven by base, depraved instincts. These individuals are commonly perceived as likely to loot property, price gouge one another, and generally behave in other selfish ways--most of which are imagined to spread from individual to individual in a contagious fashion. [For a sample of the literature outlining the disaster mythology, see Quarantelli and Dynes, 1972; Wenger, et al, 1975; Scanlon, 1978; Wenger, et al, 1980; Bryan, 1982; Aga Khan, 1983; Stallings, 1984; Wenger, 1985; Drabek, 1986; Wenger and Friedman, 1986; Johnson, 1987; Quarantelli, 1987; Rubin and Palm, 1987; Fischer, 1988(a), 1988(b), and 1989; Fischer and Trowbridge, 1992; Fischer and Drain, 1993; Fischer, 1994.]

Panic Flight

The literature on disaster mythology notes that the proverbial man in the street, as well as many media and disaster management personnel for that matter, believe that when a disaster occurs [potential] victims will panic and engage in any behavior deemed necessary at the moment to facilitate their escape. Panic flight is viewed as a natural outcome of the intense fear experienced by [potential] victims, i.e., the intense fear automatically results in irrational flight, the running in any direction without thought given to a rational escape route. Evacuations are sometimes delayed, until it is deemed absolutely necessary, because officials do not want to cause an unnecessary panic. When the nuclear incident began at Three Mile Island, near Harrisburg, Pennsylvania in 1979, certain emergency personnel and political leaders cautioned nearby residents that there was no need to panic. When an evacuation was considered and then recommended for pregnant women and preschool children, officials suggested to their citizens that the voluntary evacuation be done in an orderly manner--that there was, once again, no need to panic. The Presidential Commission on TMI later learned that there had been some hesitation to call for any evacuation as they feared the behavioral response problems which they believed would ensue.

The research literature (Drabek, 1968; Quarantelli, 1981) has established that individuals do not attempt to flee when there is not a perceived avenue for escape. When there is a perceived avenue of escape, and when the opportunity to use it is seen as diminishing, there is a rational tendency to avail oneself of the opportunity to use it. I personally lived within twenty miles of TMI when the 1979 incident occurred. When I became concerned about the impact of TMI on our two young daughters, my wife and I packed up our family of four and left for my parents-in-law who lived on Long Island (had the meltdown continued, the anticipated plume would have drifted over Long Island—sometimes you just cannot win). Those leaving the area were not mindlessly fleeing in fear, they made a rational decision to be prudent and seek a safer location. This is normative, orderly behavior. It is not panic flight.

Looting

Looting is perhaps the most expected behavioral response to disaster. Both print and broadcast media personnel report on the alleged looting incidents, on the steps being taken to prevent it, and, alternately, on how unusual it was for the community in question to not be preyed upon by looters. The National Guard is usually activated ostensibly to protect against looting, in addition to performing other tasks. Pass systems are typically developed to keep individuals from entering the stricken area in order to keep looters out. What often occurs (Fischer, Schaeffer & Trowbridge, 1992) is victims are also prevented (or at least feel harassed) from returning to their homes to quickly save what property they can.

Many people refuse to evacuate because they fear their property will be stolen. They often arm themselves and threaten to shoot any unknown person entering their property. Some drown as a hurricane's storm surge impacts their home. During Hurricane Gilbert (Fischer, 1989), one city manager took very public precautions to prevent looting. Even though he knew that looting rarely occurs, he took such precautions primarily to convince citizens that it was safe to evacuate.

Price Gouging

When Fischer and Martin (Fischer, 1989) were in Texas during Hurricane Gilbert, they were watching a local evening news broadcast which reported that a couple of local merchants had been arrested for charging an exorbitant price for the plywood that residents needed to protect their windows during the pending hurricane. The researchers immediately telephoned the city police and asked how many had been arrested for price gouging. The response: "none." The broadcast had correctly reported earlier that the local city council had passed an ordinance that day to protect against price gouging. The broadcast media focused a fair amount of its hurricane coverage on this kind of expected deviant behavior. Citizens believe it commonly occurs, media personnel report it, further reinforcing the perception, and local leaders take steps to prevent and respond to it. It rarely occurs, however. When it does, it tends to be done by outsiders who may converge to the area. Local citizens and especially local merchants rarely exhibit such behavior during a disaster event.

Contagion

It is frequently believed that those who converge to the disaster scene, while they may not arrive with malice in their hearts, may join in the looting and price gouging as the deviance is believed to spread through the crowd like a contagious disease. People are believed to be caught up in the selfish frenzy of the moment, losing control, joining the mob as LeBon (1895) had once described the emergence of collective behavior.

Martial Law

It has frequently been reported and expected that martial law is commonly declared in an effort to restore or maintain order in the aftermath of a disaster. The expected deviant behavior is viewed as rendering such a radical response as necessary and understandable. In fact, martial law has *never* been declared in the United States in response to a disaster event[1].

---

[1] Unfortunately an error appeared in the 2nd edition of this book when it was stated that martial law had been declared once in the U.S. when in fact it has never been.

Psychological Dependency

The perceived scene of the disaster area is usually one in which victims are too "out of it" to know what to do, they are often portrayed as being in need of direction. It is commonly believed that survivors are incapable of functioning at all after their experience (Fischer, 1988). For example, it is believed that residents must either be organized by outsiders in order to begin the body search, assessments of damage, assisting the injured, and beginning the cleanup. Actually, the survivors have usually been doing all of these, quite well before the emergency organizations arrive and take over. Some often feel resentful when these organizations take the credit for helping all these alleged psychologically dependent people who could do nothing for themselves (Quarantelli, 1976).

Disaster Shock

In conjunction with psychological dependency, survivors are also often perceived as being in a state of shock as a result of their experience. "Friends of a friend" of a victim often report that the survivor was so incapacitated that he sat on "the remains of his front porch for days, garden hose in hand, ready to wash the mud from the flood away, but was unable to move" (Fischer, 1988). Fischer also found other third person reports have claimed that survivors spent hours walking essentially in circles not knowing where they were, what happened, or what to do. Reporters often (mis)interpret the body language of those they observe at a disaster site. Some survivors may appear to be in shock, while they are actually exhausted and, therefore, are resting.

Evacuation Behavior

Ask a potential evacuee if he is concerned about evacuating from a city when the forecast is for a hurricane to impact the area and the likely response is:

> Yes I am concerned; I don't want to join all those crazies as they flee, they'll crowd and push each other off the roads trying to escape the path of the storm . . . why, they might even pack a gun, and worse yet, use it! (Fischer, 1989)

Once again, deviant behavior is assumed. This stereotype has emerged in American society which permeates virtually all levels of public and private life. Average citizens believe it, media personnel believe it, screen writers and movie directors believe it, government officials and even many emergency preparedness personnel believe it . . . and worse, prepare for it as if it were reality. Hollywood versions of disasters typically portray a version of the above reinforcing this misperception for all who view their work (Quarantelli, 1985).

Shelter Use

Along with the belief that citizens flee an area when told to do so, it is commonly assumed that when they do leave they go to the designated public shelters. It is further assumed that the shelters are, therefore, overcrowded with the thousands of evacuees. Some shelters are fully utilized, but many, perhaps most, go under-used. Emergency planners who are aware of this tendency develop shelter utilization plans that open shelters on an "as needed basis," i.e., when the first shelter is filling, they activate a second, and so forth. This is the pattern that Fischer and Martin (1989) observed in Texas during Hurricane Gilbert.

Death, Injury & Damage Estimates

When the Loma Prieta (San Francisco) earthquake occurred during the 1989 World Series, the first published death count was 272. This figure was broadcast and printed throughout the United States, usually as the lead story or headline. Approximately two weeks later when the final official death count was determined it did not appear on most of the evening news programs. Some newspapers did report it, but the brief stories usually were found deep inside the paper. The final, official death count was 67. The pattern of overestimating is typical. While there are those occasions, e.g., Hurricane Andrew, where underestimates occur, the more common pattern is for death, injury and damage estimates to be dramatically revised downward some weeks after the event. In all fairness, it is difficult to get accurate information. Rumor affects the count. Sometimes the same people are counted two or more times. There is, of course, an advantage to having high property damage estimates in that the site is more likely to be declared a federal disaster area resulting in federal aid or low-cost loans for rebuilding.

The disaster mythology includes a belief in looting, price gouging, panic flight, deviant and selfish behavior, the necessity of martial law, psychological dependency and disaster shock. Shelters are seen as overused and evacuations are seen as likely to contribute to panic flight. It is also assumed that the death, injury and damage estimates are essentially accurate. The research literature has established that these beliefs are largely myth, thus they are collectively characterized as the *disaster mythology*. The Federal Emergency Management Agency (FEMA), disaster researchers, and well trained emergency personnel know the mythology is something that they must be aware of in order to anticipate the public's actual behavioral response, e.g., hesitancy to evacuate due to fear that their property will be looted. Well designed disaster plans attempt to counter the public's belief in the mythology and respond to the actual behavioral response their community will encounter during a disaster.

Actual Behavioral Response to Disaster

What can we conclude then about our popular perception of how people behave after a disaster occurs? As has been explained, this perceived tendency for the depravity of mankind to emerge during disasters is not supported by the evidence. The community of individuals does not break down. The norms which we tend to follow during normal time hold during emergency time. In fact, during emergency time the "best within us" is usually exhibited as we become much more altruistic. The sociological literature on disaster documents that individuals tend to become altruistic during time of disaster. Survivors share their tools, their food, their equipment, and especially their time. Groups of survivors tend to emerge to begin automatically responding to the needs of one another. They search for the injured, the dead, and they begin cleanup activities. Police and fire personnel stay on the job, putting the needs of victims and the duty they have sworn to uphold before their own personal needs and concerns. The commonly held view of behavior is incorrect.

Examples of How Myths Do Not Hold

Hurricane Elena impacted upon Gulfport, Louisiana in September 1985 after threatening both Florida and Alabama. Gulfport has been the frequent target of hurricanes. As a result the city was probably as prepared as any impacted area has ever been. The Gulfport emergency management apparatus is very sophisticated with a state of the art Emergency Operations Center (EOC), a model written disaster plan, and highly trained emergency personnel. While the EOC responded to the hurricane's impact by managing the organizational response, there were, of course, many individual citizens who responded to their own and their neighbor's needs. After impact, the streets were flooded and blocked by debris for several hours. Electricity and water service were disrupted for several days. Normal time activities were interrupted for days or, in some instances, for weeks. While looting and price gouging were reported in the media, police records do not indicate any confirmed reports or arrests for such behaviors. The on-site disaster research field team observed that while the National Guard was called out to "prevent looting," its primary role was to direct traffic and help clear debris.

The National Hurricane Center, located in Florida, monitors the path of hurricanes which may threaten the United States. It alerts citizens of any possible impending impact in an attempt to enable potential victims to secure their possessions and find appropriate shelter either in their homes, at another site in the community or through evacuation to another area altogether. The problem with evacuations, however, is that in many communities, potential victims usually have a strong hesitancy to leave their homes for an evacuation location. Many potential evacuees risk injury or death by staying home to "ride it out." Quarantelli and Dynes (1972) note this tendency. Fischer, et al., 1993, observed the same pattern during a technological emergency when a residential community was threatened by potential toxic

gases from a major fire in Ephrata, Pennsylvania, in May 1990. Fischer observed
the same pattern during a major fire in Philadelphia in 1991.

Some areas regularly threatened by hurricanes develop a disaster subculture
whereby citizens celebrate the impending storm by throwing a "hurricane party."
These parties may involve going to the beach, beer in hand, to watch for "the big
waves to come in." They may, alternately, take a keg of beer up to a nearby lookout
to watch the winds blow in. These partygoers may become victims as the storm impacts the area. They had believed that the storm would not exceed anything in their
past experience. When it does, the partygoers may be in trouble. When the volcano
Mount St. Helens was threatening to erupt, Harry Truman, a local resident, was
interviewed by a TV newsman. "Why don't you leave, you've been advised to
evacuate in order to save yourself?" Harry responded that he had lived here for decades and never had a problem, "how bad could it be?" Harry died in the explosion
and lava flow. He is buried under the debris.

If potential victims do evacuate, they tend to relocate with relatives or friends.
The next most likely alternative is staying in a motel. Their least likely choice is the
high school gym, the usual evacuation site provided by the community.

Survivors are often believed to exist in a state of shock as a result of their experience (Fischer, 1988). Third person reports have claimed that survivors spent
hours walking essentially in circles not knowing where they were, what happened,
or what to do (Fischer, 1988). The sociology of disaster literature (see for example,
Quarantelli and Dynes, 1972), challenges this view that victims are usually overwhelmed by disaster shock and become psychologically dependent upon outsiders.
Survivors have actually been found to normally behave quite rationally and are the
first to respond to their needs and the needs of their neighbors.

Looting is perhaps *the* behavior most expected by the public and officials. Police departments usually talk about the fear and incidence of looting, the media report stories of its occurrence, and Governors call out the National Guard to "protect
against" it. Potential victims or survivors often report that they will not leave their
homes because they fear looting. They paint signs which read: "DON'T LOOT OR
WE'LL SHOOT!" While looting does sometimes occur, concern over it far exceeds
the rate at which it actually takes place. Unfortunately, excessive time and resources
are often expended on looting which could be better employed in mitigating against
and responding to higher priorities.

When the average American visualizes a disaster scene, he thinks of the depraved behavior acted out by what is commonly seen as a selfish, self-centered human species which is believed to prey upon itself when disaster victims are vulnerable. We picture the earthquake tremors, the terror of the victims and survivors, and
then the convergence of human vultures to the scene for the purpose of extracting
the personal belongings of those poor afflicted people. Our proud National Guard is
seen as the thread that holds humanity together in this hour of need. There normally
is a convergence. The first converging wave of citizens usually consists of emergency response personnel and average citizens seeking to honestly, altruistically
help the victims. The second wave consists of those seeking to observe and person-

ally survey the damage to the area. This second wave is not altruistic, but they are normally not seeking to separate property from the rightful owners. Normal time norms apparently direct many Americans to satisfy the self, but disaster time norms direct us to behave in a selfless fashion. Many confuse the two time periods and reverse the normative response evidenced by the majority of participants. Altruism is the norm during disaster periods.

Both average citizens and disaster response personnel should be relieved, as this means that in time of disaster we can expect better from one another rather than worse. We can also prepare to utilize our resources in a more efficient manner. For example, rather than emphasizing prevention of looting and price gouging, time and scarce financial resources can be more effectively used to devise strategies which will get the potential victims out of their homes and evacuated when there is truly a need to do so. During the TMI incident this author was fearful of what would happen if all of those living within the twenty-five mile radius of the power plant had been ordered to evacuate. The possibility of massive traffic congestion resulting from evacuees fleeing the area toting their guns for protection was considered real. The fear that whatever was left behind would be stolen by looters was also prevalent. Neither, however, occurred, and the research findings do not justify these concerns.

Research Findings in the Literature

In sharp contrast to the image usually perceived, survivors are not apathetic; they begin search and rescue activities themselves; they are very calm and do not panic (Perry, Lindell, and Greene, 1981:162). Looting behavior is exceedingly rare following disaster, yet the belief that it normally does occur impacts upon the behavioral response of survivors in that "when encouraged to evacuate their homes, substantial proportions of families fear looting and refuse to leave" (Dynes and Quarantelli, 1975). Perry, Greene, and Lindell (1980:446) observed that fear of looting was one of many reasons constraining potential victims and survivors from evacuating, perhaps not the primary reason, but a concern. Wenger et al., (1975:45) documented that " . . . the myths about disaster are prevalent and widespread, . . . individuals expect looting to occur, panic flight to exist, and disaster shock to be present." Further research observed that when residents in communities which experienced disasters were tested for their knowledge of disaster behavior, they "did not score very highly, averaging about thirty percent (30%) correct answers on the scale of disaster knowledge" (Wenger, James, and Faupel, 1980:89). These researchers did find, however, that "the residents of the three disaster communities do evidence higher levels of disaster knowledge than the residents from the disaster-free area (1980:89)." "The highest scores are found for those respondents for whom personal [disaster] experience or public education programs are the most salient source of information" (1980:90).

FIRST CASE STUDY: EVACUATION BEHAVIOR: WHY DO SOME EVACUATE, WHILE OTHERS DO NOT? A CASE STUDY OF THE EPHRATA, PENNSYLVANIA EVACUATION

Abstract

Evacuation is commonly used to mitigate victimization from a variety of disaster agents. It is important that authorities gain an accurate understanding of the circumstances under which citizens will evacuate. The authors sought to test the efficacy of evacuation message clarity and frequency, authority type, the accuracy of past warnings, and the impact of the presence of children in the home as viable variables in effecting an evacuation response. The evacuation response was found to be more likely to occur if the potential victim was ordered to do so, if the potential victim was contacted frequently (more than once) by the proper authority (as perceived by the potential victim), if past warnings were perceived as being accurate, and dependent children were in the home. Respondents from eighty-three households (N=83) in Ephrata, Pennsylvania (USA) were interviewed after a major fire emergency threatened residents of three neighborhoods contiguous to the site (Fischer, et al., 1995).

The Event

Shortly after midnight fire was detected at the Hamilton Distributing Company and Ephrata Paint Store in Ephrata, Pennsylvania, USA (12:20 a.m., May 1, 1990). Fifteen fire companies and ambulance crews, officials from the state Department of Environmental Resources (DER), the Pennsylvania Fish Commission, and the Lancaster County Hazardous Materials Team responded to this major fire emergency. The blaze resulted in a $1.6 million loss. A DER spokesperson indicated that their major concern with this fire was the immediate danger posed to the surrounding community and environment. The DER feared that toxic fumes were being released into the environment (air, land, water) as the paints and solvents stored in the building burned during the night long blaze which was not brought under control until 4:30 a.m. Mineral spirits, xylene and naphtha, when burned produce toxic fumes. If inhaled, these fumes can cause varied symptoms, including dizziness, drowsiness, nausea, vomiting and abdominal pain. It can also cause irritation to the eyes, nose and throat.

The concern for the impact of possible toxic fumes was particularly acute since the burning building was contiguous to three neighborhoods. Shortly after arriving on scene, emergency personnel decided to order an evacuation of one neighborhood, suggested an evacuation of another, and decided the third was not in danger. This third neighborhood had initially been downwind, but was upwind by the time the emergency crews had arrived and began to organize a response to the emergency event. Emergency personnel went door-to-door to notify each household that an immediate evacuation had been ordered (or suggested, in the case of the second neighborhood). Due to the time of day, most residents were at home and asleep when the fire began. Many had been awakened by the fire sirens and exploding paint canisters, while others were awakened by emergency personnel knocking on their door. Few slept through the entire event.

Research Focus and Methodology

The proximity of the toxic fire to residents who experienced three distinctly different responses by emergency response officials provided a unique opportunity to assess the circumstances under which potential victims are likely to evacuate. By 9:00 a.m., less than nine hours after the blaze was first discovered, a three-person field team from Millersville University of Pennsylvania (USA) was onsite to examine the nature of the emergency event, its impact on the surrounding community, and the community response to the emergency. After completing field interviews of emergency officials (fire, police, emergency management officials, HazMat officials) and numerous residents of the evacuated area, the field team decided to focus on the evacuation response. The team developed an interview guide and during the next three months it interviewed residents of the two contiguous neighborhoods which had received either an order or suggestion to evacuate. The interviewers sought to speak with an adult residing in each household to discover when and how each household became aware of the fire, how the members first responded, if they were ordered to evacuate, if and how they found out about the evacuation, and if they did, in fact, evacuate. Three attempts were made to arrange and complete an interview for each household. There were a total of 156 households in the two neighborhoods. Eighty-four (84) homes were located in the area where the evacuation was ordered and seventy-two (72) households were located in the area where an evacuation was merely suggested. Interviews were completed for eighty-three (83) households which resulted in an overall response rate of 53%. We were able to interview 67% of those households which were ordered to evacuate and 38% of the households who received only an evacuation suggestion.

After completing the interviews, the field team sought to assess the extent to which the evacuation behavior conformed to that predicted by the research literature on warning messages. Researchers have long argued that disaster warnings must be conceptualized as a social process (see, for example, Williams, 1956; Mileti, 1975; Mileti, et al., 1975; Janis and Mann, 1977; Perry, 1985; Drabek, 1986; Fischer, et al., 1995). "The initial response to a warning is disbelief," as the literature notes (Drabek, 1969 & 1986; Moore, et al., 1963; Fritz and Mathewson, 1957). If the disaster event was unexpected, e.g., the case of a rapid onset disaster agent such as a tornado, and if the level of emergency preparedness is low, most people tend to continue in their normal routine when first warned of an impending disaster, as they disbelieve the warning whether it comes from an authority or not (Quarantelli, 1980; Perry, et al., 1981). If the warning message appears to the listener as vague, their tendency to disbelieve it is increased (Mileti, et al., 1975; Drabek, 1986; Perry, et al., 1981; Fritz, 1957; Fischer, 1994; Fischer, et al., 1995).

Several variables appear to increase the likelihood of a warning being taken seriously and appropriately acted upon. These variables include the clarity of the warning message, i.e., specificity of the nature of the hazard and what the listener is directed to do in response to it (Perry, et al., 1982); the consistency of the warning message with other warning messages, i.e., media, weather services, local authorities, family members seem to all be giving the same message (Mileti, et al., 1975; Drabek, 1986; Fritz, 1957; Demerath, 1957; Fischer, et al., 1995); the frequency of the warnings (Mileti, 1975; Drabek, 1969 & 1986; Perry, et al., 1981; Fritz, 1981; Drabek and Boggs, 1968; Fischer, et al., 1995); the type of authority who is giving the message, e.g., the media is believed more than the police or fire personnel, yet the police/fire personnel are believed more than friends or family (Drabek, 1986; Fischer, et al., 1995); the accuracy of past warnings, i.e., if they accurately forecast the disaster agent's direction and impact (Drabek, 1986; Haas, et al., 1976; Foster, 1980; Fischer, et al., 1995); and the frequency of the disaster agent, e.g., if tornadoes frequently strike the area (Drabek, 1986; Anderson, 1969; Fischer, 1994; Fischer, et al., 1995).

The present study sought to assess the extent to which the literature on warning messages, and their impact on appropriate response, was applicable in explaining the evacuation response to the Ephrata fire emergency. The current study assessed the impact of message clarity and frequency, the type of authority giving the message, and the accuracy of past warnings in effecting an evacuation response.

Demographic Description of Impacted Area

The households interviewed in the Ephrata fire evacuation study consisted primarily of working class residents with three out of four heads of household (74%) holding jobs thus classified (please see Table 2.1). The respondents were primarily Protestant (81%), Caucasian (98%) females (69%) who were married (86%) with children living at home (51%) and had completed no more than a high school education (68%). They ranged in age from 18 to 86, with the average age being 49. A standard deviation of sixteen years resulted in two-thirds of the respondents falling between 33 and 65 years of age.

Fire Information Source and First Response

Most households reportedly were asleep when the fire began (81%, please see Table 2.2). More than two-thirds found out about the fire in one of three ways: they either discovered the fire themselves (37%) as they were awakened by the noise, or they were awakened by another family member (22%) within the household, or they were awakened by a neighbor (11%) who alerted them. A fourth of the households became aware of the fire only when emergency personnel came to their door to either order or suggest an evacuation. The most common response (64%) when learning of the fire was to converge to the scene. Unfortunately, this common response in such emergencies can exacerbate the very concern which motivated the DER to order or suggest an evacuation, i.e., exposure to toxic fumes. During the interview process, some of the respondents showed the interviewers burn wholes in their clothing from the hot ash that landed on them while they were at the scene of the fire. When asked why they converged and stayed to watch, several indicated they "hadn't been told to evacuate yet." Clearly, they were not considering the possible danger resulting from toxic fumes at that point.

Evacuation Information Source and Frequency of Contact

The overwhelming majority (84%) of the households did find out about the evacuation during the course of the fire (please see Table 2.3). Almost two-thirds (64%) discovered an evacuation had been ordered or suggested when emergency personnel came to their home. Approximately half of the remaining households (18%) were alerted to the evacuation from a family member, friend, or neighbor. Almost no one was alerted by the media (2%) and the remaining households (16%) never became aware of the evacuation during the emergency (most of these were not home at the time; a few slept through the event and did not hear the emergency personnel at their front door).

Almost two-thirds of those interviewed (61%) received the direct order to evacuate, approximately half of the remaining interviewed households (17%) were given the suggestion to evacuate by emergency personnel, and the remaining interviewed households (22%) were not contacted directly by emergency personnel (some heard from others, some did not hear at all). The number of times the respondents were contacted about the evacuation ranged from zero to three times. Almost two-thirds (64%) reported being contacted once, approximately one in five households (22%) were reportedly not contacted; the others were contacted two (11%) or three (2%) times.

Evacuation Behavior

More than two-thirds (69%) of the households indicated they did evacuate eventually (please see Table 2.4). Well over half (60%) waited until they were told to evacuate, before doing so. Only one in ten households (9%) left immediately after learning of the fire and before they were told to leave. Respondents who did evacuate were most likely to leave within 15 minutes (41%) of receiving the evacuation instructions; the other evacuees (27%) left within an hour, the remaining respondents did not evacuate.

The households were far more likely to leave if they had been told to do so by emergency personnel (47%) than if they had been told about the evacuation by family or friends (22%). Most of those who did evacuate (56%) stayed with family or friends. While only one in ten households (12%) evacuated to and stayed at the public shelter, a third of those who eventually stayed with family or friends did initially evacuate to the shelter. Within an hour of arriving these individuals made arrangements to stay with family or friends.

Those who evacuated tended to stay away from their home for an entire day (46%). When asked why they returned home when they did, it was not because they had been told it was safe to do so through an emergency personnel press release (17%). Respondents typically returned to the area and asked emergency personnel if it was safe to return (32%), some decided on their own it was time to return home (13%), or asked a family member if it was safe (7%). A third (31%) did not evacuate at all.

Factors Impacting Upon Evacuation Decisions

We sought to determine if evacuation behavior varied by source of evacuation information, by the number of times contacted about the evacuation order/suggestion, by the neighborhood (ordered versus suggested), if the respondent was personally contacted by emergency personnel, and if dependent children were present in the household. The type of authority (Mileti, 1975; Drabek, 1969 & 1986; Perry and Greene, 1983; Fischer, et al., 1995) has been found to impact on evacuation behavior in the following manner: the media is believed more than the police or fire personnel, while the police and fire personnel are believed more than friends or family. In the current evacuation study, it was found that media played virtually no role in providing the respondents with fire or evacuation information (please refer to Tables 2.2 and 2.3 again). This is probably due to the time of day during which the fire was occurring, between 12:20 a.m. and 4:30 a.m. The household was more likely to evacuate if the primary source of evacuation information was the emergency personnel (92%) than if it was from another family member or friends (79%, please see Table 2.5). Our finding supports the literature.

The clarity of the warning message (Perry, et al., 1982; Fischer, et al., 1995) has been found to impact on evacuation behavior, i.e., specificity of the nature of the hazard and what the listener is directed to do in response to it. Those who became aware of the emergency and the order to evacuate did evacuate (100%). Most of those who found out that the evacuation was suggested, but not ordered, chose NOT to evacuate (79%) [most of those who did not find out about the evacuation plan did not leave during the emergency (83%)]. The former indicated they clearly understood the danger and left while the latter interpreted the danger as not severe and stayed. Obviously the evacuation response is more likely when emergency officials have the authority to order an evacuation.

The frequency of the warnings has been found (Drabek, 1986; Fischer, 1994; Fischer, et al., 1995) to impact on the likelihood of evacuation. The greater the frequency of contacts, the more likely the respondent is to evacuate. The current study was found to support the literature. The overwhelming majority of those who were never contacted did not evacuate (79%), while the reverse is true for those who were contacted at least once. More than three-fourths (79%) who were contacted once did evacuate, while all (100%) of those who were contacted at least twice evacuated.

Accuracy of past warnings enhances the chance of effecting an evacuation (Mileti, et al., 1975; Drabek, 1986; Haas, et al., 1976; Foster, 1980; Fischer, et al., 1995). Again, the current study supports this finding. Most of those (87%) who had been previously evacuated for, in their view, good cause, evacuated presently while a bare majority (53%) of those who had not had this prior experience, evacuated during the Ephrata fire.

The current study found that households were more likely to evacuate if dependent children were present in the home during the time of the emergency. Most of those with children (91%) left, while a majority (54%) of those who did not have dependent children in the home failed to evacuate. This finding conforms to the evacuation behavior literature (Bartlett, et al., 1983; Fischer, et al., 1995).

Discussion

Under what circumstances are potential victims more or less likely to evacuate? Research literature has identified several variables which increase the likelihood of a warning being taken seriously and appropriately acted upon. These variables include the clarity of the warning message, the consistency of the message, the frequency of the warnings, the type of authority giving the message, the accuracy of past warnings and the frequency of the disaster agent. The current study sought to test the efficacy of message clarity and frequency, as well as authority type and the accuracy of past warnings as viable variables in effecting an evacuation response. The literature was supported. Hence, emergency personnel who are attempting to effect an evacuation would be well served to remember that an evacuation is more likely to occur if the potential victim is ordered to do so (assuming the legal authority to issue such an order), the potential victim is directly contacted frequently (more than once) by the proper authority (as perceived by the potential victim), and past warnings proved to be accurate. It should also be noted that many researchers (Fischer, et al., 1995; Drabek, 1986; Dynes and Quarantelli, 1976) have observed that evacuation almost always occurs by family units, not solitary individuals. Since the present emergency occurred after midnight, most family members were at home which probably also helps to explain the rather high evacuation rate. Research (McLuckie, 1977) has also found urban populations are less reluctant to evacuate than rural populations. The neighborhoods involved in the Ephrata evacuation were suburban. The rather high evacuation rate may also be at least partly attributed to the suburban nature of the area.

The research literature (Dynes and Quarantelli, 1976) observes that the presence of pre-school age children in the home tends to be associated with a greater likelihood of evacuation. The presence of children in the home proved to be a key determining factor in the current study. Those who had children in the home were far more likely to evacuate than those who did not. Emergency personnel may seek to provide clarity in their warning or evacuation message by focusing on the potential hazards which may come to children who are not evacuated from the area.

As one researcher (Perry, 1990) noted, older citizens do not normally fail to evacuate because they are too frail to do so. In several evacuations elderly citizens were found to be at least as likely to evacuate as other age groups. A more salient issue indirectly associated with age appears to be the effect that children have on the parents. Parental concern for their safety appears to increase the likelihood of evacuating. The older citizens are less likely to still have children living at home, and may be less likely, therefore, to evacuate. Emergency personnel may also wish to develop alternative strategies to increase the likelihood of evacuation among those with no children at home. Since this population appears to be less likely to leave, the prudent course of action must be one which addresses this problem. Perhaps all too often, practitioners tend to believe that an area has been evacuated merely because the warning or order has been given (Fischer, 1994). The current study demonstrates how such an assumption can be invalid.

TABLE 3.1: DEMOGRAPHIC CHARACTERISTICS (N = 83)

Gender		Marital Status	
Male	31%	Married	86%
Female	69%	Unmarried	14%

Race		Socio-Economic Status	
Caucasian	98%	Middle Class	13%
All Others	2%	Working Class	74%
		No Response	13%

Religion		Age	
Protestant	81%	18 - 40 Years	33%
Catholic	12%	41 - 56 Years	33%
Other/None	7%	57 - 86 Years	34%
		mean = 49 sd = 16	

Education		Children Present at Home?	
College	18%	Yes	51%
High School	41%	No	49%
Less	27%		
No Response	14%		

TABLE 3.2:	**FIRE INFORMATION & FIRST RESPONSE** **(N = 83)**

What Were You Doing When Your First Became Aware of the Fire?

| Sleeping at Home | 81% |
| Awake at Home | 19% |

How Did You Find Out About the Fire?

I Discovered It	37%
From Family Member	22%
From Neighbor	11%
From Emergency Personnel	24%
From Media/Other	6%

What Did You Do When You First Learned of the Fire?

Went to See It (Site)	64%
Spontaneously Evacuated	15%
Turned to Media Source	5%
Telephoned Someone	9%
Ignored It	7%

TABLE 3.3: EVACUATION INFO SOURCE & FREQUENCY OF CONTACT **(N = 83)**

Did You Find Out About the Evacuation During the Course of the Fire?

| Yes | 84% |
| No | 16% |

How Did You Learn of the Evacuation Plan?

From Family/Friend/Neighbor	18%
From Media	2%
From Emergency Personnel	64%
Did Not Learn of It	16%

Were You Ordered to Evacuate?

I Was Ordered to Evacuate	61%
It Was Suggested That I Evacuate	17%
No One Told Me about the Evacuation	22%

How Many Times Were You Contacted about the Evacuation Plan?

None	23%
One	64%
Two	11%
Three	2%

TABLE 3.4:	EVACUATION BEHAVIOR
	(N = 83)

Did You Evacuate?
Yes	69%
No	31%

When Did You Evacuate?
Spontaneously After Learning of the Fire	9%
When Told To Do So	60%
I Never Evacuated	31%

How Long After Deciding To Evacuate, Did You Leave?
Immediately	11%
Within 15 Minutes	31%
Within 30 Minutes	10%
Within 60 Minutes	17%
Did Not Evacuate	31%

Why Did You Evacuate?
Ordered/Suggested	47%
Family Decided To	22%
Did Not Evacuate	31%

Where Did You Evacuate To?
Relative/Friend	56%
Motel	1%
Public Shelter	12%
Did Not Evacuate	31%

How Long Did You Stay Away From Home After Evacuating?
4 - 8 Hours	23%
8 - 24 Hours	46%
Did Not Evacuate	31%

Why Did You Return Home After Evacuating?
Asked Emergency Personnel If OK To Return	32%
Media Reported It Was OK To Return	17%
Family Member/Friend Said It Was OK	7%
I Decided It Was OK To Return	13%
Did Not Evacuate	31%

TABLE 3.5: FACTORS IMPACTING ON EVACUATION DECISIONS (N = 83)		

Did You Evacuate?	Source of Evacuation Information		
	Emergency	Family	Did Not Find Out
Yes	92%	79%	0%
No	8%	21%	100%

Did You Evacuate?	Were You Ordered To Evacuate?		
	Ordered	Suggested	Neither
Yes	100%	21%	17%
No	0%	79%	83%

Did You Evacuate?	Number of Times Contacted About Evacuation?		
	None	One Time	Two + Times
Yes	21%	79%	100%
No	79%	21%	0%

Did You Evacuate?	Past Warnings Usually Accurate?	
	Yes	No
Yes	87%	53%
No	13%	47%

Did You Evacuate?	Children in Home?	
	Yes	No
Yes	91%	46%
No	9%	54%

THE "LOOTING" MYTH AND THE REALITY

The Research Literature & the Perspective Provided by Hurricane Katrina

Looting occurred after Katrina. In some instances it may be argued that inadequate preparation for housing evacuees in the Super Dome and the Convention Center in New Orleans, coupled with a slow response to their needs in the aftermath, literally caused the "looting" which may be more accurately characterized as "appropriation of property to support life." When responders used property in such a manner the term "appropriation" was self-applied (Fischer, et al, 2006), which survivors were labeled as "looters" when they appropriated property to sustain life. On the other hand, stealing a television set, stereo, fishing rod, liquor, or cigarettes is not exactly sustaining life—it is sustaining criminal behavior. And, the latter also occurred in the aftermath of Katrina. The question arises, under what circumstances does looting cease to be a myth and become a reality?

Quarantelli (2007) provides some perspective. He notes modern usage of the term "looting" probably developed as a result of the U.S. military which sponsored some social science research of disasters in the early 1950s. They had feared that the U.S. would socially disintegrate after an atomic attack and people would engage in anti-social behavior. This concern existed despite the findings of British studies that found looting was not a serious problem among their civilian population after massive air bombings of World War II. The same was observed in Germany and Japan.

As Quarantelli notes, early studies have repeatedly found that instances of looting in the disasters examined (few of these occurred in large, urban areas) were non-existent or numerically rare. These findings have stood in stark contrast to media stories of widespread looting. During the civil disturbances in large U.S. cities, looting was common—and correctly reported as occurring. "The looting in riots is frequent, overtly undertaken, aimed at specific targets, participated in by very large numbers of individuals often in social networks, and was socially supported" (Quarantelli, 2007). Urban riots emerge in a conflict environment after lengthy periods of perceived domination by elites which is usually at variance with natural disasters. Historically researchers observe community bonding, viewing themselves as a collective victim in the face of the impact of the disaster. Through the 1970s semi-systematic studies and anecdotal reports in other developed countries were consistent with the U.S. experience (Quarantelli, 2007). The generalized proposal emerged, therefore, that "looting was not a problem in modern, developed countries and that in rare instances when it occurred it had the distinct social characteristics found by the pioneer disaster researchers" (Quarantelli, 2007).

Looting has sometimes occurred in developing nations on a massive scale, e.g. 2007 earthquake in Pakistan, but not in others, e.g. 1985 Mexico City earthquake. And, since the 1970s occasional large-scale community crises have been accompanied by mass looting, e.g. the 1977 New York City blackout looting occurred in selective neighborhoods paralleling the conflict pattern of the urban riots during the 1960s. On the other hand, similar blackouts in 1968 and 2003 did not include mass looting. So we cannot draw and "obvious" conclusions (Quarantelli, 2007).

Yet again, we must consider the mass looting in St. Croix (U.S. Virgin Islands) after Hurricane Hugo impacted the city in 1985. A systematic quantitative survey of all businesses in the major shopping centers (Quarantelli, 2007) found less than 10% reported they were not totally looted.[2] Gangs operating in the city prior to im-

---

2 Author's note: methodologically speaking one must always remember that such surveys report what the respondent *states* occurred. The methodological literature is, however, replete (see Babbie, 2004) with examples of the misperceptions or outright deceit that appears in such surveys. For example, it is sometimes to the respondent's advantage to exaggerate the situation for financial gain via insurance payouts. Having said this, all indications, anecdotal as well as quantitative findings, indicate St. Croix

pact were found to initiate the looting targeting stores with large amounts of consumer goods. A second wave of looting involved those without a criminal life style
who targeted other types of stores, e.g. hardware stores. And, a third, larger wave of
citizens then occurred looting basic necessities, e.g. food from supermarkets. There
was no authenticated case of the looting of private residences, schools, hotels, industry, or resorts. No physical force was used by the looters. The overall pattern
was similar to the earlier behavior found in civil disturbances.

Quarantelli (2007) suggests that this atypical case of mass looting was associated with a major disaster or catastrophe (consistent with Fischer's disaster scale),
as opposed to a lesser disaster, and included "a concentration of extremely (economically) disadvantaged citizens exposed to everyday perceptions of major difference s in lifestyles" (or years of deprivation, classic conflict theory illustration). He
further notes several additional contributing factors, i.e. a subculture tolerant of
minor stealing and youth gangs involved in activity such as drug dealing in normal
time, and a local police force widely viewed as corrupt (and found to engage in
looting themselves).

New Orleans after Hurricane Katrina would arguably be similar to the St.Croix
experience. Pre-existing gangs, tolerance for some normal time stealing, widely
perceived police corruption, as well as some looting as appropriation by citizens for
necessities—set among a population experiencing economic deprivation for an extended period of time prior to the disaster. "The pattern of mass looting and the
social conditions generating it were the same in both cases. Looting of any kind is
rare in certain kinds of disasters in certain types of societies. The pattern of looting
in natural disasters is different from what occurs in civil disturbances. There are
occasional atypical instances of mass lootings that emerge if a complex set or prior
social conditions exist" (Quarantelli, 2007).

The Contrarian View

Some researchers continue to be fixated on looting as a norm rather than a rarity. As
Quarantelli meticulously noted above, looting does occur. In previous editions of
this book your author noted looting does occur. The argument is not if it occurs, but
how frequently is it a problem and under what circumstances is it likely to occur.
Frailing (2007) seems to suggest that because it did occur in New Orleans after
Katrina, looting is therefore something that is not a myth, i.e., normally occurs.
And, "to write off even the possibility of looting as a myth in the context of natural
disasters is irresponsible at best. It is crucial that disaster response planners anticipate looting in the wake of natural disasters and design their responses accordingly."

The literature clearly articulates that looting is a rare occurrence, yet it does
occur under certain circumstances. The argument frequently advance by your author

---

was certainly a classic example of when mass looting does indeed occur.

has been centered on the reality that there are limited resources in the aftermath of a disaster. Therefore, a planner and a responder, by necessity, must prioritize the use of those limited resources to provide the most good to the most citizens. This author has never suggested that looting never occurs or that the planner should never anticipate its possibility. This author has argued that in an environment where resources are limited and time must be used wisely, focusing a disproportionate amount of one's resources in anticipation of countering that which rarely occurs in lieu of dealing with what always occurs is a disservice to the public one is charged with serving. Fear should not drive public policy, rational and effective planning is more germane. The reader must be careful to correctly understand the findings reported in the literature along with the important distinctions and qualifications rather than ignore them. Researchers must also guard against treating rumor as fact and keep in mind that police statistics are "reported occurrences," not "actual occurrences"—as the literature on crime reporting has established there is usually great variation between the two in normal time let alone disaster time. And finally, it is imperative that we develop an acceptable disaster scale against which the research literature can be assessed and modified.

SECOND CASE STUDY: TERRORISM & SEPTEMBER 11, 2001: DOES THE "BEHAVIORAL RESPONSE TO DISASTER" MODEL FIT?

Abstract

A recent question from the research literature is addressed: to what extent does the behavioral response to natural and technological disaster model apply to terrorist events involving a WMD? Earlier work argued that the literature is applicable. Anecdotal evidence and preliminary content analysis findings from the aftermath of the terrorist attack of 11 September 2001 demonstrate the salience of the model to terrorism.

The Event

In 1998 this author was asked to write a White Paper (Fischer, 1998a) that would outline the likely behavioral response of citizens impacted by terrorism involving a weapon of mass destruction (WMD). As a result of Presidential Decision Directive 39 (PDD 39, 1995), the U.S. Defense Department (DOD) sought to obtain social science based information that would be useful in designing counter terrorism training sessions for major U.S. metropolitan areas. The White Paper was to be a social science guide for tabletop training vignettes. The White Paper merged a review of the disaster research literature on behavioral response to disaster (based upon studies of the behavioral response to natural and technological disasters) with the research literature the medical effects of nuclear, biological, and chemical (NBC) agents (for example, see Beres, 1997; Betts, 1998; Christopher, et al, 1997; Congressional Report, 2000; Fischer, 2000; Holloway, et al, 1997; Steinbruner, 1997; Tucker, 1998; Zilinskas, 1997). The argument was made in the paper that, lacking any other alternative, the disaster research literature provided the best model for predicting the likely behavioral scenarios in terrorism involving a WMD. It was also noted in the paper that we, fortunately, had not had an opportunity for a large-scale test of the assertion that it is the best predictive model. The terrorism attack on the United States on 11 September 2001 has, unfortunately, provided the opportunity to determine if indeed the model is applicable. The purpose of the current paper is to summarize what we know from the disaster research literature and compare it, at least in a preliminary fashion, to what we observe occurring in the aftermath of the attack on and collapse of the New York City (NYC) Twin Towers.

Popular Perception

What is the popular image of the behavioral response of disaster survivors and those who come to their aid? Most people in the United States believe in what disaster researchers have described as a disaster mythology (for example, see Wenger, et al, 1975; Fischer, 1998b). Most of us assume that individuals cease to act in a predictable, orderly, normative fashion. Sociologically speaking, most people expect the everyday behavior governing norms to collapse in Durkheim's anomie. Conversely, most of us assume that emergency organizations will be well prepared to immediately respond to and help us recover from the event.

Disaster Mythology

The common perception, which is myth more than reality (for example, see Fischer, 1998b), is that people will flee in panic (necessitating, it is believed by many emergency personnel, holding off as long as possible on calling for evacuations), suffer from psychological dependency (will be unable to think for themselves), and disaster shock (will be unable to act on their on). It is often believed that evacuations must not be called too soon, for fear of encountering massive, uncontrollable flight behavior. It is also commonly believed that shelters normally overflow beyond capacity and organizers will be unable to deal with a mob mentality they will invariably confront. Both survivors and those converging to the scene are viewed as being driven by base, depraved instincts. These individuals are commonly perceived as likely to loot property, price gouge one another, and generally behave in other selfish ways—most of which are imagined to spread from individual to individual in a contagious fashion. Martial law is assumed to be necessary to quell such behavior—at the very least, a patrolling by the National Guard is expected. Death, injury, and damage are often estimated to be quite high. More than 40 years of research into the behavioral response to natural and technological disasters has resulted in a consistent and clear understanding of the above, though common, perceptions to be far more myth than real. It is often difficult for lay people to believe that the disaster mythology is really myth. Why? There are several sociological reasons. First, we are commonly socialized from an early age by significant others and mass media (print, broadcast, and film) to believe in the depraved nature of behavioral response to disaster events—because such has been assumed for eons of time. And second, our experience with civil disturbances where looting, for example does commonly occur, is thought to be applicable to disaster response when, in fact, it is not. And third, so-called common sense seems to dictate that one would be panic stricken, and so-forth, in such events. [Again, please refer to Fischer, 1998b, for a detailed discussion of the mythology and reasons for belief in the common perception of myth as reality.]

Actual Behavioral Response

This perception that a disaster results in the display of human depravity, is not supported by the evidence (for a diverse examination of social science perspectives on the nature of disaster, see Quarantelli, 1998). The community of human beings does not break down. There is, instead, an emergent norm process that occurs resulting in the adoption of those behavioral guides that subscribe to the belief, or value, that humans in trouble must be helped. Actually the best within us is usually exhibited as we become much more altruistic. Survivors share their tools, their food, equipment and especially their time. Groups of survivors tend to emerge to begin automatically responding to the needs of one another. They search for the injured, the dead, and they begin cleanup activities. Police and fire personnel stay on the job, putting the needs of victims and the duty they have sworn to uphold before their own personal needs, concerns and safety. In sharp contrast to the image commonly perceived, survivors are not apathetic or panic stricken. Looting behavior and price gouging are exceedingly rare following a disaster. Survivors act on their own and respond to help that is eventually provided, i.e., they do not become psychologically dependent or go into disaster shock. Martial law is almost never declared. Evacuations are often called much later than they should be, affording potential evacuees too little time—and, decision makers are too quick to assume that their call for evacuation will be heeded rather than implement a follow-up plan designed to enhance the evacuation response. And those who do evacuate are least likely to go to shelters; they tend to, instead, go to the homes of relatives and friends or to motels. Damage, injury and death estimates are normally revised downward as we move from impact through the recovery period. [Please refer to Table 3.6 for a summary comparison of mythology versus reality.]

Who Cares?

Okay, so we find that reality and popular perception diverge—so what? Well, emergency personnel tend to plan for and respond to those events they anticipate facing before, during and after a disaster (or terrorist) event. If, as is commonly found, they plan to respond to myth, they will not be prepared to respond to reality. The result? Unnecessary suffering will likely be added to that already experienced by the victims. For example, if we plan to focus on controlling deviant behavior, which we then do not find, we are unprepared to effect a successful evacuation.

TABLE 3.6	CONTRASTING WORLD VIEWS
Myth	**Reality**
Panic Flight	Rational Behavior
Looting	Crime Declines
Price Gouging	Giving Away Needed Items
Martial Law	Normal Law
Psychological Dependency	Ability to Respond to Needs
Disaster Shock	Respond to Others
Evacuation – Don't Call Too Soon	Evacuation – Need to Start Early
Shelter Use – Fill Quickly	Shelter Use – Used as Last Resort
Accurate: Death/Injury/Damages	Exaggerated: Death/Injury/Damages

What Do We Learn from the 11 September Terrorist Attack?

The short answer to this question is as follows. We learn that the argument advanced in 1998, i.e., the disaster research model of behavioral response to disaster as applicable to terrorism events as well, is salient. While a plethora of empirical research findings are expected to emerge from the NYC terrorism experience, preliminary findings (some based upon preliminary content analyses of broadcast media live behavioral response footage and others based upon anecdotal evidence from a variety of sources) suggest that the previously reviewed findings are supported by behavioral responses observed in the aftermath of September 11. Illustrations will be shared below.

Panic

Even though the word was often used by mass media personnel and laypeople to describe the escape of many running from the twin towers as they collapsed, a careful examination (via content analysis of the live video footage) of the behavior of these survivors indicates that they were rationally moving away from the obvious danger. Did they experience grave fear? Undoubtedly. Were they in a state of panic? No! They were rationally moving from point "a" to point "b" or from danger to a safe place. Furthermore, conversations (while not a random sample) with survivors who descended the stairways in the twin towers prior to their collapse, unanimously indicate that these individuals behaved in a very orderly, altruistic fashion. They helped one another down the steps and they proceeded as according to previous evacuation plans. They were calm and followed directions.

Altruism

The Fire Department of New York (FDNY) lost many brave members when the towers collapsed. Automatically responding to the call, these firefighters ascended the stairwells in the towers—and died doing their job. Others kept coming. Fire departments from around the country sent personnel too numerous to even be used at "ground zero" (convergence behavior of an altruistic nature). Other FDNY members did not want to leave the impact area and resisted efforts to give them relief—they stayed on the job often to their own detriment.

Individual citizens throughout the United States donated financial resources to help the victims. Citizens from varied backgrounds converged to offer their help, e.g., medical personnel, counselors and therapists, average people seeking to help in any way they could. Altruism was extremely evident in the immediate post-impact period and the recovery period.

Disaster Shock and Psychological Dependency

Anecdotal evidence suggests that numerous cases illustrate that survivors assessed the information they were able to obtain as they obtained it and sought to take charge of their individual situations, not waiting for others to direct their behavior—except where it became necessary to do so. For example, one teaching assistant in a local elementary school received a cell phone call from her husband, who worked at the trade center, shortly after impact. He indicated that two planes had hit the twin towers and he had evacuated to a safe site "down the street." As she was talking to him the towers collapsed and their phone line went dead. She was not certain of her husband's fate (he survived), but refused to go home to wait for word about her husband preferring, as she said, to "stay on the job where she is needed—with the children."

Media

The major network news reporters based in NYC, e.g., NBC Today Show personnel and the NBC Evening News personnel, functioned very much as local media do generally during disaster events—suspending normal programming and focusing on providing information on local people and organizations for local citizens and organizations (live programming broadcasting from NYC were the local stations on this occasion as well as national). Accuracy was greater as long as the focus remained on live broadcasting of local responders and needs. Later broadcasting increasingly focused on reporting on behavioral issues as they, media personnel, anticipated they would be (disaster mythology), e.g., asking about panic, looting.

Martial Law

Even in this tragic event involving a WMD martial law was not declared. While the military offered to relieve the city of the burden of responding to the event, NYC officials declined the offer and continued to coordinate the organizational response. The original EOC no longer existed as it had been in one of the towers and the city had to established a new, emergent EOC. Despite all the challenges NYC faced, its response was heroic in proportions.

Local Decision Makers

Local decision makers, e.g., the mayor's office, sought to establish a command center (and, as noted above, they had to reestablish their EOC), designate a spokesperson to interact with the media, and update the community and nation at regular intervals. Perhaps benefiting from prior training sessions and drills, the mayor's office in particular mastered the ideal model of providing regular briefings to the press (feeding them) during which they delineated what they currently knew and what they currently did not know. It would appear that the mayor became a role model for future decision makers in his information gathering and disseminating.

Looting and Price Gouging

While some reports eventually appeared declaring the existence of some looting at ground zero and some price gouging by outsiders, the final data are not yet in to ascertain how accurate (versus rumor reporting which is typical of disaster events generally) these reports were. It can be concluded, however, that even if the few reported instances turn out to be true, the mayor's office has already reported that crime in general was dramatically down during the aftermath of the terrorist event. This is a pattern commonly found in the literature on behavioral response to natural and technological disasters as citizens become very altruistic in meeting the needs of others.

Estimates of Damage, Injury and Death

Happily the usual pattern of overestimating the death toll is in tack in the NYC twin tower collapse. We will have to await final tabulations for all three of these categories to know the extent of these aspects of the tragedy. But we do now know that the actual death toll appears to be less than half of the initial estimate which is consistent with research findings for natural and technological disasters generally.

Concluding Observation

While we currently only have anecdotal information to use to assess the efficacy of depending upon the disaster research literature on behavioral response to disaster as a model for predicting response needs to terrorism, early indications support the argument that this literature is, as previously suggested, applicable indeed. There has not been a single divergent element observed. While final conclusions will have to await the data analysis of ongoing research by field teams working in NYC, this author does not expect to be surprised by those findings as he views the anecdotal information as indicative of the whole.

Chapter 4

Why We Believe the Disaster Mythology

MASS MEDIA AS A SOURCE OF INFORMATION ON DISASTERS

The primary source of disaster information for most Americans is the mass media (Wenger, et al, 1975). Our images of what the survivors of Chernobyl must have had to endure have been created through our exposure to television and print news. Similarly, the mass media created our perception of the post-impact damage resulting from Hurricane Andrew in Homestead, Florida, in August 1992. If most Americans rely upon the various forms of mass media to obtain their information about what occurs before, during, and after a disaster, then the accuracy of their perception is dependent upon the media. If the media accurately portrays how citizens and emergency personnel respond, then the viewer is more likely to gain an accurate perception and vice versa. We may borrow from the symbolic interaction theory to explain the process. The looking-glass self is developed through our interaction with significant others. Our perception of ourselves is based upon our perception of their (significant others) perception of us. What is real about ourselves, in our eyes, is based upon what we think they think we are. We act as if that perception is reality which, of course, may be a misperception. Regardless of whether our perception is accurate or not, we respond on the basis of it being real. It in essence becomes reality. If we apply the looking-glass process to explaining how we come to view our perception of what occurs during a disaster, then our perception of what occurs is based upon our perception of the perception of significant others (the media in this case). Many use the media as significant others in this instance because we *assume* they know what is real as they are on the scene reporting the news, i.e., reality.

The reality Americans perceive as a result of their use of the mass media is often incorrect, i.e., a misperception. Case studies will be presented which empirically illustrate the extent to which various "significant others" misperceive and how they unwittingly perpetuate such misperceptions to the news consumer. Such misperceptions often result in the allocation of scarce resources for imaginary problems. Adequate resources are often unavailable for combating the actual problems. A working knowledge of what really occurs is needed on the part of local leaders, emergency management personnel, and the residents of the community.

One very important caveat, the mass media has greatly reduced the level of flamboyant exaggeration in what they report as typical behavioral and organizational response to disasters. Fifty years ago, you may have read of the cadaver which had three fingers cut off by a looter stealing rings from a disaster victim. Such extremely exaggerated reporting is far less likely to occur today. However, since a larger portion of the newshole is now devoted to reporting disasters, the opportunity for myth perpetuation is greater today. As a result, a less than accurate image is still commonly portrayed in both the print and broadcast media (Drabek, 1986; Fischer & Bischoff, 1988; Fischer, 1989).

Media Reporting Patterns

The results of several studies (for example, see Fischer & Bischoff, 1988; Fischer, 1989) suggest that there are several factors which may contribute to making it more or less likely that disaster myths will be reported as fact. These factors include the type of news coverage, the interview incidence within a news story, the disaster period being reported on, the size of the newshole devoted to the disaster, and the disaster type. The impact of each of these is discussed below.

Soft versus Hard News

A hard news story is one which relates the basic, objective facts to the reader, e.g., type of disaster agent (flood, hurricane, tornado, chemical spill), duration of event (storm blew through the area for four hours), how long it took to restore essential services (the electricity was out for eight hours). A soft news story is essentially a human interest story. It would include segments from interviews of local officials who are attempting to manage the organizational response to the disaster (mayor, police chief, civil defense director), victims who have survived (a woman who has lost her car to the flood waters, a man who lost his family when the house collapsed on them) and emergency personnel and bystanders who have converged to the site. These news stories often focus on the tales the survivors have to tell about their ordeal. For example, in one such news account (Fischer & Bischoff, 1988), one man related how his neighbor's house was there one minute and gone the next. Gone also were the lives of the woman and daughter who were home at the time. The police chief of the town told reporters that looting threatened to become a problem but the Guard was called out in time to forestall it. When asked how many looters had been apprehended, the chief said, "none, but many were spotted by witnesses."

It has been observed, the greater the emphasis on soft, versus hard news, the greater the likelihood that myths will appear in the story (Fischer & Bischoff, 1988). As soon as the reporter ventures into the personal experiences of those who were there, the *news* story becomes more a news *story*. When the reporter makes the mistake of accepting statements as factually correct, he unwittingly passes on myths which reinforce the view that behavioral response to disaster is characterized by the breakdown of the norms of good citizenship.

Interview Incidence

It stands to reason, then, that as the incidence of soft news interviews increases, an increase in myth reporting results. One may wonder how myths could possibly come from the mouths of "those who were there." Survivors may sometimes exaggerate, sometimes report what they believe occurred because they believe in the disaster mythology, sometimes misinterpret events, or sometimes be misinterpreted themselves. Local officials may also exaggerate, report what they believe occurred based upon reports to them, misinterpret and be misinterpreted. They also have a vested interest in their community being declared a federal disaster area making federal monies available for rebuilding. This is not to say that they would deliberately misrepresent events, but in their exuberance to do a good job it is possible to succumb to the exaggerations commonly making the rounds through the rumor mill.

Post Impact Period

When the human interest story interviews focus primarily on events which occurred during the immediate post-impact disaster period, the incidence of myth reporting is greater than for any other period. Remember there are five time periods which comprise the life cycle of a disaster: the pre-impact period, the impact period, the immediate post-impact period, the short-term recovery period, and the long-range recovery period. It is during the immediate post-impact period that officials and survivors are most prone to be excited and to exaggerate. During this stage of the disaster life cycle normal time norms are usually suspended in favor of altruism. In the spirit of openness interviewees gladly share their perceptions of their experiences. These perceptions should, however, be suspect for the reasons noted earlier.

For most types of disasters, media personnel are not able to get on-site until after impact, so the likelihood is great that the interviewing of victims will occur primarily during the post-impact time period when the media rush to publish or broadcast news of the event. Reporters are trained to seek out the most dramatic settings and stories. Thus we tend to see the building that has been damaged most severely, conveying the image that this is typical of the damage sustained in the entire community. We tend to hear the story of victims who most dramatically relate their disaster experience. Once again, we end up with the perception that the account is both true and typical of disaster events. The result? The disaster mythology is again perpetuated to an unwitting audience of readers or viewers. While the *New York Times* decries that it publishes "the truth so that it will make us free," the media, in general, may not provide us with that which does so.

Newshole Size

It should not surprise the reader to learn that when the reporter has more time or space in which to enumerate the activities reported by the survivors, the myth tally increases. When the number of mythical accounts being included in the news story increases, obviously the total number of myths portrayed will increase. Since 1944 the size of the newshole devoted to disasters has dramatically increased in news-magazines. Only a few column inches used to be allotted to a hard news account of a disaster event, i.e., reporting the type of disaster agent, the location of the event and the response of the local and state officials. Since 1945 the national print media has devoted an ever increasing number of column inches to reporting on disasters. For example, in the aftermath of the 1985 Mexico Earthquake, *Time Magazine* devoted over 200 column inches to both hard and soft news reporting in the first of three issues published after the quake. The first issue featured the Mexico quake on its cover and as the major story of the magazine that week. As noted earlier, the more space devoted to disaster "news," the more likely we are to be exposed to myths.

Variation by Disaster Type

Another variable impacting upon variation of the publication of disaster myths is the type of disaster, i.e., natural versus technological. Fischer and Bischoff (1988) found that the print media was much more likely to publish myths when reporting on natural disasters. When the disaster was technological in nature, e.g., chemical spill, transportation accident, nuclear power plant radiation leak, the media was much less likely to portray myth. To the extent that technological news stories focus on interviews of survivors during the post-impact period, myths are perpetuated. What usually occurs, however, is that the news stories focus on what happened during the pre-impact and impact time periods. There is the tendency to want to recount events leading up to the airplane crash in an attempt to explain why it occurred in the first place (blame-fixing). Similarly, when a nuclear power plant leaks radiation into the air, the media focus on what happened, why and what to do now to protect one self. Early interviews focus on what experts have to say, since the survivor cannot provide a technical explanation for what happened. Hard news reporting usually occurs as soft news reports are far less frequent. It is not until the latter part of the disaster life cycle that reports focus more on the effects of the event on local citizens. For example, the early media reports on TMI were concerned with describing the extent of the radiation venting, the degree of danger resulting from exposure to it, and what went wrong in the first place. In time, the focus of an increasing percentage of the TMI news stories focused on the emotional stress of those living within twenty-five miles of the power plant.

We can therefore expect a different response by the media depending on whether the disaster agent is natural or technological. In most cases the natural disaster will be presented in accordance with the mythical model; and, the mythical model will not be portrayed for technological disasters--unless the story's focus is on the post-impact disaster period. During this time period myths are likely to be perpetuated for the technological disaster as well.

Summary

Several variables, then, affect the likelihood that the media will present a mythical account of how people behave after a disaster has struck their area. *Expanded disaster coverage, soft news reporting and interviewing during the post-impact period all contribute to misunderstanding the behavioral response to disaster. When the media devotes a large portion of its newshole to the reporting of soft news based upon interviews conducted during the post-impact disaster period of a natural disaster, the public is more likely to believe in the disaster mythology.*

Implication

As long as the public is told that the aftermath of a disaster is accompanied by a breakdown in norms, they will continue to expect the Governor to call out the National Guard to control deviant behavior. If reporters, local officials, emergency management personnel, and the public are aware of facts surrounding our behavior after a disaster agent impacts upon us, then we should be able to get on with planning a more effective response to disasters which anticipates the problems which are most likely to befall us. Perhaps we will soon turn on our televisions or radios and open our newspapers and newsmagazines to an accurate, rather than a mythical portrayal of behavioral response to disasters.

FIRST CASE STUDY: DISASTROUS FANTASIZING IN THE PRINT MEDIA: HOW DISASTERS HAVE BEEN PORTRAYED IN NEWSMAGAZINE REPORTING OVER A FORTY YEAR PERIOD

In 1988, Fischer and Bischoff completed a content analysis of *Time Magazine's* reporting on disasters. The study was based upon the news reports published during the forty year period between 1944 and 1985. Their detailed findings are presented below to provide the reader with an empirical illustration of the factors found impacting upon incidence of mythology publication in the print media.

Students of behavioral response to disaster continually refer to the role of the media in perpetuating the disaster mythology with little supportive empirical evidence. The current study sought to assess the validity of this assumption by conducting a content analysis of disaster news stories published in a national newsmagazine over a forty year period beginning in 1944. An enumeration of the incidence of disaster myths finds that the mythology continues to be portrayed in the national print media. While "we no longer read of looters allegedly cutting off the fingers of the deceased to steal their rings" (observation made by E.L. Quarantelli in a 1988 conversation), the *incidence* of myth portrayal has nevertheless increased over the course of the forty year period under study--at least for one representative national print media publication. The primary determinants in myth portrayal appear to be the size of the newshole devoted to disaster reporting, the type of news story (hard versus soft), interview incidence, the disaster period being reported on, and the type of disaster (natural versus technological). The media tends to publish post-impact human interest stories which are based upon victim and local official interviews. The tendency for the media to publish unconfirmed statements made to them by their interviewees who tend to embellish their stories or pass along rumor appears to result in mythology perpetuation in the case of natural disaster news stories. Since the media tends to focus on technical aspects of pre-impact and impact time in technological disaster stories as part of the blame-fixing process, it is far less likely to pass along the disaster myths commonly reported in the post impact time period.

Emergency management personnel must take their constituent's perception of behavioral response to disasters into account when making such decisions. If the citizenry expects looters to descend upon the streets, then they expect the competent manager to counter such deviance by seeking to have the National Guard called up to protect against such behavior. If the citizenry expects a massive exodus of would-be victims to fill the roadways leading from the impending disaster area, then they expect the competent manager to counter provide safe evacuation routes and adequate shelter to house the fleeing masses.

The Research Questions

The research questions, then, become, to what extent do the media perpetuate the mythology? How has its perpetuation changed over time? Is there any difference between how behavior is portrayed before impact versus after impact? Is there any difference between how behavioral response is portrayed in natural versus technological disasters? These questions form the basis of the current study.

Methodology

While the above issues need to be addressed across all media forms at all levels, i.e., newspapers, newsmagazines, radio and television both at the local and national levels, we focused on the national newsmagazine. This methodology expands our knowledge base. Most previous research reported in the literature focuses on local media.

To maintain consistency of comparison, one of the three major newsmagazines (the one with the largest circulation during the time period studied) was selected for a content analysis. It was reasoned that the best newsmagazine to analyze would be the one which has the widest readership and, therefore, the one which potentially influences the largest audience. The content analysis sought to identify the number and type of myths portrayed, the column inches of the article, the disaster time period(s) reported on, the number and type of interviews conducted, the focus of the news story (soft versus hard news), and the extent to which behavioral response appeared to be mythical rather than accurately portrayed. News stories were examined which were based upon a disaster or major emergency incident occurring between 1945 and 1985. This provided the opportunity for measuring change in myth incidence and type over time. For purposes of the current study, a disaster event or emergency incident was defined as "any event which disrupts, in any manner, the normal time activities of the human beings found in the vicinity of the incident site." We realize that this definition does not conform exactly to Fritz (1961), but we sought to examine any event that provided the opportunity for the media to activate the disaster mythology. This approach yielded 80 news stories in a forty year period which reported on either a natural or a technological disaster or emergency. Natural disaster news stories included one earthquake, twenty-two floods, thirteen hurricanes, five tornadoes, and one tsunami. Technological disaster stories included six fires or conflagrations, twenty-nine air and railway transportation accidents, and three hazardous materials accidents. Since every story published between 1945 and 1985 was included in the study, it was not possible to obtain an equal number of news stories for each type of disaster incident.

Hard news stories are defined as those which focus primarily on the technical facts of the incident, e.g., weather conditions, number of passengers on the plane, the chemicals being transported, the years of pilot experience. Soft news stories are defined as those which focus primarily on the human interest story, i.e., stories based upon interview information gathered about survivors, victims, emergency personnel, onlookers, and so forth. Soft news interview information includes behavioral observations made, emotions articulated, and so forth. Some stories included elements of both hard and soft news. The story was judged to be soft or hard, in this case, based upon its overall slant.

For purposes of content analysis, a disaster myth was assumed to be portrayed if behavior described in the news story conformed with that found in the literature on disaster myths (for example, see Wenger, et al., 1978; Drabek, 1986). The news reports of death, damage and injury were compared with confirmed figures published in other sources such as *The World Almanac* (1988). In the case of other myths such as looting, we assumed the literature is accurate in claiming such instances are very rare and viewed reporting of such as mythical.

Findings

Descriptive Overview

By examining Table 4.1 we can see that half of all the news stories contained at least one myth, in fact, some had as many as twelve myths. No news articles contained reports of contagion. Mass evacuations were reported more often (by 24% of the news stories) than any other disaster myth. Panic (10%), looting (11%), disaster shock and psychological dependency (7%), as well as selfish behavior (7%) were reported to have occurred in approximately one tenth of the stories.

TABLE 4.1:	DESCRIPTIVE OVERVIEW (N = 80)		

Myths Present		Disaster Agents	
Yes	50%	Earthquake	1%
No	50%	Flood	28%
		Hurricane	16%
		Tornado	6%
Disaster Type		Tsunami	1%
Natural	52%	Fire	8%
Technological	48%	HazMat	4%
		Trans Accident	36%
Year			
1944-1964	34%		
1965-1985	66%		
		Myth Type**	
Disaster Period			Yes	No
Pre-Imp/Impact	60%	Panic	10%	90%
Post Impact	40%	Martial Law	1%	99%
		Dependency	7%	93%
		Looting	11%	89%
News Type		Selfish	7%	93%
Hard	57%	Hi Evacuate	24%	76%
Soft	43%	Hi Death	10%	90%
		Hi Damage	16%	84%
		Hi Shelter	6%	94%
Human Interest Interviews		Contagion	0%	100%
Yes	60%		
No	40%	*Some 50% 50%*
		**Add left to right=100%

The reporting split evenly between types of disasters. Approximately half of the news stories were written about natural disasters (52%) and half about techno-logical disasters (48%).

The incidence of reporting on disaster incidents increased over time, ap-proximately two-thirds (66%) of the news stories appeared in the newsmagazine since 1965 while only a third (34%) appeared between 1944 and 1964. Some-what more than half (60%) of the news stories focused on events reportedly oc-curring during the pre-impact and impact time periods, while the remainder (40%) reported on behavior to have occurred during the post-impact time period. Slightly more than half (57%) of the stories were primarily hard news stories and the other half (43%) focused on soft news items such as the so-called human interest stories about the trials and tribulations reportedly experienced by some survivors and relief workers. More than half of the news accounts (60%) included interviews of survivors, local officials and eye witnesses. And, finally, the natural disaster agent most often reported on (28% of the stories) was the flood, while the technological agent most often reported on (36% of the stories) was the air or rail transportation accident.

Myth Incidence Variation

Under what circumstances does myth occurrence seem to vary? If we examine Table 4.2 we can observe that the reporting of the disaster mythology appears to be associated with *natural disasters* (77% of the natural disaster news stories contained at least one myth while 91% of the technological disaster stories contained none). In the *post-impact disaster period* 88% of the news stories contained myths while 75% of the pre-impact and impact period stories were free of myths. The *soft news* story (88% of the soft news stories contained myths and 78% of the hard news stories contained none), and the presence of cited *interviews* of victims, emergency personnel and eyewitnesses (60% of the news stories containing such interviews reported at least one myth while 66% of those which did not contain such interviews reported no myths).

TABLE 4.2	MYTH INCIDENCE VARIATION (N=80)							
	Disaster		**Period**		**News**		**Interviews**	
Myths	**Nat**	**Tech**	**Pre**	**Post**	**Hard**	**Soft**	**Yes**	**No**
Yes	77%	9%	25%	88%	22%	88%	60%	34%
No	23%	91%	75%	12%	78%	12%	40%	66%

Why might disaster type, disaster period, news type, and interviewing impact upon the incidence of myth incidence? We suggest that the disaster mythology is much more likely to be reported in natural disasters because the media tends to focus on the post-impact period in their reporting. It is during this time period that most of the current media interest is directed. The substance of the news story seems to be centered on the behavioral aftermath of the event, e.g., what people are doing to cope. Much of each news story is devoted to interviews of reported victims, local officials and eyewitnesses. Local officials may exaggerate as a result of being caught up in the excitement of the event. Survivors may embellish their stories for the same reason. The media may unwittingly relay such unconfirmed reports to the public, thereby reinforcing the mythology. A few of the many examples found in the news stories examined include:

Hurricane Betsy, 1965
One surviving resident stated, "little looting was reported, but I heard that one thief fell out of his boat while looting and drowned." And, "I heard that merchants were charging $1 or more for a loaf of bread, and $5 for a block of ice . . . !"

Hurricane Agnes, 1972
A neighbor reported "one man finished all the cleanup then sat in front of his house for 3 days with the hose in his hand, not moving."

Xenia Tornado, 1974
One victim reported seeing "one terrified elderly victim sitting wrapped in a blanket in a rocking chair for hours refusing to say a word."

It appears that in the aftermath of technological disasters the media are more likely to focus on blame-fixing, e.g., why did the Henderson Plant blowup? Who was at fault? How recent were the safety inspections? How accurate were they? Were the identified violations addressed? Hence, in technological disasters it appears that the emphasis is on pre-impact and impact time. When a technological disaster occurs, the media tend to focus on technical events and human failure with respect to these events. News reporting tends to become much more hard news oriented than for that reported during the aftermath of a natural disaster. Interviews are less frequent and, to the extent that they do occur, they focus primarily on technical experts, e.g., FAA investigators, presidents of airlines, and so forth. Victim interviews are less frequent, one reason perhaps being the lower frequency of victims who survive a technological event such as a plane crash. To the extent that post-impact behavior of survivors becomes the focus, the number of column inches devoted to soft news dramatically increases along with the incidence of published myths.

Variation by Disaster Type

As noted earlier, over three-fourths (77%) of the natural disaster news stories contained at least one myth while most (91%) of the technological disaster stories were myth free (see Table 4.3). Over half (57%) of the natural disaster stories focused on the post-impact period while almost four-fifths (79%) of the technological disaster stories focused on either the pre-impact or impact periods. Furthermore, approximately two-thirds (64%) of the natural disaster stories were basically soft news reports while over four-fifths (82%) of the technological disaster stories were hard news reports. And finally, almost three-fourths (71%) of the natural disaster stories used human interest story interviews, while over half (53%) of the technological disaster stories did not. What is not revealed in the table is the finding that of those technological stories which did use human interest stories, many (70%) did contain myths. The pivotal finding, then, is the observation that the nature of the disaster, natural versus technological, appears to impact upon the nature of the reporting.

TABLE 4.3	VARIATION BY DISASTER TYPE (Note: add columns left to right = 100%; N = 80)						
Disaster	**Myths** Yes No		**Period** Pre Post		**News** Hard Soft		**Interviews** Yes No
Natural	77% 23%		43% 57%		36% 64%		71% 29%
Tech	9% 91%		79% 21%		82% 18%		47% 53%

Longitudinal Variation

A final research question remains. Has myth incidence varied since 1944? The answer is *yes* (please see Table 4.4). Three-fourths (74%) of the news articles appearing before 1965 did not contain disaster myths while more than four-fifths (82%) of those published since 1965 contained myths. Most (85%) of the pre-1965 stories focused on the pre-impact and impact time periods while over half (53%) of the stories published since 1965 focused on the post impact period. Most (89%) of the pre-1964 stories were hard news oriented while over half (58%) of those stories appearing since that time were primarily soft news. The use of the human interest interview dramatically increased over the years. Before 1965, three-fourths (74%) of the stories contained none of these interviews, while the reverse (77% of the stories) is true for those published since 1965. Not only does Table 4.4 reveal that there has been a tendency for the media to become more mythical in their reporting over time, but this data gives further support for the assumption that focus of time period, news type, and the use of interviews impact upon the chances of the disaster mythology being perpetuated.

TABLE 4.4	LONGITUDINAL VARIATION (Note: add columns left to right=100%; N = 80)						
Year	**Myths** Yes No		**Period** Pre Post		**News** Hard Soft		**Interviews** Yes No
1944-64	74% 26%		85% 15%		89% 11%		26% 74%
1965-85	38% 82%		47% 53%		42% 58%		77% 23%

Conclusions and Caveats

What can we conclude from the current research effort? The national print media does indeed continue to perpetuate the disaster mythology. The reported myths are less exaggerated, but they are reported more frequently. There appear to be circumstances under which this perpetuation is more, versus less, likely to occur. In the case of the natural disaster, the disaster mythology is more likely to appear due to the media's apparent tendency to focus on the stereotypical behavioral response reported by victims, local officials and eyewitnesses interviewed during the post-impact time period. This reporting forms the basis of the soft news typical of natural disaster news stories. An increase in soft news reporting and interviewing during the post-impact period are associated with myth appearance in the news stories.

It should be noted, however, that the current findings were based upon a content analysis of news stories of the disaster events or emergency incidents published over a forty year period in only one national newsmagazine. We cannot generalize the findings to other forms and levels of media reporting. In addition, the present findings are based upon a plethora of flood, hurricane, and transportation accident news stories. We do not know if the mythology is as prevalent for other disaster agents.

PUBLISHED DISASTER EVENTS/EMERGENCY INCIDENTS, 1944-1985	
YEAR	**EVENT(S)**
1944	Midwest Tornado, New England Hurricane
1945	NYC Plane Crash, New Jersey Flood, Florida Hurricane
1946	Chicago Hotel Fire, Hawaiian Tsunami
1947	Texas Chemical Plant Fire
1948	New Jersey Train Crash
1950	Detroit Plane Crash, Illinois and Ohio Train Crashes
1952	Southern Tornado
1956	New Jersey Plane Crash
1958	Nevada Plane Crash, Massachusetts Plane Crash
1959	NYC Plane Crash, S. Dakota Fire, Pennsylvania Floods
1960	N. Carolina Plane Crash, N.J. Blimp Crash, Ill. Flood
1961	Hurricane Carla
1964	2 California Plane Crashes, Northwestern U.S. Floods
1965	NYC Plane Crash, Midwest Tornadoes, Hurricane Betsy, Betsy Floods
1967	N.C. Plane Collision, Ohio Plane Crash, Alaskan Floods, Hurricane Beulah, Beulah Floods
1969	Nebraska Train/Chem Spill, Midwest Floods, Hurricane Camille
1971	Southern Tornado
1972	Chicago Train Collision, Chicago Plane Crash, S.D. Flood, Hurricane Agnes, Agnes Floods
1973	Mississippi Floods

1974	Xenia Tornado
1975	NYC Plane Crash
1976	N.D. Flood, Colorado Flood
1977	Indiana Plane Crash, R.I. Dorm Fire, Kansas Flood
1978	Tennessee Train/Chem Spill, Calif. Plane Collision
1979	Pennsylvania TMI Nuclear Power Plant Accident, Chicago Plane Crash, Mississippi Flood, Hurricane Frederick, Hurricane David
1980	Hurricane Allen
1981	Massachusetts Conflagration
1982	Washington D.C. Plane Crash, NY Radioactive Spill, California Brush Fire, Louisiana Train/Chem Spill, Louisiana Plane Crash
1983	Southern Floods, California Earthquake, Utah Flood, Hurricane Alicia
1985	Texas Plane Crash, Hurricane Gloria

SECOND CASE STUDY: HURRICANE GILBERT:
THE MEDIA'S CREATION OF THE STORM OF THE CENTURY DURING SEPTEMBER 1988

It has been previously established that the average American citizen believes in a disaster mythology and that this belief is facilitated by the mass media's portrayal of disaster events. The national print media, for example, appears to participate in this process. The question is why? Why do they do it? Do they deliberately seek to deceive their readers in order to grab their attention--and, hence, their money--with wild headlines? Or, is there a process at work rooted in the organizational production of the news during a disaster and facilitated by the media's belief in the disaster mythology? The following case study (Fischer, 1989) seeks to answer these questions.

Abstract

A two-person field team spent five days taping local and network news broadcasts, obtaining copies of local newspapers and interviewing local officials and media personnel during the pre-impact, impact and post-impact time periods of Hurricane Gilbert's march toward the south Texas Gulf Coast in September 1988. The research objectives were (1) to determine the incidence of the media's mythical versus accurate portrayal of the behavioral response to Gilbert and (2) to explain why the media's portrayal was mythical or accurate. The team worked in Houston, Corpus Christi, Brownsville and Galveston. They also briefly visited Matamoros, Mexico.

Upon returning from the field, the researchers conducted additional telephone interviews of local officials and media personnel. An analysis of the information gained during the interview process, combined with that gained from a content analysis of the broadcast and print media news stories on Gilbert, has resulted in the following findings. First, the media was fairly accurate in their overall portrayal of the behavioral response to the threat posed by Hurricane Gilbert. They were particularly accurate when it came to portraying rational behavior in preparation for the storm, in portraying the usual disaster subculture behavior, and in portraying the usual altruism. Second, the media was found, however, to exaggerate the evacuation rates, shelter populations, and the gravity of weather changes. Third, the disaster myths which were most often perpetuated were looting, price gouging, and panic. And fourth, variation in accuracy was observed between the various media forms. Reasons suggested for this variation center around three themes. (1) Most news personnel subscribed to the disaster mythology. Their belief in the mythology influenced their view of what constituted reality. Their news gathering and reporting was influenced by their perspective, i.e., the mythology was reality to them which. The story they sought to gather news on, conformed to their view of reality, i.e., myths. Variation in organizational approaches to gathering and reporting news affected the extent to which the belief in the disaster mythology framed the accuracy of news reporting, however. (2) Norms governing local versus network news gathering and reporting affected accuracy, in that the local media were more altruistic while the network organizations were more self-serving. (3) Differences between the organizational approaches to news gathering and reporting resulted in greater or lesser control of what constituted news, and hence, affected accuracy. The greater the control by myth believers in the framing of the news story, the greater the inaccuracy, for control resulted in managing the news to reflect the (mythical) perception of the behavioral response to Gilbert.

Local media personnel were governed by a norm which defined their role as being the information gatherer and disseminator to help save their community (an example of the altruism typically experienced by most would-be victims). Local news organizations tended to serve as a conduit for disseminating the information the local emergency management officials wished the public to have. These news organizations would broadcast the entire press conferences held by local emergency management officials. The local print media would devote major stories to reprinting the transcripts of these press conferences. Accuracy was therefore dependent upon the degree to which local officials subscribed to an accurate or mythical view of the behavioral response to disasters.

The network organization personnel functioned as pack animals, i.e., they traveled together when gathering the news, focusing more on avoiding being scooped than on getting the scoop. They would often set their cameras and satellite dishes away from the EOC and other emergency response organizations, preferring more picturesque settings like the sea coast. Once their satellite dishes were set in place they tended to bring interviewees to their location. This practice gave greater control of the newsmaking process to the networks. Network personnel were governed by a norm which defined their role as that of managing the news to provide a good picturesque story for their viewers. The news they created tended to conform to their perception of the behavior they expect during a disaster. Greater control over news management resulted in greater inaccuracy.

The Research Question

Disaster researchers seek to determine why the disaster mythology continues to be the definition of the situation, i.e., the explanatory model, for the vast majority of Americans (for example, see Wenger, et al, 1975). Why does belief continue in the common occurrence of widespread panic flight, the declaration of martial law, psychological dependency, convergence to the scene by non-victims for the purpose of looting and other forms of deviant behavior, immoral competition for necessities and price gouging, the mass evacuation of the majority of potential victims, a massive number of personal injuries and deaths, massive property damage, the occurrence of disaster shock, contagion behavior, and the mass sheltering of a majority of the would-be victims? Some researchers have suggested (Quarantelli, 1980) that Hollywood movies may play a roll in forming our frame of reference. Perhaps the expectations of deviant responses to disaster come from the presentations of self developed by the celluloid approximation of reality.

Disaster researchers frequently return from the field noting that the media's portrayal of disaster events and the reported behavioral response has not been altogether accurate. Some (Wenger and Friedman, 1986; Fischer and Bischoff, 1988) have suggested that the media actually perpetuates the community breakdown model. Until recently, little empirical research had been done to assess the accuracy or inaccuracy of disaster media coverage. Scanlon, et al, (1978) and Goltz (1984) found such coverage to be highly accurate in the local broadcast and local print media. Wenger and Friedman (1986) found the coverage to be mixed, both accurate and inaccurate, in the local print media's coverage of Hurricane Alicia. In studies of the "national print media" (newsmagazines) Fischer and Bischoff (1988) observed many inaccuracies which tended to perpetuate the disaster mythology. Hence, a debate exists among disaster researchers (Quarantelli, 1987). The central question around which the debate has emerged is essentially: to what extent do the media perpetuate the community breakdown model? If it does, why does it do so? If not, why not? Furthermore, does accuracy vary by media type, i.e., local versus national media and print versus broadcast media?

The focus of the current field research was (1) to empirically determine the extent to which the local media (print and broadcast) perpetuate the mythology surrounding behavioral response to disaster and (2) to determine why this mythology is perpetuated, to the extent that it is, during emergency time. The objective of the field work along the Texas Gulf Coast in September 1988, was to gather data which would provide empirically based answers to these questions.

Methodology

On-Site: In the Field

Shortly after its inception in the Caribbean, Hurricane Gilbert was dubbed the storm of the century by the national weather service as it became a category five hurricane. With this declaration, the American media began to flood the airwaves and printed page with predictions of what one could expect in terms of damage, devastation and behavior in response to such a storm. A massive convergence of media personnel commenced to the Texas Gulf coast. Local, regional, national and international news personnel took their positions in Houston, Galveston, Corpus Christi and Brownsville.

Our two-person field team monitored Gilbert's progress through the Caribbean, across the Yucatan, and into the Gulf. After consultation with the Natural Hazards Center and disaster research colleagues around the country, we decided to depart for Houston so that we would arrive on-site by noon Thursday September 15, 1988, which would be (according to NOAA predictions) twenty-four to thirty-six hours before impact. At the time of departure for the field, the National Hurricane Center felt the most likely impact area would be between Corpus Christi and Galveston. Since we were doing a media study, we felt that it would be most prudent to be on-site before, during and after impact since this was "the storm of the century." We would be able to gather data on the media's portrayal of behavioral response to Gilbert across all three of these emergency time periods.

As soon as we arrived in Houston, we set up our equipment in our hotel room. We recorded the local television and radio broadcasts about Gilbert before going to the Houston EOC late Thursday night (it became too difficult, however, to tape both television and radio broadcasts, as well as conduct interviews in the field, so we had to abandon our plan to systematically record radio news broadcasts and settle for a sporadic sample which did not enable us to conduct a proper analysis when we returned from the field). While the EOC visit secured our safety, we were there primarily to interview the EOC and media personnel who came and went during our visit. By late Thursday night the forecast had changed. Impact was not expected until late Friday and Gilbert had still not made his expected turn north toward our location. We returned to our hotel room and resumed taping and began telephone interviewing.

Friday morning we continued to record media broadcasts, as well as obtain copies of local newspaper coverage of Gilbert. Impact predictions continued to change, Gilbert was expected to reach landfall further south. Landfall was now expected to occur between Brownsville and Corpus Christi. Our field team decided to move closer to the expected impact area to gather data on local media portrayals. We spent the remainder of the day, Friday, September 16, recording broadcasts, buying newspapers and interviewing local officials and media personnel in Corpus Christi. When the prediction of landfall changed again, to the area between Brownsville, Texas and northern Mexico, we moved again. We spent the remainder of Saturday, September 17, recording, obtaining newspapers and interviewing media personnel and officials in Brownsville. Gilbert reached land south of Matamoros, Mexico. On our fourth day in the field, Sunday, September 18, the team returned to Houston to tape the post-impact media portrayal, to do some interviewing and prepare to enter Galveston on day five (Monday, September 19) to interview officials and media personnel. Late on the fifth day we returned to our research center.

When we interviewed local officials we had to assume the role of the researcher to facilitate entree. We tended to follow our interview guide fairly closely, adding questions as they seemed pertinent to do so. When interviewing media personnel, however, we frequently assumed the role of an interested bystander, not acknowledging our research role. We found this approach highly beneficial, for we believe the information we obtained was far more honest than would have been forthcoming otherwise. We had the feeling that the media personnel were distrustful of anyone who might seek to make them "look bad," in the words of one interviewee who we had apprised of our research mission. By playing the role of a "would-be groupie," the media personnel were flattered and highly cooperative. We had to be very flexible in our questioning and go with our instincts in this interview mode, hence, we did not follow the interview guide closely when interviewing media personnel in the field (telephone interviewing conducted after returning from the field was similar to that done with local officials both on-site and off-site, the guide was followed more closely and the interviewee knew of our mission--and was far more guarded).

Off-Site: Back at the Research Center

After returning from the field, the team conducted follow-up telephone interviews to media personnel and local officials. We spoke with those who were important to the study but were unable to meet with us while we were in the field. A complete analysis of the videotapes, audio tapes, newspaper reports and interview data was then completed. We developed two content analysis forms. One form was for use in analyzing the television news broadcasts, the other for analyzing the newspaper news stories. Telephone interviews were conducted to determine the reporter's prior disaster experience, belief in the disaster mythology, and news gathering strategy. These interviews were conducted with the aid of an open-ended question guide (this question guide was employed when interviewing in both the field and by telephone afterward). Each of these research tools will be briefly described below.

Content Analysis

A primary objective of the content analysis was to determine the incidence of myth portrayal by both the local broadcast and print media. We were guided by the disaster literature reviewed earlier and sought to identify media portrayal of instances of: panic flight, disaster shock, price gouging, looting, convergence of other forms of deviance, declaration of martial law, exaggerated estimates of the number of evacuees and those sheltered, as well as exaggerated estimates of the extent of damage, injuries and deaths. We decided to also examine for exaggerations of the weather conditions, since we wondered about some of this coverage prior to leaving for the field. The traditional definitions of what constitutes each of these, as viewed in the disaster literature, were employed in the study.

To determine if a "disaster myth" had been portrayed, e.g., a looting incident, we interviewed records personnel in the police departments of the cities we visited. We interviewed to determine such things as actual arrests for looting, price gouging and means for estimating the number of evacuees and so forth. In this way we could ascertain, for example, if verified instances of looting had occurred and if evacuee estimations were reasonably derived. We found the disaster literature served as an accurate predictor of what actually occurred during the behavioral response to Hurricane Gilbert.

The first evening in the field we were watching and recording a local news broadcast in which the reporter stated that two merchants had been arrested for price gouging. I immediately turned to the phone and called the Galveston City police records office, told them what I had just heard on the evening news, and asked for confirmation. The officer stated there had been no arrests for such behavior. Several days later, however, we read in the Galveston newspaper that two Houston citizens, *who were not merchants*, purchased truck loads of plywood and converged on Galveston to sell each sheet at a 300% markup. They were reportedly arrested. When I contacted the city police records office again, the record keeping process had been updated and they confirmed that the newspaper had the correct story. The television broadcast did leave the impression that price gouging is a common occurrence in disaster settings and that it was being done by Galveston merchants. The local newspaper was accurate while the television broadcast was not. This pattern will become familiar to the reader when the findings of this study are shared in detail.

We also sought to determine the extent to which behavioral response to disaster was accurately portrayed. For example, when *burglaries* were discussed rather than *looting,* we categorized this reference as an accurate portrayal. The burglary rate was usually qualified in those media reports as being lower than during normal time. Furthermore, the term burglary carries a much different connotation than that of looting. We also looked for instances where citizens were portrayed as behaving rationally (purchasing supplies in anticipation of power outages), engaging in typical disaster subculture behavior (surfing), and behaving altruistically (helping others prepare for the storm).

We also sought data which would identify the news source (which local newspaper, television station, or network), the reporter, the disaster period being reported on, the news type (soft, hard, mixture), the orientation of the news story (behavior, weather, human interest, damage, information dissemination, organizational activities, hurricane history, or a mixture), and the location of the story (headline, page one story versus page 13 story or lead off broadcast news story versus an item buried later in the news program). The location of the story proved to be a valuable piece of information, for we found that the information gathered by the traditional content analysis format examining for disaster myth incidence, yielded an incomplete quantitative picture of the substance of the news stories we examined. By comparing the location of the news story which contained mythical versus accurate portrayals of behavior before, during and after Gilbert, with media type, i.e., print versus broadcast, we found what we believed to be a much more accurate quantitative picture. The emerging picture was compatible with the anecdotal evidence we gathered in the field.

Interview Guides

In interviewing local officials and media personnel we had two primary objectives. The first was to ascertain the extent to which the portrayed behavior may or may not be mythical in the case of Gilbert. The second objective was to determine the reasons why the mythology was perpetuated in the media, to the extent that it was found to be doing so. We sought to determine the extent of prior disaster experience for both local officials and the media personnel we spoke with. We also sought to determine if the interviewee believed in the disaster mythology or subscribed to a more accurate definition of the situation. For example, we would approach a broadcast reporter and start what appeared to be a casual conversation just after he or she completed a live feed, by asking, "you seem very experienced in dealing with storms like this, I'm curious what kind of behavior do potential victims usually engage in?" The answer to this question fit a rather uniform pattern: the average reporter believes the disaster mythology is not mythology, but reality. One exception was two newspaper reporters who had been exposed to the mythology information during an educational or training experience. The accuracy of their writings was far superior to that of other broadcast and print media personnel who believed in the mythology.

We sought to obtain an understanding of how the various media forms (local print, local television and network television reporters and crews) approach covering such a news story in order to determine variations in organizational structure which may explain variations in news content, slant, and so forth. We observed distinct differences in how the various media forms manage the story. We believe that these differences were instrumental in producing different pictures to the viewing and reading audience. One's perception of the behavioral response to the "Storm of the Century" may have depended upon one's chosen source of information.

Findings

Hurricane Gilbert's Life Cycle and Path of Destruction

Gilbert's destructive life cycle lasted approximately one week, from Friday, September 9 through Friday, September 16, 1988. It reportedly was responsible for several hundred deaths and caused billions of dollars of damage. On Friday, September 9, 1988, the storm which was to be Gilbert, had not yet been classified a hurricane. It passed by the Windward Islands (St. Lucia, St. Vincent, and Dominica) causing a reported $750,000 in damages to the banana crops on each island.

On Saturday, September 10, the storm sufficiently increased in strength to become a hurricane. The northern edge of the newly dubbed Hurricane Gilbert crossed over Puerto Rico causing power outages and an estimated $200,000 in crop damage. Other nearby islands reported flooding and agricultural damage.

On Sunday, September 11, five deaths were attributed to Gilbert in the Dominican Republic. One hundred families were reported to be homeless and there was widespread agricultural damage.

On Monday, September 12, Haiti reported 10 deaths due to Gilbert, serious agricultural damage, and many fallen buildings. Jamaica took a direct hit. There were reportedly 26 dead, an estimated 500,000 homeless, and $8 billion in damages. Reportedly, 80% of Jamaica's homes were damaged, 20% were destroyed.

On Tuesday, September 13, Gilbert hit the Cayman Islands with 130 mile per hour winds. Widespread flooding was reported and between 5% and 10% of the houses were estimated to have been destroyed.

On Wednesday, September 14, Mexico's Yucatan Peninsula was directly hit by Gilbert with 180 mile per hour winds and 18 foot waves. There were 17 reported deaths and millions of dollars in reported damage.

On Thursday, September 15, the day the field team left for the southern Texas Gulf coast, Gilbert was believed to be heading for the Galveston-Corpus Christi-Brownsville area and was expected to regain strength up to category 5. News broadcasts all along the coast urged citizens to prepare their homes for impact and many were asked to evacuate. Galveston, for example, called for an evacuation of the entire island. The National Hurricane Center indicated that impact was possible anywhere along the Texas Gulf Coast.

On Friday, September 16, Gilbert maintained winds of 120 miles per hour and made landfall at approximately 5:35 p.m. Central time, 120 miles south of Brownsville, Texas. It primarily impacted along the Mexican coast in an area almost totally devoid of people. Fortunately, the Texas Gulf Coast was spared. The torrential rainfall did cause flooding in areas further inland such as Monterrey, Mexico, which reportedly killed over 200. Tornadoes were spawned by Gilbert in Mexico and Texas. Damage was reported to have resulted from them, but no deaths. Gilbert, the media dubbed "storm of the century," was not.

Assessment of Actual Behavioral Response

As previously noted, certain behaviors are commonly assumed to occur during disaster events. These are: panic, looting, price gouging by local merchants, declaration of martial law, disaster shock, massive evacuations, and large shelter populations. During our on-site research in Brownsville, Corpus Christi, Galveston, and Houston, we sought to determine the degree to which any of these occurred. While we did not collect the specific numbers of, for example, the sheltered, we visited shelters, police stations and so forth to observe and interview appropriate personnel.

We found no verified instance of panic, looting, or disaster shock. Martial law was not declared. The evacuees and the sheltered appeared to follow the normal pattern, i.e., 10% evacuation rate and most evacuees stayed with relatives, friends or in motels/hotels. A small percentage of evacuees appeared to actually stay at shelters. A few out-of-town citizens, not merchants, did converge to Galveston to sell truck loads of plywood at inflated prices (300% above normal). There were two arrests for such in Galveston (broadcast media mistakenly reported that these were local merchants which perpetuated the myth, the local print media accurately reported the story). There were no verified instances of price gouging by local merchants or local citizens generally. In fact, examples of altruism were abundant as were examples of very rational preparatory behavior and the usual disaster subculture activities. The most common disaster subculture activities observed during Gilbert included surfing, hurricane (beer) parties, and converging to the beach to watch the tide rise. In each city, burglary rates declined from that which occurs during normal time. While weather is not included in the list of disaster myths, we do want to note that the only time we experienced any mildly severe weather was on Friday, the night of September 16, when we were along the Gulf coast in Corpus Christi. Wind gusts were between 50 and 65 miles per hour. On all other occasions whether in the motel, on the road, in an EOC, walking along the beach, interviewing media personnel, and so forth, we had difficulty believing we were in a hurricane area. The winds were actually quite calm, the rain was light, and the ocean waves were only slighting more threatening than normal. When we watched CNN reporters broadcasting live from the cities we were in, we sometimes went to our motel door and opened it to make sure we were not missing something-- the news report did not correspond with our own experience, we wondered if we were talking about the same event.

The Media's Portrayal of the 'Storm of the Century'

A hurricane has a slow onset time. It is, therefore, possible to monitor its development, follow its life cycle, attempt to predict landfall, and prepare for its impact. When Gilbert began its march of destruction through the Caribbean, the growing ferocity and size of the storm (a category five storm which was approximately 500 miles across at its peak) captured not only the attention of the National Hurricane Center, weather personnel generally, and Gulf Coast emergency management personnel and residents; it also captured the attention, and sometimes the imagination, of the mass media. Local television, radio, and print media personnel in the various coastal communities noticed. Local television, radio, and print media personnel in various communities throughout the nation noticed. Network television and nationally oriented print media personnel noticed. And media personnel from around the world prepared to cover the event. Our research team spoke with television and print media reporters and crew personnel from numerous Texas communities, as

well as from communities in California, Oklahoma, New York and Florida. The
national networks and media from other nations such as Holland, Japan, and Australia were represented. Media personnel converged onto the southern Texas Gulf
coast. Friday evening we stood along the coast in Corpus Christi, for example, and
saw an endless line of tripods strung along the sidewalks, parking lots, streets and
marinas. Mass media had invested heavily in covering this "Storm of the Century."
With such an opportunity at hand we decided to also gather data on and analyze
network news coverage of Gilbert in addition to the local broadcast and print media
coverage.

Our analysis of the media's coverage of Gilbert was based on our analysis of
243 television news broadcast stories or segments, 311 local newspaper stories, and
53 interviews. We interviewed local emergency management personnel, local government officials, local residents (evacuees and non-evacuees), local media personnel, and national media personnel. Interviews were conducted both on-site face to
face and by telephone, as well as off-site by telephone.

Broadcast Media. We recorded 243 news stories broadcast by the local Texas Gulf
coast television stations (Houston, Corpus Christi, and Brownsville) and the networks (ABC, CBS, CNN, and NBC) during our five days on-site. While we were
not able to record every broadcast made by CNN, which broadcasts continuous
news twenty-four hours a day, we were able to record virtually every Gilbert-related
news story broadcast by the other networks. We also recorded all the local television news programs which were broadcast while we were on-site during the pre-
impact, impact and post-impact time periods. We recorded and analyzed a total of
95 local television news stories and 148 network stories (see Table 4.5). This dis-
parity reflects the continuous coverage given Gilbert by CNN, which virtually
ceased normal broadcasting during the immediate pre-impact, impact, and immediate post-impact time periods. The other networks devoted the majority of there
normal evening news broadcasts to Gilbert during these time periods, but provided
little more than occasional minute updates. The local television stations continued
normal programming throughout Gilbert's life cycle. Some listed shelters which
were open by superimposing announcements across normal programming during the
day; otherwise, the only coverage given Gilbert was through devoting their normal
evening news broadcasts to storm coverage.

As previously mentioned, we were able to record 243 Gilbert news stories, 148
from the networks and 95 from local stations. Of the 95 locally broadcast news stories, 9 were from Brownsville, 23 from Corpus Christi, and 63 from Houston
(please see Table 4.5). In perhaps a crude fashion, this variation is indicative of the
attention given the storm over its life cycle. We were recording in Houston during
pre-impact (and somewhat during post-impact), in Corpus Christi during impact and
immediate post-impact, and in Brownsville and Houston during post-impact.
Broadcast media attention to Gilbert gradually increased through the pre-impact
period which extended over the better part of a week. The incidence of this coverage peaked just prior to impact. Coverage during impact was intense but the impact

period lasted for only a few hours. Coverage gradually declined during the post-impact period. This process is illustrated (in Table 4.5) by the fact that we recorded 126 broadcasts during the pre-impact period, 54 during impact, and 63 during the post-impact period.

With regard to the type of news (soft versus hard) being broadcast, two out of three news stories broadcast were thoroughly intertwined with both soft and hard news. Of the remaining third, soft news was broadcast over hard by a margin of approximately two to one (see Table 4.5).

TABLE 4.5:	BROADCAST NEWS DESCRIPTORS (N = 243 unless otherwise noted)	
News Source		
	Local TV	39% (95)
	Network TV	61% (148)
Broadcast Origin		
	Brownsville	4% (9)
	Corpus Christi	10% (23)
	Houston	25% (63)
	Network TV	61% (148)
Disaster Period		
	Pre-Impact	52% (126)
	Impact	22% (54)
	Post-Impact	26% (63)
News Type		
	Hard	13% (32)
	Soft	24% (59)
	Mix	63% (152)
Story Orientation or Slant		
	Behavior	42% (103)
	Weather	28% (68)
	Human Interest	1% (3)
	Damage	16% (39)
	Information	4% (10)
	Organizations	3% (6)
	Storm History	3% (8)
	Mix	3% (6)

The focus of the stories varied (see Table 4.5). However, the greatest plurality (42%) concentrated on the behavioral response to Gilbert before, during and after impact. Approximately a fourth (28%) of the news stories focused on weather reporting, while less than a fifth (16%) focused on reporting the damage created by

Gilbert. The remaining news stories (14%) focused on various items including public information (e.g., shelters available, how to prepare), organization activity (e.g.,
Red Cross, City Officials), the history of previous encounters with hurricanes in the
area (e.g., the worst hurricane death toll in U.S. history--the 1900 Galveston experience where 6,000 are believed to have died), and various human interest stories
(e.g., the hurricane travel experiences of one reporter).

Examining the results of the traditional aspects of our content analysis which,
as noted earlier, does not tell the whole story, we find that the television news stories were pretty accurate in their portrayal of the behavioral response to Gilbert (see
Table 4.6). We examined 243 news stories for evidence of mythical versus accurate
portrayal of 10 behavioral categories: panic flight, looting or other forms of storm
related deviance, price gouging, evacuating, sheltering, injury and death tolls, damage estimating, acting rationally, engaging in disaster subculture behavior, and behaving altruistically. There were a possible 2,430 instances of such behavior being
reported (243 stories multiplied by the 10 behaviors for which we examined).

TABLE 4.6: INCIDENCE OF DISASTER MYTHS IN BROADCAST MEDIA NEWS
(N = total across the rows)

	Accurate	Myth	Nothing
Panic	0% (0)	1% (2)	99% (241)
Looting	0% (0)	5% (13)	95% (230)
Price Gouging	0% (0)	2% (5)	98% (238)
Evacuation	8% (20)	14% (33)	78% (190)
Sheltering	3% (7)	5% (12)	92% (224)
Injury/Death	3% (8)	0% (0)	97% (235)
Damage	19% (46)	3% (7)	78% (190)
Act Rational	19% (46)	1% (1)	80% (196)
Subculture	7% (16)	1% (2)	92% (225)
Altruism	3% (8)	0% (0)	97% (235)

Most of the time (in 2,204 instances) the myths were not addressed in the story.
In 226 instances (103 stories) the myths were addressed in some way--either accurately or inaccurately. In the latter case (see Table 4.6), we find that two out of three
times the behavior is described accurately, e.g., potential victims are behaving rationally and not fleeing in panic flight. In only one third of the cases is the disaster
mythology perpetuated, e.g., fear of looting. On the basis of these numbers alone,
one could conclude that the broadcast media provided knowledgeable coverage of
the behavioral response to Gilbert.

This traditional approach to doing a content analysis fails to take into account
that the existence or occurrence of every mythical portrayal or accurate portrayal
does not influence the viewer (or reader in the case of a newspaper) equally. We
argue that it is reasonable to assume that the headlines and stories on page one of a

newspaper or the lead off story(s) of the evening news are more influential in forming reader/viewer perceptions of the behavioral response to a disaster than those
which appear later. We are not saying that the appearance of accurate or mythical
portrayals anywhere in the story do not influence the viewing or reading audience.
What we are suggesting is that impact can be rank ordered. Lead off stories and
headline stories are more likely to influence perceptions than those which appear in
a later story or are buried on page 33 of a newspaper. An examination of the results
of a traditional content analysis will suggest that there are few differences between
media type and accuracy versus error in the news stories. As researchers who were
on-site and who have thoroughly examined the data, and as consumers of the news
stories about Hurricane Gilbert, we felt we "knew" better, however. We used an
alternative approach to categorize the data in conducting our content analysis
which, we believe, is more qualitatively revealing of the potential impact the news
stories may have on forming accurate versus erroneous perspectives of the behavioral response to disaster.   First, we looked at each news broadcast (and each issue
of a newspaper) as a unit of analysis (instead of the story itself). A viewer sits down
to watch the evening news or a reader sits down to read a newspaper. We then tried
to view the data from the perspective of a potential news consumer, i.e., we looked
at the nature of the lead off story(s) (or headlined articles on page one of a newspaper). We categorized such stories in three ways: as either prominently displaying
myths or exaggerations, as non-prominently displaying myths or exaggerations (by
placing them late in the news program or buried in stories in the newspaper on, say,
page 13), or as being myth free. This analytical approach yielded some very interesting results. The lead stories on the network news (see Table 4.7), especially
CNN, portrayed elements of the disaster mythology (deviance and exaggerations) in
a majority (53%) of their news programs, while less than a fifth (18%) of the local
news programs contain elements of the mythology in their lead off stories. Conversely, one fourth of the network news programs were myth free and almost two-
thirds (64%) of the local news programs were as well. Anecdotal evidence will be
cited throughout the report to illustrate the qualitative differences between the *network* and *local* news coverage of Gilbert and to exemplify the reasons we believe
we found which explain why this variation exists.

TABLE 4.7: ANALYSIS OF BROADCAST NEWS PROGRAMS		
	Network TV	**Local TV**
Myths Prominent	53% (10)	18% (2)
Not Prominent	21% (4)	18% (2)
No Myth Appearance	26% (5)	64% (7)

Local Versus Network Television News Stories. The total story of the television
coverage of Hurricane Gilbert is not told by a traditional content analysis. The limi-

tation inherent in reducing human behavior to numerical analysis often loses something valuable in the process. The same is true for the current analysis. The field team, both while in the field and while reviewing the television news video, detected a clear, unmistakable difference in the focus of the local news from the national news treatment of Hurricane Gilbert. The interview process substantiated what we felt we saw but which was not as clearly revealed by the traditional content analysis format. By examining Table 4.8, we find that the story line of a majority (54%) of the news stories focuses on behavioral responses to the hurricane while approximately a third (35%) of the local stories do the same. On the other hand, approximately a third (32%) of the national news stories also focus on weather aspects of the hurricane while less than a fourth (22%) of the local stories do this. And, approximately a fifth (21%) of the national news stories focus on hurricane damage, while less than one in ten (8%) of the local stories do. There is a subtle, but distinct difference between local and national Hurricane Gilbert news reporting indicated by our content analysis. Local news tends to focus more on behavioral response and information giving, while national news focuses more on weather and damage.

TABLE 4.8: STORY LINE DIFFERENTIATED BY BROADCAST NEWS SOURCE (Total N = 243 unless otherwise noted)		
	Network TV	**Local TV**
Behavior	54% (51)	35% (52)
Weather	22% (21)	32% (47)
Damage	8% (8)	21% (31)
Info/Organizations	12% (12)	3% (4)
Misc	4% (3)	9% (14)
	100% (95)	100% (148)

This trend was also evident in the predominant settings for the background video shown during reporter's comments. We do not have hard data to support our observations we instead draw from our anecdotal information compiled during analysis of the taped news broadcasts. Local news broadcasts tended to be filled with reports from on-the-scene roving reporters reporting live from city hall, an evacuation shelter, a beach, a damaged home, a police roadblock, and so forth. National news broadcasts, on the other hand, tended to be filled primarily with reports that appeared to be on the scene, but were not . . . at least not to the same extent as the local news reports were. The network news rotated from one coastal city to another to get a live, on the scene report from their man or woman "in the field." In virtually every case, the reporter was physically stationed along the beach with rising tide pictured in the background. To the unsuspecting television viewer the reporters appeared to be doing a credible job reporting on the progress of the hurricane. The waves and wind would be expected to increase and mess the reporter's hair. The viewer had no reason to suspect otherwise. Since we were on-site, we could observe the behind the scenes activity of the news organizations and interview relevant news personnel. A picture emerges which points to a very different normative and social structural-organizational approach to how the local and national organizations covered Hurricane Gilbert. The local news crews are familiar with the local officials and the local organizations charged with responding to the emergency at hand. In some cases they were on a first name basis with these officials. In many instances they knew who they could trust to get an accurate assessment of the situation. The local news organization was acting as an extension of the local political and emergency structure. To be sure, the local news organization is a separate entity, and often a critical one at that, but local norms seemed to dictate that it willingly join in the mission to get out the *information* to help the people in their community.

The traditional content analysis format does not reveal the slant of the news stories. The above observation, i.e., the combined normative mission of the local emergency organizations and the local news organizations, was revealed to us through anecdotal data gathered both on-site and during the analysis of the news broadcast. Through our interviews of local news media personnel it became apparent that the dominant norm governing their behavior during an emergency event was to get out the *information that will help their community*. Yes, they were trying to get good stories. While each reporter may secretly hope for the story that will win a Pulitzer, their primary quest was to provide information which would help the viewing audience, e.g., in deciding to evacuate or not, what to do and where to go if they do evacuate. The norm of getting good information for the community audience was reinforced by the belief that this audience was motivated to watch their broadcast for the information that may govern their decisions.

The national news reporters, however, operated from a very different normative mission. Our interviewing of reporters and anchors for network news organizations, combined with our observations of their news presentation activities, led us to conclude that the driving norm of the national news organization was to get a picturesque *story*. The story was expected to be attention grabbing, with *dramatic* footage which will motivate the viewing audience to stay tuned rather than change stations. The national news organization did not see itself as broadcasting to a localized audience which was attempting to get information that may impact upon its decision-making processes. Instead, the national organizations were more engaged in a ratings battle, hence the quest for the good picturesque story. A good *story* and good *news* is not the same product.

To offer an example of the normative process the national news personnel went through, in variation to the local organizations, we will share a synopsis of several interviews and some personal observations. The evening we were in Corpus Christi we informally interviewed several members of a network news team preparing live satellite feeds from Corpus Christi. The crew members, who did not know the nature of our work, shared, in response to various questions, their observations on the preparation of the live reports their anchor and reporters made. The unanimous view of the interviewees was something like:

> A great deal of creativity (read: imagination) goes into these newscasts. He (anchor) positions himself in front of those palms and out in the rain for effect . . . high drama, all drama. . . we spent the day driving all up and down the coast looking for something exciting to tape for background video tonight, nothing, there was nothing (the storm is a fizzle here). They (network) put so much money into this thing, we have to report something. . . so, drama, high drama.

While our sources were talking, we observed a reporter preparing for a live feed to the network by moving from the protection of the hotel overhang to a drizzly location in front of a palm tree whose branches appeared to move most freely and dramatically when the wind blew. He then messed his hair just before air time ("drama, high drama").

The local organizations did not exhibit this quest for drama. As noted earlier, the norm governing their news gathering and reporting behavior appeared to be distinctly different: to gather the news that relayed a precise description of the behavioral response, organizational response and weather in their community in order to facilitate local preparation for and recovery from impact. These organizations appeared to feel a responsibility to their community and sought to be an active part in the preparation and cleanup activities by doing what they could to aid in the situation, i.e., gather and disseminate information. Just as altruism governs much of the behavior of individual survivors to disaster, we detected an air of altruism on the part of the local news personnel, at least when compared to the national news media.

In addition to normative variation, we detected a structural difference between local and national news organizations which we believe impacts upon the variation in the reporting product. The local news personnel, as previously noted, are more likely to know some of the key decision-makers in the local emergency response organizations. *They travel to the officials* they seek to interview in order to provide information directly to their audience. Local officials tended to plan their news conferences with the local news broadcast hour in mind. The local news could provide live coverage for the emergency management official who wanted to get up-to-date information directly out to the citizenry. The altruistic norms governing the local media resulted in their cooperation in this process by essentially turning their access to the airwaves over to such officials. While the national news personnel attend some staged, previously announced press conferences and also do some additional on-site interviewing, they appear to have a greater tendency to *bring those they want to interview to their location.* This may appear to be an insignificant difference, but we argue that it impacts dramatically on the slant of the news broadcast. Interviewees are brought to the location of the network's satellite dish for the live feed. This location is usually one which provides the most drama for the video considerations, e.g., Corpus Christi coast with rising tide and blowing palm leaves in the background. By bringing selected local officials to this location specifically for an interview, the network has greater control over what is broadcast. They are selecting who will speak for the community. Those selected are more likely to tell the story from the perspective the news personnel *believe* to reflect the situation accurately. The network producer and director, as well as the reporters, are in control here. For example, if the news personnel believe in the disaster mythology, they may be inclined to select interviewees who report observing or fearing such activities. The reporter *believes* he is accurately reporting on disaster events. Since the interviewees are flattered to be on national television, they are often willingly led by the reporter.

The *local* media, on the other hand, functioned in their communities as a conduit. While they sought interesting stories, local officials were usually broadcast (live) reading their prepared statements. Interviews focused more on individuals with whom they had a prior working relationship and in whom they trusted to provide "the truth."

National news personnel tended to be more follower than leader in that they would arrive on-site and would locate, for example, where the press was meeting local officials for interview purposes and press conferences (following or acting like the pack animal, as Scanlon, 1988, describes it). A national network crew announces their presence and begins interviewing the official who appears to know what he or she is talking about. The judgment as to who is knowledgeable is *not* made on the basis of a prior working relationship. It is made on the basis of who has the greater command presence. For example, when we were interviewing the Corpus Christi city manager, a television crew from another city arrived and asked to interrupt our interview. I readily agreed seeing this as an opportunity. During this interview I interjected some information I had which the city manager had not yet received. I had my credentials on to facilitate entree, so I looked very professional, knowledgeable and, I think, my presentation of self was somewhat authoritative. The television reporter took notes as if what I was saying were Gospel. I believe I could have told her anything and it would have been believed or at least reported.

To further exemplify the pack animal nature of the national media, when we arrived in Corpus Christi, we were amazed at the number of tripods and satellite dishes lining the coast. Crews from across the country and from around the world were side-by-side, block after block along the coastal highway. Many major hotels were on this road, the crews were staying in these hotels and were set to report from literally right outside their hotel rooms. They were on-site in that they were in the city which was expected to be impacted by the hurricane, but they did not conduct interviews where their sources were originally located. Network people did drive through the city, but they sought sources who agreed to come to their coastal site in the evening to do an interview during a live network feed. It was quite a sight to see television equipment and reporters lined shoulder to should, block after block. Were they *getting* the scoop or trying *not to be scooped*? Since they looked like pack animals, we think the latter is more accurate than the former.

These anecdotal observations are shared in order to provide what we think is an accurate analytical focus to the qualitative differences that do exist between the local and national news broadcasts (remember Table 4.7). We noted above that the differences in story line did not tell, in our view, the complete story of these differ-

ences. And, the variation in accuracy versus myth in the presentation of panic, looting, price gouging, evacuation estimates, sheltering estimates, injury and death estimates, damage estimates, description of rational behaviors, disaster subculture
behavior, and altruism, needs the analytical focus just provided in order to explain
the differences in accuracy that we observed. Hence, we argue that the normative
and social structural differences between local and network news gathering and reporting result in differences in accuracy.

Variation in Broadcast Accuracy. By looking at Table 4.9, we can see that 80% of
the local news stories accurately portrayed references to the disaster myths while
only 52% of the network news stories contained accurate references. Conversely,
38% of the network stories contained mythical references while only 22% of the
local news stories did. It appears that the local news stories were more accurate
overall than the network stories.

There was little difference in accuracy or myth rates between local and network
news when it came to their treatment of panic, looting, price gouging, and injury
and death estimates. The most striking differences concerned the handling of
evacuation, sheltering and damage estimates, as well as the emphasis on rational
behavior, disaster subculture behavior and altruism.

Disaster researchers (see Quarantelli, 1987 for example) know that the number
of evacuees is usually overestimated by local officials. In most instances, approximately 10% of the potentially affected population evacuates. In the case of the cities
of the southern Texas coast during Hurricane Gilbert, we suspect the evacuation
rate may have been higher than the norm given the previous experience that these
communities had suffered during other recent hurricanes. There is no evidence,
however, in our view to support the claims of the network news reporters that the
towns along the coast were "ghost towns, with most people having left--all but a few
stragglers who refuse to go." When we drove up and down the streets of these cities
we found the neighborhoods full of people preparing for the storm. They flooded
shopping centers to buy batteries, other supplies, and food. They were in their yards
securing lawn furniture and boarding up windows. We do not believe the (news)
reported estimates that between 60% and 80% were leaving. We suspect that 20%
would be closer to reality.

The network "stage setting" results in exaggerated evacuation estimates. More
than one network reporter stood in the deserted streets, sometimes at 3:00 a.m., cit-
ing the empty backdrop as evidence of the massive evacuation of the city. When the
downtown stores are closed so that employees can go home to prepare for the storm
and possible evacuation, it is unlikely that shoppers would be downtown window
shopping during an impending hurricane. It is quite rational for those shoppers to be
at home--not only to prepare for the impending hurricane, but also because most
people do not window shop even during non-emergency time at 3:00 a.m. What
struck the analysts as even more remarkable was that such claims of massive
evacuation were frequently followed by news footage showing hundreds of locals
strolling the beaches, surfing and otherwise engaging in typical disaster subculture

behaviors. The contradiction usually escaped the reporters. To be sure, local reporting also included some broadcasts which overestimated evacuation figures, but their
level of accuracy was distinctly greater than the networks (14% of the news accounts dealt with evacuation estimates accurately versus only 5% for the network
reporting, please see Table 4.9).

TABLE 4.9: INCIDENCE OF MYTHS DIFFERENTIATED BY BROADCAST NEWS SOURCE (Total N = 243 unless otherwise noted)				
	Local TV (N=95)		Network TV (N=148)	
	Accurate	Myth	Accurate	Myth
Panic	0%	2%	0%	0%
Looting	0%	5%	0%	5%
Price Gouging	0%	2%	0%	2%
Evacuation	14%	11%	5%	16%
Sheltering	3%	2%	3%	8%
Injury/Death	5%	0%	2%	0%
Damage	11%	0%	24%	5%
Act Rational	30%	0%	12%	1%
Subculture	10%	0%	5%	1%
Altruism	7%	0%	1%	0%

The literature on behavioral response to disaster (see Dynes, 1970) observes
that most evacuees do not go to shelters but stay with relatives, friends or rent mo-
tel/hotel rooms instead. In conjunction with the exaggerated estimates of evacuees,
the numbers of those sheltered were usually exaggerated. Some local and network
broadcasts exaggerated the sheltered population as well. We visited some shelters in
Corpus Christi during the impact and immediate post-impact periods only to find
less than two hundred people in shelters. The director of the shelter indicated that
few shelters were opened in the city, for their disaster plan stipulated that as one
shelter fills up, another will be opened. Even if every shelter had been opened and
filled to capacity, the total sheltered population would not have equaled the estimates being broadcast.

The network news was more inaccurate than the local news in two ways. First,
the estimates were even further inflated on the network news than the local news.
Second, a higher percentage of network news stories dealt inaccurately with these
estimates (7% versus 2%, see Table 4.9). We suspect that this greater inaccuracy on
the part of the network news is the result of two influences. Most network news had
a distinct flavor of exaggeration which we tie to the norm governing their reporting
behavior: get good video, offer us a good story. And secondly, the pack animal nature of the network news personnel leads to a kind of "whisper down the lane" phe-
nomenon. For example, one CNN reporter stated on air that "someone around here
said that perhaps as many as 60,000 are housed in shelters." The individual he was

referring to was a fellow reporter from an affiliate. The direct live feed facilitates such inaccuracy in our opinion, for the normal time editing process is short-circuited as Wenger and Friedman (1988) observed. The rumor-based story is more likely to go directly over the airwaves during a disaster while the editing norms are more closely adhered to during normal time broadcasts.

Networks commonly exaggerated the weather conditions. For example, a CNN reporter stated that the "wind is picking up now" and suddenly stepped backward as though to catch himself from falling in response to a wind gust. The wind gusts were not exceeding 35 miles per hour at that point (far below hurricane strength) and the wind had, in fact, not been picking up before, during or for hours after that broadcast. The crew members we interviewed suggested that "when you broadcast continually and invest this much equipment and personnel in a story, there *will* be a story."

Accurate Portrayal of Behavioral Response. We now turn our attention away from myths and to three areas that the literature (see, for example, Quarantelli, 1987) identifies as typical behavior so a comparison can be made. Victims and potential victims tend to behave in a very rational manner. They prepare themselves if time permits by purchasing bottled water, food, flashlight batteries and so forth. Many localities that are frequently affected by disaster events, such as hurricanes, tend to develop what Wenger (1980) labels "disaster subcultures." Citizens in such locales will sometimes throw hurricane parties and surf in the big storm created waves. And thirdly, most victims and potential victims tend to not respond to disaster events selfishly (as looters or price gougers), but tend to demonstrate altruism. They help one another, give food away, organize search and rescue groups long before emergency organization personnel arrive on the scene.

In our content analysis we sought to assess the extent to which the local and network broadcast media portrayed rational behavior, disaster subculture behavior and altruistic behavior in an accurate way. We once again found local news reports to be far more accurate than the networks (see Table 4.9). Rational behaviors were pictured and articulated on 30% of the local news reports, while only 12% of the network reports did so. Disaster subculture behavior was accurately portrayed by the local news 10% of the time while only 5% of the network news reports contained such references. And altruistic behaviors were accurately portrayed in 7% of the local newscasts while the networks did so only during 1% of their reports.

Impact of Organizational Structure. Our interviewing of local and network personnel suggests the primary reasons for these differences are tied to the structural variation in the two levels of television news broadcasting. Almost all news personnel believed the disaster mythology. I "played dumb" and asked reporters, for example, "how do people usually behave during these things? Since you have seen so many you must have a clear picture?" To a person, they gushed forth with a complete description which formed the essence of the mythology: looting, price gouging, antisocial behavior generally, "crazy behaviors," very selfish, panicky, and an inability to respond (shock) to the events that follow. Reporters frequently asked public officials if there has been any looting, price gouging, and so forth. One anchor asked a reporter who was broadcasting live (from in front of his hotel), if there had been "any crazy behavior, looting and price gouging . . . ." The reporter responded that local officials felt that they "had things under control and did not expect such to occur." Even if they reported that these behaviors did not occur, the questions were asked and answers reported in such a way that would lead one to believe that such things usually did occur during disasters. The accuracy of the local news was held hostage to the knowledge limits of the local officials who spoke for their emergency organizations. In most instances, we found the local officials and emergency management personnel in the Texas coastal communities to be fairly knowledgeable and accurate in their perception and understanding of the typical behavioral response to disasters. This observation is, however, qualified in that we are referring only to the designated spokespersons for these organizations. Individuals within the organizations were often found to be far less knowledgeable and more likely to believe in the mythology. For example, in one area the city manager repeatedly went on local television warning citizens to prepare to leave the area rather than wait for an official evacuation declaration. He acknowledged the difficulty in getting people to leave. He stated, through the media, that roadblocks and police patrols were in place to "guard against looting in those areas where citizens have evacuated." When we interviewed this city manager, he spontaneously acknowledged that looting does not normally occur during disasters but he had to "convince the people that steps were taken to prevent it, otherwise they would never leave, but would stay to protect their property against imagined looters." Of course, in communities where officials believe the mythology, the "news" they broadcast may be erroneous, even though the altruistic norm of getting information out to save the community still may govern local news personnel behavior.

Local Print Media. We analyzed 311 Hurricane Gilbert news stories published in the *Brownsville Herald*, the *Corpus Christi Caller Times*, the *Galveston Daily News*, and the *Houston Chronicle*. We were able to obtain copies of every issue of the Galveston newspaper published for the pre-impact, impact and post-impact periods. We were not able to obtain every issue of the remaining newspapers which were often sold out before we were able to reach those cities. Most (88%) of the news stories were written by the newspaper staff while approximately a tenth (12%) of the hurricane news stories were written by AP or UPI staff members (please see Table 4.10).

A majority (57%) of the news stories were devoted to pre-impact activities; slightly more than one tenth (13%) were devoted to impact activities; a quarter of the stories (25%) focused on post-impact activity; and the remaining 5% of the stories reported on a mixture of activity occurring during two or more disaster time periods. The observed variation is to be expected. Hurricanes are slow-onset events; the pre-impact period is often the longest time period of the storm's life cycle. Therefore, the print media has a longer time to write about the storm, thus generating more articles for this time period. The impact period, on the other hand, is the shortest time period of a hurricane's life cycle. One would expect fewer stories to be written about activity during this period. In contrast to television news stories, which primarily consisted of soft or mixed news, the local print media focused primarily on hard news (60%). Only a third (34%) of the hurricane stories were soft with the remaining 6% being a mixture of the two (see Table 3.10). The print media was similar to the local broadcast media in that it seemed to be governed by the altruistic norm of gathering and disseminating information that would be helpful to saving the local community. The depth of detail is, of course, much greater in the print media since local staff reporters are not competing to offer the best thirty second sound bite. A newspaper article is by design a vehicle which facilitates the relaying of information to a more thorough extent than is possible in the current format of the television news story.

TABLE 4.10:   PRINT MEDIA NEWS DESCRIPTORS
            (N = 311 unless otherwise noted)

News Source
Staff   88% (273)
Network TV   12% (38)

Newspaper Origin
Brownsville   11% (33)
Corpus Christi   14% (42)
Houston   39% (122)
Network TV   36% (114)

Disaster Period
Pre-Impact   57% (178)
Impact   14% (42)
Post-Impact   25% (77)
Mix   4% (14)

News Type
Hard   60% (187)
Soft   34% (105)
Mix   6% (19)

Story Orientation or Slant
Behavior   29% (89)
Weather   10% (30)
Human Interest   5% (16)
Damage   11% (34)
Information   13% (41)
Organizations   29% (89)
Storm History   1% (3)
Mix   2% (9)

There was a greater range of news stories published in the print media. Returning to Table 4.10, we find observe the number of stories focusing on behavioral response to the storm is equal to the number of stories reporting on storm related organizational activities (29% each). While the broadcast media also focused on storm related behavior, it did so far more often (42%) than the print media (29%). The broadcast media had fewer stories (3%) about organizational activity than the print media (29%). The print media also devoted more newsprint to pure information dissemination (where shelters were, etc.) than the broadcast media (13% for the print media versus 4% for the broadcast media).

We found the print media's stories to be very accurate in their portrayal of the behavioral response to Gilbert (please see Table 4.11). We examined 311 news stories for evidence of mythical versus accurate portrayal of the ten behavioral categories. There were 3,110 possible instances of such behavior being reported (311 stories multiplied by the 10 behaviors for which we examined). Most of the time (2,806 instances), the behavior was not addressed in the story. Behavior was addressed in 304 instances. The behavior was described accurately three-fourths of the time (77%). In less than one fourth (23%) of the stories myths were perpetuated, e.g., fear of looting. The news stories were rather accurate in the portrayal of the behavioral response to the storm. To the extent that there were inaccuracies, they were centered upon the perpetuation of the looting and price gouging myths. Inaccuracies occurred slightly less frequently than they did in broadcast media news stories. And, the print media reporting was distinctly more accurate in their published estimates of evacuees, the sheltered and damage. The print media parallels the local broadcast media in that both will likely have working relationships with key leaders and can discriminate between those who are knowledgeable versus those who were not, unlike the network news personnel.

TABLE 4.11: INCIDENCE OF DISASTER MYTHS IN PRINT MEDIA NEWS (N = 311 totaled across the rows)			
	Accurate	Myth	Nothing
Panic	1% (4)	4% (13)	95% (294)
Looting	2% (7)	7% (21)	91% (283)
Price Gouging	2% (6)	3% (10)	95% (295)
Evacuation	13% (39)	3% (8)	84% (264)
Sheltering	3% (8)	3% (10)	94% (293)
Injury/Death	9% (28)	0% (0)	91% (283)
Damage	15% (46)	1% (1)	84% (264)
Act Rational	19% (59)	2% (5)	79% (247)
Subculture	6% (18)	0% (0)	94% (293)
Altruism	6% (20)	1% (1)	93% (290)

Even when myths about deviant behavior were portrayed in the print media, they were usually found either in articles buried in the newspaper (not headline news) or buried in an article receiving essentially passing notice. On the other hand, the broadcast media tended to highlight behavioral responses to the storm that perpetuated the mythology. To be sure, most print reporters, but not as many as among the broadcast media, believed in the disaster mythology. The focus of their stories, however, was less sensational than in broadcast media stories. The norm governing their news gathering and reporting behavior was not "get the equivalent of *good video*," but "report on the varied activities of individuals and organizations in preparation for impact and cleanup." A hard news orientation coupled with organizational norms in variance to the broadcast media, and particularly the networks, led, in our view, to a more even-handed and accurate presentation of the behavioral response to the "storm of the century."

If we examine Table 4.12, we find the print media followed a pattern similar to that of the local broadcast news. Most (78%) of the newspapers either did not prominently display articles which contained behavioral myths or they were myth-free. Only 22% of the newspaper editions prominently displayed articles which portrayed aspects of disaster mythology. If we compare network news broadcasts with both types of local media combined, we find an indication of the extent to which there was divergence between the national news and local news coverage. While a majority (53%) of the national news programs led with stories that perpetuated the disaster mythology, the opposite was true for the local media (21%). We observed earlier that local broadcast media behavior appeared to be more altruistic. It sought to help the community. This may result from the fact that the local broadcast personnel lived in the area and defined themselves as potential victims along with the other local residents, while the network personnel are outsiders converging to the scene to get the story which will promote their career.

TABLE 4.12: BROADCAST NEWS PROGRAMS & DAILY NEWSPAPERS

	Network TV	Local TV	Print
Myths Prominent	53% (10)	18% (2)	22% (4)
Not Prominent/None	47% (9)	82% (9)	78% (14)

	National	Local Media
Myths Prominent	53% (10)	21% (6)
Not Prominent/None	47% (9)	79% (23)

The network media devoted most of its air time to live feeds from their reporters in the coastal cities. The local broadcast media devoted most of its air time to reports on multifaceted storm related activities from various settings within their community. The local print media devoted the bulk of its newsprint to an even greater variation of storm related activities. In viewing the network news one feels excitement or hype; when reading the newspaper accounts one feels he is exposed to a cross-section of the experience of preparing for and living through the threatening storm in the locale.

Local Staff Writing Versus Wire Service Writing. We compared local newspaper writing with that from the wire services. By examining Table 3.13, we find the story line of a plurality of the staff stories focuses on behavioral and organizational responses to the storm (31%) and organizational responses (31% each). On the other hand, the wire stories focused on storm damage (26%) and weather.

TABLE 4.13: STORY LINE DIFFERENTIATED BY PRINT NEWS SOURCE
(Total N = 311 unless otherwise noted)

	Staff	Wire Services
Behavior	31% (85)	11% (4)
Weather	8% (22)	21% (8)
Damage	9% (24)	26% (10)
Info	13% (35)	16% (6)
Organizations	31% (84)	13% (5)
Misc	8% (23)	13% (5)

Most of the wire service stories did not have a byline published with the story, so we were not able to interview wire service writers. We did, however, interview staff reporters from each newspaper. These reporters shared the same belief in the mythology as the broadcast media reporters, thus the occasional focus on resident fears of looting and price gouging. These reporters also shared the same approach to news gathering as the local broadcast media, which we believe was directly responsible for the high degree of accuracy in reports on other behavioral responses to the storm, i.e., being part of the local social fabric, these news people had previously developed working relationships with numerous community leaders. The reporters used their contacts during such emergency events, seeking those they believed were most accurate. Of course, just as with the local broadcast media, the print media reporters were dependent upon the actual accuracy of these local officials. Since we found many local officials in the cities threatened by Gilbert to be rather knowledgeable with respect to the behavioral response to disasters, the perpetuation of the mythology was limited. Many reporters still asked leading questions which reflected their own belief in the mythology, but since the local officials were fairly knowledgeable and since the reporters were essentially acting as an information disseminating extension of the local emergency officials, the print news stories were accurate (some reporters even wrote articles stressing the fact that the burglary rate actually decreased). The print media assumed the local officials were their best source for the most complete picture of what was occurring in their community, this perception on the part of the media could be characterized as an example of what Quarantelli (1981) calls the command post view of disasters. The press assumes the validity of the command post view which, of course, may not always be a safe as-sumption.

Variation in Print Media Accuracy. While the stories published in local newspapers were rather accurate, there were lapses in this accuracy, as noted above. Deviant behavior, e.g., looting and price gouging, was the most common myth to appear. This inaccuracy was counter-balanced though with attention given to the rational behavior, typical disaster subculture behavior and altruism that occurred. There were differences, however, between the degree of accuracy found in local staff writ-ing versus that published from the wire services (see Table 4.14).

Table 4.14: Incidence of Myths Differentiated By Print Media News Source (Total N = 311 unless otherwise noted)				
	Staff (N=273)		**Wire Service** (N=38)	
	Accurate	**Myth**	**Accurate**	**Myth**
Panic	2%	5%	0%	0%
Looting	3%	7%	0%	5%
Price Gouging	2%	3%	0%	3%
Evacuation	14%	2%	5%	5%
Sheltering	3%	3%	0%	5%
Injury/Death	8%	0%	16%	0%
Damage	15%	0%	16%	3%
Act Rational	21%	2%	5%	3%
Subculture	7%	0%	0%	0%
Altruism	7%	0%	5%	3%

Articles written by the local staff tended to be more accurate than wire service articles when it came to evacuation estimates (14% versus 5%), descriptions of ra-tional behavior (21% versus 5%), and disaster subculture behavior (7% versus 0%). Wire service articles were found to focus more on damage, death and injury report-ing than behavior. Both staff and wire service articles reflect a high degree of accu-racy in these areas.

Concluding Summary and Observations

We believe that a rank-ordering of the news sources analyzed for accuracy in re-porting on the behavioral and organizational response to Hurricane Gilbert, yields the following: the local print media was the most accurate, followed by the local television broadcast media and then the network news reporting which was judged to be the most likely to exaggerate. When myths were portrayed, those most likely to appear in any medium were myths perpetuating belief in an increase in deviance during disaster such as looting and price gouging. The behaviors most likely to be reported accurately were those dealing with the rational preparation, clean-up activities engaged in by individuals and their families, the typical disaster subculture activities such as surfing, and instances of usual altruism, e.g., search and rescue activities. Typical exaggerations centered on evacuation and shelter population estimates. Degree of accuracy did vary by media type.

To summarize our findings and observations on the local and network television news broadcasting on Hurricane Gilbert, we found the television news, generally, to be relatively accurate. There were some references to panic, looting, price gouging and other imagined forms of deviant behavior which perpetuated the mythology. Property damage, injury and death estimates were also judged fairly accurate. The usual exaggerations in evacuation and sheltering estimates were observed to occur. Altruism, instances of typical disaster subculture behavior and the rational behavior of local citizens preparing for, and cleaning up from the storm, were all portrayed.

An underlying cause of the myth perpetuation which did occur was the widespread belief in the disaster mythology among news personnel. Their mistaken definition of the situation frames their news gathering and reporting perspective. Even when officials are not mistakenly reporting such behaviors, reporters frequently asked if any had occurred, implying that their occurrence is normal and to be expected.

Differences in accuracy were observed between local and network reporting. The news gathering and reporting behavior of local news personnel was primarily governed by an altruistic norm. They sought to gather and disseminate the information their community needed in order to adequately prepare themselves and to protect the community from impact. Even though most local news personnel believed in the mythology, the accuracy of their reporting was enhanced by their organizational approach to the news. They tended to devote large portions of their coverage to the prepared statements of emergency management spokespersons. Hence, the accuracy of their news depended upon the accuracy of these sources. They were found to be accurate in the communities under study.

The news gathering and reporting behavior of network news personnel, on the other hand, was primarily *not* governed by an altruistic norm, but by a self-interest norm. They were not part of the community, but converged to it for the purpose of covering the storm. As it became clear that the storm would not impact directly on the Texas coast, they had to go ahead and gather "good pictures" and portray the drama they expected of such an event. They were there to cover the big story, and they created, staged, and broadcast as big a story as they could. Weather impact, evacuation rates and the number of the sheltered were all reported to be much higher than the final determination. They staged events that they thought were indicative of what was really happening. The trouble with their organizational approach was that they were wrong about what they thought typically occurs.

To summarize, we found the print media to be very accurate. There were some references to panic, looting, price gouging and other imagined forms of deviant behavior. Property damage, injury and death estimates were fairly accurate. And, the usual exaggerations in evacuation and sheltering estimates were observed to occur. Altruism, instances of typical disaster subculture behavior and the rational behavior of local citizens preparing for, and cleaning up from, the storm were all portrayed.

As with the broadcast media, print media personnel believe in the disaster mythology which frames their news gathering and reporting perspective. Myth perpetuation is the direct result. Even when officials are not mistakenly reporting such behaviors, print reporters asked if any had occurred, implying that their occurrence is normal and to be expected. The print media stories were far more diverse than broadcast news, particularly network news. A more complete picture of the behavioral and organizational response to Gilbert was obtained from the printed stories. The news broadcasts were generally rather superficial and the network news was often more fable (as Nimmo, 1984, observed) than fact.

The network media particularly functioned as pack animals (Scanlon, 1988) and gathered in herds along the coastal beaches of those southern Texas cities deemed most likely to be impacted. They tended to bring interviewees to their satellite locations and sent film crews around the area to obtain dramatic video which they would use as a backdrop for their summarized versions of the behavioral and organizational response to Gilbert. The network productions were far more staged than the local news. Print media stories were more focused on getting out information that would be helpful to the local citizens. The network audience was seen as being more global and an entertainment ethic seemed to be the primary focus of those reporters who converged on the south Texas coast.

While reporters from all mediums sought the command post view (Quarantelli, 1981) of the disaster, local reporters (both broadcast and print) devoted more of their reporting to what the local officials were saying than the network reporters did. In the case of Gilbert, this facilitated greater accuracy, as many of the officials were very knowledgeable. The network crews sought to manage their news to present the story that they believed accurately portrayed what occurs in such a disaster. Their creative efforts, however, tended to result in greater inaccuracy. Their erroneous definition of the situation, coupled with the organizational structure which allowed them to stage what they sought to broadcast, produced the more fabled version of the news story.

Chapter 5

Organizational Response to Disaster

While the public often believes the behavioral response to disaster is deviant and chaotic, it tends to believe emergency organizations are prepared to respond fairly effectively. The behavioral response, as previously noted, is actually very altruistic. Ironically, the organizational response is often quite chaotic. The effectiveness of the organizational response may depend upon the level of prior planning, the extent to which emergency plans are rehearsed, and the degree of prior disaster experience. For example, in 1988 a small mid-western city ordered an evacuation for about 800 people who lived near a burning warehouse which housed toxic substances. Evacuees were not found to panic, engage in looting, or exhibit any of the other behaviors which constitute the disaster mythology. However, when I called the local emergency manager's office I was told that they "think he is at the fire." They had been unable to reach him and were not sure where he was. I found him at the temporary command post about a half mile from the burning building. Then when I called the mayor's office, he said that he had been sitting there for "the last hour and a half answering the phone, I cannot call out and find out what is going on because every time I finish an incoming call another one comes before I can call out." It is typically difficult for those attempting to respond to a disaster to quickly communicate with one another and obtain accurate information. For this reason many emergency personnel resort to the media, just as the average citizen does. When asked how many were asked to evacuate, the mayor replied: "I really don't know, *our best source of information has been the local radio* which has people on the scene." If the media is the best source, then one hopes that the media *is* a very accurate source of information during the disaster. This source, as discussed in the previous chapter, can sometimes be very inaccurate.

EMERGENCY ORGANIZATIONS

What constitutes an emergency organization? An emergency organization is charged with the responsibility of responding to emergency and disaster incidents such as fires, chemical spills, floods, and hurricanes. The Federal Emergency Management Agency (FEMA) believes that the model community will have a written comprehensive disaster plan which stipulates which office will coordinate the community's disaster response (Wenger, Quarantelli & Dynes, 1987). Depending on the community, the local emergency management agency, the fire department, the police department, the sheriff's office, the public safety director's office, the mayor's office or the county commissioner's office may be designated as the disaster coordinating agency or one may emerge after a disaster occurs. Regardless of who coordinates the response, most, if not all, of these organizations respond to an emergency by completing their specialized mission. Emergency medical services (hospitals, ambulance, rescue squads), the Red Cross, and the Salvation Army also offer their skills. The media (radio, television and print) become part of the emergency response by gathering and disseminating information.

Actual Organizational Response

Emergency organizations often strive to convey the image "that everything is under control." What occurs in most post-impact communities is closer to organized disorganization. Accurate information is difficult to obtain; decision-makers often have a hard time communicating with one another; the written disaster plan (if one exists) is often ignored during a real emergency; the pre-impact designated disaster coordinator may not emerge as the actual post-impact leader; individual organizations are likely to carry out their self-defined mission without coordination with the other emergency organizations; decisions are often made based upon disaster myths and inaccurate media information, and turf battles often result in less than complete cooperation between the various emergency organizations (Fischer, 1989). The aftermath of a disaster is usually nothing like that which the organizations had anticipated (Fischer, Schaeffer & Trowbridge, 1992). Its massive disruption of normal time activities requires much more organizational flexibility and interorganizational cooperation than had been previously expected.

For example, in the aftermath of Three Mile Island (TMI), local leaders, the Governor's office, the Nuclear Regulatory Agency (NRA) and the (U.S.) President's office all sought to learn what had happened, why, and what to do about it. They were interested in managing the damaged reactor and protecting the affected population. Emergency managers and political leaders, as well as the populace, had a very difficult time trying to obtain accurate information about what had happened at the power plant, what to do about it, and how to best protect people in the area. The national media reported everything from a meltdown to a leak of a small radioactive cloud into the atmosphere. The implications of these two events vary greatly. A complete meltdown would be a catastrophe for at least hundreds of thousands of people, while a radioactive leak may possibly become a problem for a few hundred or few thousand people. "Nearly a quarter of the reporters had a single expert on tap . . . the rest of the reporters made *themselves* into experts--fast" (Sandman and Paden, 1979:54; see also Scanlon, Dixon, and McClellan, 1982:29, 30). "Many reporters had no scientific background. . . and had difficulty presenting this information to the public in a form that would be understandable" (President's Commission on the Accident at Three Mile Island, 1979:58).

An Effective Response

Disaster researchers (for example see Wenger, Quarantelli, and Dynes, 1987; Kreps, 1978:80; Mileti, Drabek, and Haas, 1975:81 & 95) have observed various conditions under which emergency organizations are more likely to respond effectively to a disaster event. One important factor is the *degree of recognition* the local emergency office has before a disaster event occurs. If it is recognized as *the qualified disaster coordinator before an event,* then it is more likely to have the *autonomy* it needs to coordinate the response. The more autonomy this office has to warn of an impending disaster, to order an evacuation, to begin search and rescue activities, to direct damage assessment, to receive and distribute information, to initiate sheltering, to activate security measures, to restrict convergence activities (e.g., the flood of sightseers), to oversee the restoration of essential services, and to coordinate local decision-making, the more effective the organizational response is likely to be. The more extensively involved this office is in preparing for and activating the above response activities, the more effective the organizational outcome.

The effectiveness of inter-organizational communication, i.e., obtaining and distributing accurate information, contributes to the effectiveness of the organizational response (for example see Gray, 1981:361; Scanlon, 1977). A huge convergence of information impacts upon those organizations trying to respond to a disaster. Most communities have the technological capacity to communicate effectively, but they fail to do so because the various emergency organizations do not freely share information with one another. For example, the fire department is very experienced in responding to a fire and taking charge of the situation. However, it is very unlikely that the fire department has any experience responding to an actual nuclear meltdown. A nuclear disaster is much broader in scope and magnitude than a fire emergency. While very experienced in responding to and coordinating the response to everyday emergencies, the fire department would normally lack experience responding to any disaster of such magnitude.

A *fully functioning emergency operating center* (EOC) aids in the *communication of information* and the *coordination of decision-making.* An ideal EOC houses the technological equipment for communicating with the various responding organizations, similar to, but more extensive than a police station's radio or communication room. It includes work space for representatives of the various emergency organizations so that they may all be housed together in an effort to better facilitate information flow and decision-making. The EOC in Hamilton County, Mississippi, serves as an example. This EOC provides a separate work station and phone for a representative from every emergency organization conceivable, e.g., fire, police, Red Cross, Salvation Army, and public safety. It also is the center from which the local emergency management director seeks to *coordinate* the community response to a disaster. This EOC is designed to serve as an information hub, with updated information flowing into and out of the EOC. Needs assessments and decisions are ostensibly completed much more effectively through the use of the EOC communication network.

If a local emergency management organization has the *authority and ability to procure and distribute human and material resources,* as well as *delegate and coordinate necessary tasks,* then an effective response is more likely. Many communities suffer from the lack of a clear emergency time authority structure which has been tested through prior disaster experience or regular, realistic drills. When I was in a Virginia community as part of a field team during the post-impact period following a 1987 flood, I found the designated local emergency manager to be essentially powerless. A local government official with prior disaster experience and the confidence of the mayor behind him, emerged to take control of what had been a less viable response (in the opinion of researchers on the scene and apparently the local government officials as well).   Just as it is important to coordinate the disaster response among the various local emergency organizations, *coordination with outside private* as well as with *state and federal organizations* increases the likelihood of an effective response. *Maximizing use of the resources available* has already been noted as a contributing factor. Whether they are local, state or national resources, their effective coordination contributes to an effective overall response.

As the *cooperation between the emergency management organizations and mass media increases,* the chance of an effective disaster response increases. An effectively managed emergency management organization is more likely to be able to gather accurate information. If accurate information is freely shared with the media, accurate reporting is enhanced which better serves the public. Cooperation also increases the likelihood that response activities will be based upon real, not mythical, needs. When the disaster myths are not activated, an effective response is more likely. Remember the previously mentioned small mid-western city mayor who was depending upon the local media for information to help him make appropriate disaster response decisions? His decisions would only be as effective as the available information were accurate.

Summary

Emergency organizations are more likely to have trouble responding effectively to a disaster than individuals are to become deviant in the aftermath of an incident. Prior disaster experience, the presence of a clear authority structure, accurate information gathering and dissemination, a fully functioning EOC, appropriate procurement and distribution of human and material resources, proper task delegation and coordination, cooperative coordination of information flow with the mass media organizations, coordination with outside private as well as state and national organizations, and response activities based upon real rather than mythical needs all contribute to an effective community response. Disaster research continues to play a role in helping FEMA, as well as state and local emergency managers, develop strategies that facilitate effective organizational response to disasters.

FIRST CASE STUDY: LEMA MYTH SURVEY: HAS ANYTHING CHANGED IN 20 YEARS? WHAT THE PROFESSIONALS BELIEVE & THE ROLE OF EXPERIENCE

Local emergency management agency (LEMA) coordinators are gaining an increasingly accurate understanding of the actual behavioral response to disaster. There are still many, however, who continue to adhere to the mythology. Fischer and Drain (1993) argue that organizational response to disaster is based upon the problems which the LEMA director expects to encounter during a disaster. If he believes in the disaster mythology then the prepared response will reflect mythical problems--resulting in an increased risk of loss of life and property. The following case study empirically illustrates how belief in the mythology has decreased over the last twenty years, while still remaining unacceptably high.

Abstract

Fifty-four local emergency management agency (LEMA) directors from the state of Ohio responded to a mail-questionnaire which sought to demographically describe LEMA directors, to enumerate their disaster and job experience, to determine how accurately they understand behavioral response to disaster, to determine which disaster myths are most often believed, and to determine if education, disaster experience, and EMS experiences are associated with a more accurate understanding of the behavioral response problems commonly encountered during a disaster. The typical LEMA director was a 50 year old male who earned $25,000 in 1990. He has completed high school and then completed several college courses during his EMS career. He has been employed in EMS for 14 years, seven of which have been served as LEMA director. He has attended 8 training seminars (one every 2 years), participated in 5 disaster drills (one every 3 years), and has worked through 2 disasters (one every 7 years) during his career. The respondents performed better on a disaster knowledge scale than did their predecessors a decade earlier, which suggests that education and training have had an encouraging impact. They still averaged only a 65% (the equivalent of a "D") on the disaster knowledge scale. *Education, training,* and *experience* were found to be associated with a more accurate perception of the behavioral response to disaster. A response rate of 61% was attained after two mailings.

LEMA Disaster Response

The Federal Emergency Management Agency (FEMA) was established to coordinate the federal response to disasters. Virtually every state has a state emergency
management agency to coordinate their state response. Local governments usually
have their own local emergency management agencies (LEMA) to coordinate the
local response. These local agencies are typically charged with the responsibility to
develop written disaster plans, organize disaster drills, hold or attend training seminars, educate segments of the community on how to prepare for and respond to disasters. They are often expected to take the lead in coordinating the response to a
disaster during the immediate post-impact period (Drabek, 1986). When devising
disaster response plans and, then, when actually responding to a disaster, the planning and response will be strongly influenced by the accuracy of the perception the
LEMA's have of the typical problems they are likely to encounter during the immediate post-impact disaster time period. As Hultaker and Trost (1978:9) observed,
when "disaster planners base their efforts on misunderstandings about how humans
behave during disasters then planners will plan for difficulties which will not occur
while they will disregard the real difficulties" that will occur. Hultaker and Trost
further state that "the greater the degree that disaster plans reflect myths about social behavioral responses, the greater the likelihood they will be ineffective." The
literature also notes that emergency organization officials also tend to subscribe to
the disaster mythology. They did not have as strong a mythical view, however, as
the general public. Wenger, James, and Faupel (1980:91) discovered that while
mythology was prevalent within the belief system of local emergency organizational
officials, it was less so than among the public at large. That is, more officials (43%)
gave correct responses on their disaster knowledge scale than did the public (30%).
"The lowest scores were found for local police, fire, military, and medical authorities while the highest levels of insight were held by directors of local Offices of
Emergency Preparedness [LEMA's] followed closely by local government officials" (cited in Drabek, 1986:31). When LEMA officials have been found to believe
in the disaster mythology, they have been found to make disaster response decisions
that may adversely affect the public good. Information about danger which should
be disseminated to the public to facilitate their evacuation is often withheld "because of a fear that people will panic" (Dynes, Quarantelli, and Kreps, 1972:31). It
would be more effective to assume "that persons in a disaster-impacted area will
actively respond to the emergency and will not wait for community officials to tell
them what to do" (Dynes, Quarantelli, and Kreps, 1972:32).

Study's Focus: Has anything changed in 20 years?

The cited literature on the impact of the disaster mythology upon disaster planning
and response is, in many instances, between ten and twenty years old. The current
project was conceived to determine if there has been any change during this time,
i.e., has LEMA belief in the disaster mythology further declined? Presumably, the

training and other educational efforts over this time would have an impact resulting in a more accurate perception of the behavioral response problems encountered during time of disaster. The focus of the current project was to examine the extent to which LEMA directors believe in the disaster mythology, identify those myths which are most versus least frequently believed, and to examine variables which may explain variation in myth subscription. The project was also designed to provide a demographic description of the typical LEMA director, at least as found in the mid-western state studied.

How the Study Was Conducted

A mail-questionnaire was completed by the local emergency management agency directors of a mid-western state in which entree had been gained. The state of Ohio frequently experiences both technological and natural disasters. The questionnaire contained both closed-ended and open-ended questions. The usual demographic data was sought for gender, age, education, and race. Work experience data was also sought, e.g., years worked as LEMA director as well as years worked within the emergency management field generally, the number of training seminars and disaster drills participated in, and the number of major emergencies or disasters experienced. A disaster knowledge scale was devised for the questionnaire. The questionnaire was mailed to the emergency manager in each county of the state. Since there were eighty-eight counties in the state, there were eighty-eight possible respondents for the survey. A second mailing was conducted involving those who had not responded to the first one. The response rate was 61% which is considered adequate (Babbie, 2004). Those who responded to the survey were observed to not significantly differ from the total population of interest. Appropriate statistical analyses were conducted on the data.

Demographic Characteristics

Information on gender, age, education and income were obtained from the respondents (refer to Table 5.1). The typical LEMA director was a 50 year old male who earned $25,000 in 1990. He completed high school and then completed several college courses during his EMS career. Each demographic variable is described below.

Gender and Age. The position of LEMA director is apparently still a male domain in that the vast majority (85%) were men; less than two in ten LEMA positions (15%) were held by women. The director's age ranged from a low of 31 to a high of 77 years of age. The mean and median age was 50 years. A third (33%) were between the age of 31 and 45, another third (37%) were between 46 and 54, while the last third (30%) fell between ages 55 and 77.

Education and Income. The average LEMA director was a high school graduate who has completed several college courses. Approximately one third (30%) graduated from high school. More than one-third (41%) completed at least one college course. Therefore, more than two out of three directors (71%) did not graduate from college while less than a third (29%) did. Reported income had a wide distribution range. The lowest paid director received less than $15,000 a year while the highest paid director reported an annual income of $70,000. The average income was $25,000. Approximately one-fourth (24%) of the directors reported earning this average. Almost one third (31%) reported earning less than the average and almost another third (29%) reported earning between $30,000 and $40,000 a year. Less than one in six directors (16%) reported earning more than $40,000 a year (but not more than $70,000). It appears that the position of LEMA director is not a highly paid one for most of those holding it.

Table 5.1:	Selected Demographic Characteristics Population N = 54		
Gender		**Education**	
Male	85%	High School	30%
Female	15%	Some College	41%
		College Graduate	29%
Age		**Salary**	
31-45	33%	Less than $20K	31%
46-54	37%	$20K - $30K	24%
55-77	30%	$30K - $40K	29%
mean = 50		$40K - $70K	16%
		mean = $25K	

Job Experience

The respondents were asked to indicate how long they have worked in emergency services, how many years they have served as LEMA director, how many disaster training seminars they had attended, how many disaster drills they had participated in, and how many major emergencies or disasters they had worked (refer to Table 5.2). We found that the typical director had been employed in emergency management for fourteen years, seven of which he had served as LEMA director. The typical director reported attending eight training sessions, participating in five disaster drills, and experiencing two disasters during his career. He attends a training seminar once every two years, participates in a disaster drill once every three years, and responds to a major emergency or disaster once every seven years. The range of job experience is described below.

Years in EM. The average respondent had worked 14 years in emergency management. Half (50%) of the respondents reported working less than 12 years in the field. Approximately one in ten (13%) were new to the job, working less than a year. A third (33%) worked 6 years or less. Another third (34%) worked between 7 and 15 years, the final third (33%) worked at least 16, but no more than 42 years.

Table 5.2: Disaster Experience, Job Experience, & Mythology Belief
N = 54

Disaster Experience		LEMA Director Experience	
0 Disasters	20%	0- 2 Years	30%
1 Disaster	23%	3- 5 Years	22%
2- 3 Disasters	24%	6- 9 Years	28%
4-20 Disasters	33%	10-40 Years	20%
Mean = 3 Median = 2		Mean = 7 Median = 5	
EM Experience		Training Seminars	
0 - 6 Years	33%	0 - 3 Seminars	24%
7 - 15 Years	34%	7 - 8 Seminars	26%
16 - 42 Years	33%	9 - 17 Seminars	26%
Mean = 14 Median = 13		18 -100 Seminars	24%
		Mean = 13 Median = 8	
Disaster Drills		Disaster Mythology Score	
0 - 2 Drills	24%	0 - 11	33%
3 - 5 Drills	26%	12 - 14	39%
6 - 11 Drills	26%	15 - 20	28%
12 -100 Drills	24%	Mean = Median = 13	
Mean = 10 Median = 5			

Years as LEMA Director. While directors ranged from being new to the job to being very experienced, with 40 years experience as director, the average number of years served as director was seven. Almost one quarter (22%), however, were new to the job. A plurality of respondents indicated they were new to the job which suggests a somewhat inexperienced workforce. Almost one third (30%) had served as director for less than two years. Half (52%) of the directors had served no more than five years, further demonstrating the limited experience as director on the part of so many respondents. The remaining half (48%) are scattered from between six years of service to 40 years. Only two, however, had served more than 18 years. Since only two served more than 18 years, the average for the length of service is some-what exaggerated rendering the median (5 years) as a more appropriate indicator of the service of the typical director.

Training Seminars. The average number of disaster training seminars reportedly attended was thirteen over the career of the respondent. The number reported ranged from zero to 100. Hence, the median is a more useful indicator of the degree of training. Half (50%) of the respondents reported attending no more than eight seminars. A full 90% reportedly participated in as many as 30 training seminars. If the typical respondent had attended eight seminars and had worked in EMS for 14 years, he was attending a seminar once every two years.

Disaster Drills. There was great variation in the number of disaster drills the LEMA director participated in during his career. Only six had never participated in a drill. One respondent reported having participated in 100 drills. The average was 10, but actually half (50%) of the respondents participated in no more than five drills rendering the median (5 drills) a more useful indicator of the experience of the typical director. Approximately two-thirds (63%) participated in no more than eight drills. If the typical respondent had worked 14 years in EMS, he had participated in approximately one drill every three years.

Major Emergency & Disaster Experience. More than half (57%) of the respondents reported participating in no more than two major emergencies or disasters during their EMS careers. A fifth (20%) participated in no such emergencies or disasters. Two out of every three respondents (67%) experienced no more than three. Almost all (94%) experienced no more than eight. Only three respondents reported more experience: one person reported 10 and two individuals reported 20. Hence, the typical director responded to a major emergency or disaster approximately once every seven years.

Has Anything Changed in 20 Years? Answer: A Qualified Yes

Belief in Disaster Mythology

The respondent was asked to respond to a series of Likert scaled statements which comprised our disaster knowledge scale (see Table 5.3). These statements were developed to test belief in the disaster mythology, e.g., the extent to which looting on the part of local citizens would be a major problem needing attention after a disaster impacts a community. The respondent was asked to indicate the likelihood of each of twenty items being problematic during a disaster event. He was asked to scale his response as "very likely," "likely," "unlikely," or "very unlikely." We then coded the respondent's answer as "0" if he rated a myth from the disaster mythology as very likely or likely to occur or as "1" if he rated a myth as not (very) likely to occur. Conversely, we coded the respondent's answer as "1" if he rated an accurate statement as very likely or likely to occur or as "0" if he rated an accurate statement as (very) unlikely to occur. The summed, scaled responses could range from a low score of zero (meaning he completely believes in the disaster myths) to a maximum of twenty (which suggests that he has a completely accurate perception of the behavioral response during a disaster). In this study, the scores ranged eight to eighteen. The mean score was thirteen. As noted earlier, Wenger, James, and Faupel (1980:91) discovered that the LEMA professionals scored better on their disaster knowledge scale (43% correct answers) than the general public (30% correct answers). Both scores, however, would constitute a failing grade if 43% and 30%

were grades earned on a classroom exam. In the current study, scoring a mean of 13 is equivalent to a 65% which suggests there has been a positive change. A score of 65% is significantly better than 43%. It would appear that the educational training is having a positive impact. This observation is good news. However, if a student were to score a thirteen out of twenty on a quiz, the accompanying grade would be a "D" (65%). This is still hardly an excellent outcome. If preparation for disaster response is dependent upon one's perception of the anticipated problems, then we need to do better.

Which Myths Are Believed and Which Are Not?

By recoding the responses to the disaster knowledge scale to identify the respondents' answer as "accurate" or "mythical," we were able to rank order the disaster behavior items on the scale from *most* accurately perceived to *least* accurately perceived. Please refer to Table 5.3 to examine the frequency distributions for each. Each item of the disaster knowledge scale is examined below.

Most Accurate. Almost all (98%) of the respondents correctly understood that emergency workers will usually behave in an unselfishly. They normally place community needs above personal concerns. They also understood that survivors usually are the first to engage in search and rescue activities (85%). The respondents accurately perceived (83%) that local leaders do not normally panic and that local residents tend to help one another during a disaster (80%). Three-quarters (76%) of the respondents indicated that they were aware of the tendency for outsiders to converge to the disaster area, often resulting in heavy traffic congestion. Similarly, approximately three-fourths (74%) correctly perceived that local residents often converge to the (potential) impact area as well. Three out of every four respondents (74%) reported knowing that survivors do not normally engage in price gouging their fellow victims. Approximately the same number (72%) knew that local merchants do not usually engage in price gouging the members of their community.

Table 5.3:   Disaster Knowledge Items - Listed Most to Least Accurate
N = 54
total 100% from left to right

	Myth	Accurate
Most Accurate		
[1] Emergency Workers Will Not Be Selfish	2%	98%
[2] There Will Not Be Volunteers Shortage	15%	85%
[3] Local Leaders Will Not Panic	17%	83%
[4] Local Citizens Will Help Each Other	20%	80%
[5] Outsiders Converge to Area	24%	76%
[6] Local Convergence for Sightseeing	26%	74%
[7] Local Citizens Do Not Price Gouge	26%	74%
[8] Local Merchants Do Not Price Gouge	28%	72%
Less Accurate		
[9] Local Residents Refuse to Evacuate	32%	68%
[10] EM Workers Will Not Leave Posts	32%	68%
[11] Survivors Will Not Behave Selfishly	33%	67%
[12] Shelters Will Often Be Under-Used	37%	63%
[13] Residents Will Be Looting	39%	61%
[14] There Will Not Be Too Few Shelters	46%	54%
Least Accurate		
[15] Citizens Will Not Panic	50%	50%
[16] Residents Will Not Behave Irrationally	54%	46%
[17] Survivors Will Know What to Do	61%	39%
[18] Damage Estimates Not Initially Accurate	61%	39%
[19] Death/Injury Estimates Not Accurate	63%	37%
[20] Residents Will Prepare Before Impact	69%	31%

Less Accurate. Barely more than two-thirds (68%) of the respondents reported knowing that residents often refuse to evacuate before or after a disaster. Two-thirds (68%) also knew that emergency workers do not usually leave their posts to check on their families. And, two-thirds (67%) knew that victims and survivors are often altruistic rather than selfish during disasters. A majority (63%) were aware of the tendency for shelters to actually be under used, with evacuees preferring to stay with relatives, friends, or at a motel. Similarly, a majority (61%) of the respondents realized that looting rarely occurs before or after a disaster. And, slightly more than half (54%) knew that, in most cases, enough shelters are opened and/or available if needed.

Least Accurate. Half (50%) the respondents realized victims or potential victims usually do not panic during a disaster. Less than half (46%) knew that survivors usually do not behave irrationally due to the shock of the experience. Approximately one-third of the respondents realized that survivors will not be so traumatized that they will be incapable of responding (39%), that initial damage estimates will tend to be inaccurate (39%), that initial death and injury estimates will be inaccurate (37%), and that potential victims will often prepare if forewarned that a hurricane, for example, is nearing impact (31%).

Education, Training, & Experience Make A Difference

Training, Disaster & Work Experience as LEMA Director: Yes

Three of the experience variables appear to influence how accurately the director perceives behavioral response. Turning to Table 5.4, we find that a majority (59%) of those who had taken part in more than the median number (eight) of training seminars had a more accurate perception of the behavior response problems. These respondents earned a score that was greater than the mean score of thirteen. Conversely, a majority (56%) of the respondents who participated in fewer than the median number of training seminars scored below average on the mythology scale. A similar pattern was observed between disaster experience and belief in disaster myths. A majority (58%) of those who had experienced at least two disasters (the median) had a more accurate view of behavioral response, i.e., their score was higher than the average. A majority (57%) of those who had either no disaster experience or who had experienced only one disaster, earned a low disaster mythology score (one which was below average). And finally, a majority (58%) of the more experienced LEMA directors, i.e., those who had been in this position for longer than the median of five years, had a more accurate understanding of behavioral response patterns. A majority (54%) of the less experienced directors, on the other hand, held a less accurate understanding as they scored below average on the disaster mythology scale.

Table 5.4: Education, Training, & Experience Make a Difference Total 100% Down Columns							
	Education			**Training**		**# of Disasters**	
	High Sch	Some College	College Grad	0-7	8+	0-1	2+
MYTH 1-13	56%	50%	37%	56%	41%	57%	42%
SCORE 14-20	44%	50%	63%	44%	59%	43%	58%
	Years Director		**Drills**			**EM Years**	
	1-5	6+	0-5	6+	1-12	13+	
MYTH 1-13	54%	42%	48%	48%	44%	52%	
SCORE 14-20	46%	58%	52%	52%	56%	48%	

Drills & Work Experience in EMS: No.

The findings for the other two experience variables were somewhat surprising. The number of disaster drills in which the respondent had participated apparently had no influence on how accurately he perceived behavioral response to disaster (refer to Table 5.4 again). Essentially half of the respondents believed in the myths (48%) and half did not (52%) regardless of their level of disaster drill experience. Perhaps the impact of the disaster drill is dependent upon how accurate the drills portray behavioral response patterns and the organizational response required. Increased experience, if defined as years worked in the disaster field, does not appear, in itself, to make it more likely that the respondent will gain an increasingly accurate perception of the behavioral response problems encountered during disasters. While a majority (56%) of the less experienced respondents did not subscribe to the disaster mythology, a slight majority (52%) of the more experienced directors had a less accurate understanding of how citizens behave.

Education: Yes.

Education plays a significant role in making it more likely that the LEMA director will more accurately understand the behavioral response problems. The greatest change from myth subscription to myth rejection was observed when we compared those who had no more than a high school education with those who had completed at least a bachelor's degree. Only two in five (44%) high school graduates held an above average understanding of behavioral response problems, half (50%) of those who had completed some college course work held an above average understanding, while almost two-thirds (63%) of those who had graduated from college held an above average understanding. Education had a greater impact than disaster experience, or any of the job experience variables (training seminars, drills, years on the job, and years in the field).

Summary

The current study had several objectives. (1) To determine if LEMA directors were more or less likely to believe in the disaster mythology than twenty years ago. (2) To identify which myths are most likely to be believed. (3) To assess the impact of training, experience and education on belief in the mythology. In his 1980 study, Wenger found the average disaster knowledge score for EMS personnel to be 43%, while the current study observed an average score of 65%. While we were encouraged that the LEMA directors scored 22% higher than their predecessors twelve years earlier, we must also note that a 65% is equivalent to a "D" on a classroom exam. If EM personnel have an accurate understanding of these patterns, then we believe that their disaster response planning and mitigation adjustment activities will be pertinent to the challenges they are likely to confront during the various disaster time periods. If, for example, the director believes that he must be careful when to call for an evacuation for fear that people will panic, then he will have a tendency to plan to evacuate later than is really desirable. If he does not realize people hesitate to evacuate when told to do so, he will be unprepared to facilitate an effective evacuation. Disaster planning will be driven by the perceptions held by the planner. The more accurate the perception of disaster needs, the more accurate the preparation to meet them. It is encouraging to find that education, job and disaster experience contribute to increasing the respondent's disaster knowledge. Those who were better educated, had more job experience (as director), and greater disaster experience scored higher on the disaster knowledge scale. These findings suggest that emphasis on increased education and training will yield dividends. Perhaps hiring individuals with a college degree and then involving them in an on-going EM training program is optimal. The LEMA director and other EM personnel may attain a more accurate understanding of the behavioral response patterns common to disaster settings. Again, continued improvement in disaster planning and response should follow.

Caveats

First, the mail-questionnaire, as a methodology, always has its own limitations. The problems related to the "self-report" nature of such survey research has been documented frequently by Babbie (2004) and others. Second, the response rate was fairly good, but not excellent. The respondents, however, did not appear to vary significantly from what is demographically known about LEMA directors. Third, we selected, as our population of study, the LEMA directors of one U.S. state. We cannot, therefore, generalize with certainty to all LEMA directors in the United States or their colleagues outside of the U.S. We do argue, however, that our findings, i.e., the role of formal education, training, and disaster experience, are instructive for all who work in EMS.

Future Endeavors

The numerous case studies developed through meticulous field work have made, and will continue to make, great contributions to the literature. We also need to continue to investigate the answers to the various research questions posed by the literature through methodologies that will facilitate generalization beyond the individual cases studied. Hence, we would like to see disaster researchers continue to employ survey techniques which will enable such generalization. Field work resulting in case study generation is valuable, but we must also move beyond case studies at some point in order to determine if the findings are applicable to the population of interest. And, although disaster research falls within what academics define as applied research, theory needs to increasingly be employed in order to broaden our explanatory understanding of the human response, both that of victims and the professionals who plan for and respond to, disaster events. Unfortunately, all indications suggest greater need for such understanding in the future as more and more humans are residing and vacationing within disaster prone areas.

SECOND CASE STUDY: MEDIA'S IMPACT ON EOC RESPONSE
EOC PREOCCUPATION WITH MEDIA: DOROTHY'S EXPERIENCE

As previously noted, one indicator of an effective organizational response is LEMA-Media cooperation. This second case study illustrates how difficult it can become to establish cooperation. The agenda of the disaster response coordinator and the media may sometimes follow divergent paths. The result can be conflict.

Abstract

A three-person field team devoted four days to gathering data in Andover, Kansas, after a tornado devastated the Golden Spur Mobile Home Park on April 26, 1991. The research focus was to assess the extent to which the media's reporting of the local emergency management team's response to the disaster influenced the team's subsequent decisions. The researchers functioned as participant observers in the EOC, informally interviewed principal EOC members and media personnel, and obtained copies of media news stories (television and newspaper) which reported on the organizational response to the disaster. An assessment of the observations and interview data as well as the content analysis of the news stories, suggests that the EOC team devoted a considerable portion of their time to responding to the negative press they received centering around two issues: pre-impact warning and post-impact debris clearance. Some of the media's news stories sought to engage in blame assignation. The EOC members developed strategies to attempt to limit the emerging media-driven public relations problem. The relevant disaster research literature will help explain the response of both the EOC personnel and the media.

Andover (Kansas) Tornado Impact: April 26, 1991

What would Dorothy have found if she had returned from Oz on Friday, April 26, 1991? The answer depends on the time of day. If she had arrived at 6:00 p.m. she would have found the residents engaged in their normal activities. If she had arrived after 6:39 p.m., she would have been confronted by the horror of what looked like a reenactment of the bombing of Hiroshima.

The Event

On Friday, April 26, 1991, the work week was ending, the community's children and their parents were looking forward to the weekend. For the residents of Andover, however, this would *not* be a normal weekend. Thirteen lives would end, 175 others would be injured, 840 individuals would lose their homes, and seven million dollars in damage would be sustained by a Kansas community of 4,047 before the day was over.

The Golden Spur Mobile Home Park is located just east of one of the main traffic arteries leading into the central business district of Andover, a suburb of Wichita. The park had contained 241 mobile homes housing approximately 1,000 people. The residents represented a cross-section of the citizens of Andover: newly weds, singles, young families, middle-aged couples, retirees, and so forth. The town's police chief numbered among the residents of the mobile home park. The city government offices are housed approximately one mile north of the park. The central business district of the community is located approximately two miles north of the Golden Spur.

On the evening of Friday, April 26, some residents of the Golden Spur were not yet home from work, others had gone out for dinner or to run errands, many others were at home. By 6:00 p.m. a tornado watch had become a warning. Local radio and television stations broadcast this warning for the Wichita/Andover area. Unfortunately, numerous residents did not have their radio or television turned on when these warnings were being broadcast. Many people had no idea a tornado was approaching their community. To make matters worse, the neighborhood "civil defense" siren which was supposed to sound the warning, apparently did not work when it was activated. Furthermore, when a local police officer risked his own life trying to warn the park residents by driving up and down the streets of the Golden Spur sounding his police car siren just minutes before impact, many residents did not know (or remember) that such police action is a warning to take shelter.

At approximately 6:39 p.m. a tornado did impact the Golden Spur trailer park destroying virtually every trailer in the park. Thirteen people died and 175 were injured. More deaths and injuries had been averted for two reasons. First, many residents were not at home. Second, 200-300 residents had heard the tornado warning and went to the underground shelter located in the center of the park. They watched in horror as the tornado crushed their mobile homes. The park sustained an impact from an unusually large and powerful tornado. The police chief was in the shelter watching his own home being destroyed. He was in constant radio contact with the police station while the tornado continued its destruction. Listening to recordings of his messages to police headquarters provided a chilling indication of what the victims were experiencing. The destruction was so massive and total that FEMA certified the Andover site as a federal disaster area.

Research Goal and Methodology

The Natural Hazards Research and Applications Information Center's "Quick-Response Grant" program (University of Colorado) supports research which is focused on questions best answered through gathering data during the immediate post-impact period of a disaster event. A three-person field team from the Social Research Group (SRG—which has since evolved into the Center for Disaster Research & Education, CDRE), Millersville University of Pennsylvania, was supported by such a grant when it proceeded to the Andover site within forty-eight hours of impact. The team sought to assess how the media's reporting of the LEMA response influenced subsequent LEMA decision-making. The research literature notes the contribution made by the media in warning the public of an impending disaster and in disseminating helpful recovery information (see, for example, Drabek & Stephensen, 1971, for a discussion of the radio as a warning source; and Quarantelli, 1980), but less is known about the role of the media in influencing the LEMA decision-making process.

The research director and two research assistants remained in the field for four days functioning primarily as participant observers in the temporary emergency operating center (EOC). The team informally interviewed virtually every member of the EOC team, e.g., the mayor who served as the emergency response coordinator, a county commissioner, city councilmen, various city workers, and police personnel. The field team also observed and interviewed several print and broadcast media personnel who were working on news stories of the event. The field team sought to gain an understanding of what the EOC was attempting to coordinate and how they prioritized their actions pursuant to meeting the needs and desires of their various constituencies, e.g., victims, volunteers, city workers, and the larger public.

The members of the research team easily gained entree to the EOC. The research director had spoken with one of the LEMA personnel by telephone prior to leaving for the field. This LEMA official was receptive to our research participation and indicated that he would serve as our "sponsor." When we arrived in the field we asked for our contact and presented our credentials. The EOC personnel invited our complete participation. In fact, we had to make it clear that we were not there to advise, but merely to observe and gather information that could be helpful to others as they develop their future disaster plans. We functioned as participant observers. We were free to enter and leave the EOC as we wished. We observed virtually all EOC meetings during the four days of our field work. We completed informal, one-on-one interviews, during non-busy periods. The principal EOC personnel were very candid about their situation, i.e., the problems they were facing in trying to coordinate a response, their perceived failures, and their irritation at the media. They were very frank during their EOC meetings in discussing the details of how they should respond to the media and various community constituencies. The completeness of our entree became readily apparent to us during our second and third days in the field when they were openly discussing how they should react to the media's blame-fixing. Local officials were coming under increasing criticism in the broadcast and print media for allegedly not adequately warning the Golden Spur residents.

An interview guide was committed to memory by the field team members prior to entering the field. This informal guide contained open-ended questions designed to obtain the respondent's perspective of what problems they were encountering in responding to the disaster, how these problems were being addressed, by whom and when. We sought to ask what individuals and what organizations were involved in the response. We sought to ask the EOC personnel what they thought they would do differently (or similarly) should they face such a situation again. And, we intended to ask them to describe their perspective on the media's activities in helping or hindering the response process.

After entering the field and observing EOC activities, the team realized the limited utility of the interview guide. We found it far more useful to just observe every conversation, meeting, and discussion that we could. We tried to inconspicuously take notes. We used our tape recorders to dictate notes and to sometimes record interviews. Most of our interviews became conversations which helped us to piece together the decisions made by the different emergency organizations. We were trying to understand the interactive decision-making process of this emergent (EOC) group.

We interviewed every member of the EOC team. The team was comprised of personnel from local government agencies and volunteer organizations. We also interviewed leaders and workers in volunteer organizations which had no direct affiliation with the EOC, e.g., the Mennonite Disaster Services, and we interviewed local print and broadcast media personnel. We completed a total of 32 interviews while in the field.

The field team obtained copies of the local newspapers published during the first month of the post-impact and recovery periods in order to determine types of stories and the slant of the stories being published about the EOC's disaster response. While in the field the team also video-taped news broadcasts of two of the local television stations for later content analysis.

Did Media Reporting Influence EOC Decisions?

What We Found Upon Our Arrival

We immediately assumed the role of observer. We conducted interviews when possible. The EOC personnel appeared to be pleased to be of help to our research effort and to contribute to helping other communities who will plan for such events in the future.

The community did not have a written disaster plan. There was no full or part-time local emergency coordinator. The mayor emerged during the immediate post-impact period to function as the coordinator of the city's response to the tornado. Various other local elected officials emerged to function as a committee of advisors to assist the mayor. Community, church, and volunteer organizations converged to assist the elected officials in coordinating the cleanup. The field team found the EOC located in an empty store front in a small strip-mall adjacent to the destroyed mobile home park. The EOC contained a conference table with enough chairs to seat approximately fifteen people. A felt-tip writing board was mounted on a wall on which information was written, e.g., problems needing attention, names and phone numbers of key personnel, the mayor's next scheduled press conference. A typewriter, telephones, and eventually a television and a photo-copying machine were installed. Almost everything in the EOC, including the store it was housed in, was donated by local businesses.

EOC security was maintained by the local police department which numbered five uniformed police officers. Within thirty-six hours of impact a security badge system was in place. No one was allowed into the EOC area without a security badge. A communications bus was positioned directly in front of the store (EOC location). A Red Cross Canteen was located in the parking lot near the communications bus. Various additional volunteer organizations, e.g., ham radio operators club, were working out of other vacant stores or vehicles in the mall parking lot.

Anyone from the EOC wishing to visit the disaster site could simply walk to it within a few minutes. The field team made numerous such trips. The National Guard was on-site to prevent anyone who did not have a security badge from entering the trailer park. They were called to Andover to "prevent looting and to assist in traffic control." There was a problem with converging sightseers clogging the roads. Search and rescue activities were slowed due to this convergence. Residents who were not home during impact as well as the relatives of victims or survivors found it difficult to reach the site. Volunteers were also hindered by the convergence. The trucks carrying debris had a difficult time getting to and from the site.

Emergent Issues Reported in the Media

Debris Clearance

When we first arrived, EOC personnel were divided over when debris clearance in the trailer park should begin. It had been less than forty-eight hours since impact, but there were those who wanted to give the go-ahead to the city engineer, his crew, and the crews donated by area businesses, to initiate debris clearance. The primary reason given for starting the cleanup as soon as possible was that the businesses which donated the crews and equipment would not be able to do without them indefinitely. Their withdrawal was anticipated within days, especially if they were sitting idle. A second reason, provided by the owner of the mobile home park, was that the victims would not be able to obtain, install, and move into new mobile homes in the park until it had been cleared of the storm debris. Hence, the park owner and those who were responsible for debris clearance, lobbied the EOC to keep the survivors out of the park so debris clearance could be completed immediately.

Those opposing immediate action were concerned that the survivors needed much more time to locate valuables that were among the ruins, e.g., family photos and mementos. Members of this camp made frequent visits to the trailer park to speak with the surviving residents who were combing through the debris. These EOC officials would return to relate the pleas and frustrations these citizens expressed in asking for "a couple more days" to find their irreplaceable keepsakes.

Most local print and broadcast media focused on reporting the extent of damage, the death and injuries, the sources of help for victims, the types of aid needed, where to send it, and the locations for volunteers to meet to help victims. One local television station, however, and one local newspaper focused on blame-fixing. Blame assignation occurs more commonly after technological disasters, but has been known to occur after natural disasters such as tornadoes (Chandessers, 1966). A few reporters repeatedly interviewed victims who were very vocal about their frustration with the city's initial decision not to allow them to return to their damaged or destroyed home to obtain valuables and with the city's initial announcement that debris clearance would begin shortly. The slant of the news stories of these reporters essentially portrayed the EOC as being inconsiderate of the needs of those they were supposed to serve. The reporters believed their blame-fixing stories helped the victims obtain the additional time they requested. The news stories did indeed succeed in postponing debris clearance activity. As researchers, however, the field team sought to understand the dynamics of the EOC-media conflict. This conflict consumed a lot of the EOC personnel's time as they planned how to respond to the mounting criticism where it appeared. While the EOC was attempting to coordinate the community's response to the disaster, it devoted much time to determining what it considered to be the best response to this criticism. The debate over when to complete the debris clearance continued throughout our four days in the field. Deadlines for victims to finish their salvage efforts were set daily, then pushed back as a result of complaints by the victims and the media's portrayal of such complaints. The clearance was finally set to begin the day the field team was leaving town.

The Mennonite Disaster Services (MDS) also contributed to the EOC's continual delays. Early each morning the MDS would send a large crew to the trailer park to sift through the debris. The MDS operated separately from the EOC and resisted virtually all EOC efforts to coordinate their activity. The MDS essentially ignored any decision by the EOC when it would indicate that search activities would be discontinued to begin clearing the park. Between the media's criticism and the MDS's ignoring of EOC decisions, it became impossible to begin clearing the park. EOC personnel realized any stronger attempts to prevent the MDS from doing their work would only further exacerbate the EOC's emerging public relations problems. The field team concluded it was obvious that the media's involvement had a definite impact on the EOC decisions. It influenced how the EOC utilized its time. It also influenced the EOC's decision as to when to begin the final phase of the debris clearance. Virtually every EOC decision was held hostage to the desire to limit media damage.

Warnings

Shortly after our arrival, we also discovered the EOC team was bristling at the blame-fixing suggesting that the city did not do an adequate job warning the park residents about the tornado's impending impact. Even though there was a difference of opinion within the EOC over when to initiate debris clearance, there was unanimity of resentment toward those who sought to criticize their pre-impact efforts. Virtually all of the EOC personnel had not slept since impact forty-eight hours earlier. They felt they had been totally devoted to doing the best job they could to coordinate the community's restoration. In private conversations with the research team, some EOC personnel suggested that perhaps everything they had done may not have been perfect, but "we are only human . . . had no prior experience, no written (disaster) plan, no prior training, and are doing the best we can, making this up as we go along." They indicated that they were in frequent contact with a neighboring community which had recently experienced an emergency. The Andover EOC used this community's emergency coordinator as a consultant. Media attention still continued to focus on why the city, allegedly, had not taken adequate steps to warn the residents prior to impact.

The first such issue centered on criticism of the police department's attempt to warn the mobile home residents by sending a patrol car through the park's neighborhoods sounding its siren. The city stated this procedure was standard operating procedure during a tornado warning. From the city's perspective, they risked the life of an officer to give the warning just minutes before impact. From the point of view of those who criticized the police effort, it was a meaningless effort. In the view of one survivor: "why not at least use a bull horn to warn those who were walking on the street? How were we supposed to know what it meant?" The EOC decided to release a videotape they had of the police officer's effort. Andover had recently mounted a video camera on each police cruiser. City officials stated that these cameras were to be used to record arrests, to provide evidence for drunk-driving offenses and to protect the police officer from false charges of police brutality. By chance, the officer who sounded the alarm in the mobile home park had inadvertently recorded his attempt to warn the park residents. The EOC decided to call a press conference in order to play the videotape as a strategy for reducing the criticism. Many in the media saw it differently, however. They recoiled when they watched the police officer drive past a resident who was walking her dog, apparently unaware of the impending disaster. They thought the officer should have stopped to inform the resident of what the siren meant and tell her to seek shelter. It was seen as quite possible that she could have had time to get to the shelter if he had stopped. It is also quite possible that (a) she may have decided not to go to the shelter, (b) she may not have had enough time anyway, and/or (c) the police officer may have run out of time to save himself . . . and died. A second criticism of the city's alleged lack of adequate warning emerged. A debate raged as to whether or not the community (civil defense style) siren was actually activated during the pre-impact period. The media and the EOC continued the debate throughout the post-impact period. Many residents were quoted in the press as stating they had not heard a siren, some said they had. EOC personnel stated that it had been inspected recently and had been found to have been in good working order. One employee reportedly claimed the siren had been repaired with used parts until funds could be found to purchase the new parts. To counter the increasing negative feelings being generated in the community, the EOC decided to hold another press conference which proved to be no more successful than the first one.

The pattern was clear. While the EOC was busy responding to the post-impact needs of the trailer park, it was also spending an increasing amount of their limited time trying to determine how to respond to the media's criticism. The field team concluded the media's reporting had an impact on the EOC decision-making.

Content of Media's Reporting

While the EOC team believed the media had treated them unfairly, we found most of the print and broadcast media reporting to be either very supportive or at least neutral. Most of the reporting dealt with damage estimates, death tolls, and human interest stories about survivors. The media was a real asset as the primary or only source of disaster information for the community (as observed, for example, by Wenger, 1980-- while Wenger's focus was quite different, the point is applicable here). Only two reporters, one television and one newspaper reporter, engaged in blame-fixing. The EOC devoted a quite a bit of time and effort responding to the negative press. Some EOC personnel became increasingly antagonist toward anyone from the offending television station or newspaper. They also became increasingly distrustful of the media in general.

For example table 5.5, summarizes the results of our content analysis of the local news reports. Please note both the print and broadcast media negative reporting constituted less than one in ten stories. Most television news stories (91%) were either positive or neutral while most newspaper accounts (93%) were also either neutral or supportive of EOC efforts.

Table 5.5:	Type of Reporting by Media Format	
	Media Form	
	Broadcast	Print
Reporting		
Supportive	91% (120)	93% (141)
Critical	9% (12)	7% (10)

Recovery

During the weeks that followed the disaster event, the clearing of the park was subsequently completed. Rebuilding was begun and attempts were made to return the community to normal time activity. The media sought new stories and the victims continued to struggle with what would be, for them, a long term process of rebuilding their lives. Those local leaders who comprised the post-tornado emergent EOC staff began a soul searching process to assess what should be done to be better prepared for any future disaster.

Literature Based Analysis & Discussion of the Findings

Researchers have long argued that disaster warnings must be conceptualized as a social process (Williams, 1956; Mileti, 1975; Mileti, Drabek, and Haas, 1975; Janis & Mann 1977; Quarantelli, 1980; Perry, 1985; Drabek, 1986). "The initial response to a disaster warning is disbelief" (Drabek, 1986; see also, Drabek, 1969; Moore, et al., 1963; Fritz & Mathewson, 1957). If the disaster event was unexpected, e.g., a tornado, and if the level of emergency preparedness is low, most people tend to continue in their normal routine. When first warned of an impending disaster, they disbelieve the warning even if it comes from an authority (Perry, Lindell, & Greene, 1981; Quarantelli, 1980). If the warning message appears to the listener as vague, their tendency to disbelieve it is increased (Drabek, 1986 & 1968; Mileti, Drabek, & Haas, 1975; Perry, et al., 1981; Fritz, 1957).

Several variables appear to increase the likelihood of a warning being taken seriously and appropriately acted upon. These variables include the *clarity* of the warning message, i.e., specificity of the *nature* of the hazard and what the listener is directed to do in response to it (Perry, Lindell, & Greene, 1982); the *consistency* of the warning message with other warning messages, i.e., media, weather services, local authorities, family members seem to all be giving the same warning message (Demerath, 1957; Fritz, 1957; Mileti, Drabek, & Haas, 1975; Drabek, 1986); the *frequency* of the warnings (Mileti, 1975; Fritz, 1961; Drabek & Boggs, 1968; Drabek, 1969 & 1986; Perry, Lindell, & Greene, 1981); the *type of authority* who is giving the message, e.g., the media is believed more than the police or fire personnel, yet the police/fire personnel are believed more than friends or family (Perry & Greene, 1983; Drabek, 1969 & 1986; Mileti, 1975); the *accuracy of past warnings*, i.e., if they accurately forecast the disaster agents direction and impact (Mileti, Drabek, & Haas, 1975; Haas, Cochrane, and Eddy, 1976; Foster, 1980; Drabek, 1986); and the *frequency of the disaster agent,* e.g., if tornadoes frequently strike the area (Drabek, 1986; Anderson, 1969).

During the pre-impact period, an attempt was made to warn the residents of Andover. First, the community officials attempted to activate the civil-defense siren system. It apparently failed to operate in the normal fashion. Even if it had, it should be noted that Hodler (1982) studied the response of the residents of a community to a tornado warning and found that less than half of the affected residents who heard the civil defense warning sirens sought a location of safety, even though they were tested briefly on the first Saturday of each month. Dependence on a siren system appears to be an ineffective means of warning the population.

The community utilized two additional medium to warn the residents. First, radio and television stations broadcast the tornado watch, then the warning for the Wichita-Andover area. Because a tornado is a rapid-onset disaster agent, it is difficult to expect the warning to provide sufficient time for the total population to complete the social process of digesting, confirming, and acting upon the warning prior to impact. As noted above, the media has been found to be the most believed source of disaster warning information and Wenger, James, and Faupel (1980) found that most citizens tend to obtain their information about disasters from the media. Furthermore, not all residents have a radio or television turned on when such warnings are being given. This appeared to be the case for many Andover residents. Also, there remain the issues of clarity, consistency, frequency, previous accuracy, and frequency of tornadoes in the area. The broadcast messages were clear to the extent that they indicated the nature of the threat--a tornado, and the response the listener was being directed to follow--seek appropriate shelter. As is the nature of the state of the art of tornado forecasting, the path of the tornado and subsequent impact area is vague enough to enable many listeners to assume that they will not be the actual target. Previous experience, even in an area prone to tornadoes, tends to reinforce this perception of the validity of the warning to many listeners. And, the opportunity to broadcast frequent warnings is reduced by the rapid-onset of a tornado, unlike the slow-onset generated opportunities a hurricane provides for giving frequent warnings not only in the broadcast, but also the print media.

The remaining attempt to warn the area was the attempt by the Andover Police Department to alert the residents of the Golden Spur Mobile Home Park by sending an officer to quickly drive up and down the streets of the mobile home park with his siren activated as a warning. When it became apparent to the city that this area was in the direct path of the tornado, there were minutes to act. The patrol car was dispatched to the park; the officer had less than ten minutes to drive through the park and then return, at speeds exceeding 80 miles per hour to the station house shelter which was approximately two miles from the park. If the officer had attempted to go door to door to warn residents he would, in all likelihood, have become a victim of the storm himself. Post-storm criticism which suggested that the officer could have used a bull horn to at least warn those who were milling outside their homes, as well as the criticism which suggests that the residents "had only themselves to blame since they did not heed the warnings," assume the clarity of vision that comes with hindsight. The literature, as noted above, has observed the tendency for those who even hear the warning to disregard it, unless the message is very clear, frequently and consistently given, and is not perceived as having been unnecessarily given in the past. We can account for the response of at least 388, perhaps 488 of the Golden Spur Mobile Home Park residents. Between 200 and 300 of them heeded the warning and went to the shelter in the park. They were safe. Thirteen people died and 175 were injured. Presumably these 188 individuals either did not hear the warnings or did not heed them. We did not know the whereabouts of the remaining residents, between 512 and 612 individuals. Most, if not all of them, were apparently not home at the time. Some of them heeded the warning and left for safer locations out of the area. Many had not returned from work yet and others had gone out for the evening. Apparently, few stayed in their mobile homes and walked away unharmed. Apparently more than half of the residents we can account for did respond to the warning which is far better than what Hodler (1982, discussed previously) observed. The citizens of Andover conformed to the usual behavior patterns. The response of the relevant community organizations, e.g., the media and local government, also conformed to patterns previously observed in the research literature. For example, their attempts to warn the residents, the civil-defense siren, media warnings, and police warnings are very typical means of alerting citizens to act for their own safety.

If the Andover experience is not atypical of the research literature, then why did we observe the blame assignation process among local residents as reflected in the media? Drabek (1968) notes that searches for "the guilty" do follow some disaster events. Chandessais (1966) discovered that citizens do sometimes seek a scapegoat in the aftermath of a tornado. Singer (1982), similarly, observed a tendency to direct blame toward civic officials. Wolensky and Miller (1981, as reported in Drabek, 1986:293) noted "the generalized belief that formal authorities in local government were [seen as] unresponsive to the needs of specific citizens . . . there existed a 'gap' between what was expected and what was delivered." Drabek and Quarantelli (1967, as reported in Drabek, 1986:292) suggest that such blame assignation may "help give the illusion that corrective action of some sort is being taken." While blame assignation is more likely to occur in conjunction with a technological disaster than with one that is caused naturally (Drabek & Quarantelli, 1967), the scapegoating experienced by the Andover government officials during the post-impact and early recovery periods was *not*, therefore, totally unprecedented.

The appropriate question to address presently seems to suggest itself automatically: under what circumstances is a community likely to become more effective in responding to such disaster events? Beyond those which have already been implied above, several suggested by the literature will be offered below.

Concluding Observations

What *would* Dorothy have found if she had returned home to Kansas on that fateful Friday in April 1991? She would have found a trailer park totally destroyed by an extremely large and powerful tornado. She would have been pleased to find so many survivors resulting from the 200-300 residents wisely heeding the warning and evacuating to the underground shelter. She would have found a divided, but earnest, EOC trying its best to respond to the events that had befallen them, without a written disaster plan or training to guide them in their decision-making. She would have found a very well organized, very competent, if very independent, group assisting the victims in their determination to find irreplaceable possessions. Dorothy would have found broadcast and print media news stories which were often supportive of the community's attempts to recover from the tornado. Yet, she also would have found stories which were critical of the town's response. These latter stories were of sufficient concern to the EOC to influence their decision-making during the immediate post-impact and early recovery periods.

Since Dorothy knows "there's no place like home," she would be interested in suggesting how things could possibly be improved in the event another tornado comes to town. Therefore, the field team offers several suggestions as Andover and other communities seek to continue to improve the service they give to their public during a disaster.

Disaster Plan

A written disaster plan would assist present and future individuals who find themselves with the unenviable task of having to respond to a disaster agent's impact (see Drabek, 1986; Quarantelli, 1984; Dynes & Quarantelli, 1975; Dynes, Quarantelli, & Kreps, 1972 for a discussion of the merits of such planning). The process of constructing the written plan would be of great benefit to the organizations who must respond to such emergencies. Other communities, the state emergency management office, and FEMA would all be sources for guidance in developing such a plan.

Community Education Effort

The local government could engage in an ongoing effort to educate the community about the needs, problems, and procedures associated with disaster events. For example, school children could be taught the importance of evacuating or seeking shelter when the community and/or police siren is activated. Of course, additional warning activities could be considered to facilitate gaining the awareness of community members that an emergency is taking place.

Disaster Training & Drills

EOC personnel would receive great benefit from training seminars. Such training would not only give direction to the individual role responsibilities, but should also give some assistance in writing and updating a community's disaster plans. In addition to being taught disaster response skills, regular disaster drills would test the readiness of the individuals and their organizations. Drills should benefit the community in assessing the adequacy of their written disaster plan as well.

EOC Design

While it may not be economically feasible for every community to maintain a permanent EOC, the disaster plan could designate an emergent EOC structure which should alleviate some of the trial-and-error decision making that accompanies organizational response to a disaster. Even an EOC that does not exist until a disaster strikes, needs some written guidelines which outline what roles need to be fulfilled, what tasks commonly need to be addressed and in what order, and what problems can be expected to arise during the life cycle of the recovery period. Of course, any written plan is only useful if it is actually implemented.

Mutual Assistance Agreements

Perhaps the cooperation of organizations such as the Mennonite Disaster Services could be attained if the community developed and maintained, as part of their implemented written disaster plan, a relationship with the organizations during normal time. The community and organizations like MDS could mutually educate each other about their mutual needs, procedures, and so forth. If an emergency develops in the community, it would, thereby, be in a better position to respond in concert with the various organizations.

Developing a Relationship with the Media

Investigative reporters may by definition view their role as adversarial. It is arguably good that this is the case at times, since the Golden Spur Mobile Home Park resident's desire to have more time to reclaim their property was essentially fulfilled through the role the local media played on their behalf. The rebuilding process can be hurt, however, if local politics and personality clashes interfere with EOC attempts to respond effectively. A good disaster plan, when implemented properly, could assist those who would perform EOC functions during emergency time, if it provides for mechanisms for developing an effective relationship with key personnel in print and broadcast media during normal time. The media could become involved in the planning process and gain an understanding of the valuable role they can play disseminating information to the local community during a disaster. The media can be a very valuable aid to a community struck by disaster. Life saving information can be disseminated with the help of newspaper, television and radio reporters. If those who would fulfill EOC roles during disaster time seek to educate the media as to how they can give valuable assistance to the recovery effort, then perhaps the emergency coordinators can devote more of their time to the primary task of responding to the disaster rather than to the media's criticism. By developing a working relationship with the media, EOC personnel may gain insight into the most effective approach to involving media personnel as team members who are jointly attempting to serve the community rather than as adversaries.

THIRD CASE STUDY: The Role of Education & Experience in Mitigation Planning

Emergency management organizations implement their disaster response plans during the disaster time periods. During normal time the emergency response coordinator engages in mitigation planning and implementation. In order to reduce the incidence of victimization when a disaster strikes the community, the coordinator may initiate activities such as building a flood wall or teaching the community members how to most effectively evacuate the city should an evacuation become necessary. Fischer and McCullough (1993) completed a national survey of LEMA coordinators in order to determine the mitigation activities currently preferred and to assess the role of experience in influencing which mitigation activities were employed. The next case study shares their findings.

Abstract

A representative national (USA) sample of local emergency management agency (LEMA) coordinators (N=178) completed a mail-questionnaire which sought to identify their mitigation activities and to determine if mitigation strategies vary by eight experience variables: education, training background, major emergency experience, disaster experience, years worked as LEMA coordinator, years of EMS experience, training and disaster drill experience.

The typical LEMA coordinator employs the following mitigation strategies, in descending order of preference: disseminate response information through the schools and the media, seek zoning law changes, urge citizens to purchase insurance, attempt building code changes, engage in HazMat identification and relocation planning, and seek the building of physical appurtenances. The *only* variable observed to be associated with mitigation strategy decisions was *education,* college graduates being more likely to adopt any of the 7 activities than non-graduates. Chi-square tests were utilized. The response rate was 53%.

Introduction

During the last five years, the United States has experienced three successive, media dubbed "storms of the century." Hurricane Gilbert threatened the Gulf Coast in September 1988, then Hurricane Hugo created massive destruction in Charleston, South Carolina, and related areas in 1989, and Hurricane Andrew devastated Homestead, Florida in the fall of 1992. The prevalence of such events suggests the need for emergency response agencies to continue their quest to more effectively mitigate against and respond to disasters. And the ever growing number of citizens who not only vacation, but permanently reside in hurricane prone areas, further underscores the need for continued enhancement of community mitigation and response efforts.

Questions

To address the aforementioned need, several questions must be answered with certitude. First, what types of mitigation activities are currently most likely to be employed in the USA? Are communities currently more likely to enact zoning laws to limit habituation in disaster prone areas, to adopt building codes which require new construction to withstand a disaster agent's impact, to construct flood walls to repel future flood waters or tidal storm surges, to educate the community on disaster preparation and evacuation procedures, or to encourage residents to purchase disaster insurance to replace losses resulting from a disaster?

Second, under what circumstances is a community more, versus less, likely to make mitigation adjustments? For example, if the local emergency management agency (LEMA) coordinator has a great deal of experience, is he more likely to implement mitigation policies? If so, what type(s) of experience is most salient in predicting mitigation adoption: the number of years served as LEMA coordinator, the number of years worked within the emergency response field, the number of emergencies or disasters to which he has responded, or the number of training seminars and disaster drills in which he has participated? Or, is the amount of formal education the coordinator has completed the operative variable? In order to assess answers to these questions, we first surveyed the relevant literature and then completed the current study.

Types of Mitigation Activity

Mitigation activities tend to fall into one of four categories; (1) those which limit *access* to disaster prone areas, (2) those which create *physical appurtenances* to protect the community, (3) those which *educate* the populace *to take action* which will reduce the likelihood of their victimization, and (4) those which seek to *replace property* lost during a disaster. For example, governments have enacted zoning laws which limit habitation in areas frequented by disasters and building codes which require new construction to be able to withstand a Category III hurricane. Hurricane Andrew clearly illustrated the need for stronger adherence to these codes. In addition, communities subject to frequent flooding sometimes construct flood walls to protect against the tidal storm surge or rising flood waters. Some communities seek to enhance their evacuation response by educating elementary school children on evacuation techniques in an attempt to get this information home to their parents. Also, individuals have increasingly sought to protect themselves against possible financial loss by purchasing disaster insurance (Drabek, 1986).

Trends

During the 1960s and 1970s there was a major shift in mitigation emphasis in the USA. While the construction of physical appurtenances such as flood walls continued to be a worthwhile strategy under appropriate circumstances, policy makers increasingly emphasized the adoption of various non-structural techniques. Under the Carter Administration, the Federal Emergency Management Agency (FEMA) accelerated the trend toward non-structural approaches in 1979. The philosophy changed from attempting to control the ravages of nature to creating policies which reduce the likelihood of victimization. "Rather than proposing that more dams be built experts argued for rezoning floodplains and providing flood insurance" (White & Haas, 1975). "Insurance is one of the most significant non-structural approaches to disaster mitigation that has been tried within the USA" (Drabek, 1986). Insurance purchasing generally increases after disasters (Britton, et al., 1983). "While beneficial to individuals suffering from a disaster, it can also [however] indirectly cause more damage by encouraging individuals to reside in an area frequented by disasters--and where they might not otherwise choose to live" (McComb, 1980). "The insured homeowner . . . believes that he is the master of his own fate," (Brauman & Simms, 1978) now capable of surviving even nature's fury.

Educating the general public, through public service announcements on television and radio as well as through education efforts in the schools, is another nonstructural mitigative approach which has been increasingly utilized with positive results. For example, "during a [1974] tornado outbreak in the United States, a seventh grade teacher reviewed severe weather safety rules with his class. After school, as one of the buses was taking pupils home, a tornado appeared in its path. The driver did not know what to do, but one of the recently briefed students did. He convinced the driver to pull over, get everyone out and far enough away so that the bus could not roll onto them. All passengers sought safety in a ditch. Although the tornado destroyed the bus, none of the pupils were injured" (Foster, 1980).

Factors Affecting Adoption

For those seeking to expedite mitigation adjustment, a reasonable question is: under what circumstances are communities more, versus less, likely to engage in mitigation adjustment? Some communities devote relatively few resources to mitigation activity. Most communities are afflicted by many other problems, such as drugs and crime, which demand their attention and scarce resources on a daily basis. The possibility of a disaster may seem remote. Consequently, funds are allocated to disaster mitigation policies which are viewed as cost-effective and relevant to their community (Fischer, 1990).

Drabek (1986), in reviewing the relevant literature, identifies several factors which may impact upon the likelihood of mitigation policy adoption. These include tax base affluence, level of political activism, degree of conservatism, and extent of urbanization. An affluent community which is politically liberal, politically active and diverse, and is somewhat urbanized, is more likely to engage in mitigation adjustment (Drabek, 1986).

The Impact of Experience

The literature has attempted to assess the role *disaster experience* plays in mitigation adjustment. Its role is not clearly defined (see Fischer and McCullough, 1993). For example, "one community with a history of frequent coastal storms has paid minimal attention to mitigation, while another community, also subject to coastal storms, though far less frequently, did take a number of significant, mitigative steps" (example found in Drabek, 1986). Why the difference? We do not know.

Some researchers claim that adoption of mitigative adjustments is adversely affected by the presence of *disaster subcultures* (Wenger, 1978). The development of disaster subcultures sometimes results in increased victimization, primarily because the community is not properly prepared for the disaster. For instance, communities that are frequented by hurricanes may construct physical appurtenances which will sustain an impact at least equal to that previously experienced. The next hurricane may exceed the force of any storm previously weathered. A false sense of security may lead some community members to "wait out the storm" or even throw a "hurricane party" rather than evacuate. Such experiences make mitigation adjustment more difficult to attain.

The *decay curve* works to reduce the likelihood of a community adopting mitigation measures. Over time, the effects of the event are no longer as salient and individuals become less concerned with the possibility of a disaster striking their community again. While "disaster events do open up the constraint structures that typically restrain the adoption of mitigative adjustments, such effects are temporary. What we do *not* know is how temporary. Available evidence is limited to notions of enhanced invulnerability - we have weathered past storms - and a suggestion of gradual erosion and questioning of mitigative actions that were adopted when memories were fresh" (Drabek, 1986). "Soon codes for improved building standards are questioned on the grounds of additional costs" (Oliver, 1975).

Summarizing the literature, we find that mitigation adjustment is thought to vary by *disaster experience.* After a disaster the decay curve is found to limit the initial interest in mitigation plans to avert another disaster. Mitigation activity is also found to be greater for affluent communities as they have the means to fund it. Politically active, liberal, urbanized communities appear to be more likely to support mitigation planning as well. Unfortunately, most of the mitigation literature is based upon case studies or anecdotal evidence. Empirical research is required to determine if these findings can be generalized.

How Was the Study Conducted?

Since, the literature continues to exhibit a paucity of empirical research into mitigation adjustment we sought to redress this grievance by designing a study that would assess the mitigation activities of a national sample of local emergency management agency (LEMA) coordinators in the USA. The sample of LEMA coordinators was obtained by utilizing a computer based random number generator to randomly select the sample from a LEMA population of 2,562 (four U.S. states did not comply in providing us with mailing lists). To avoid the time delays inherent in successive mailings, we sampled with replacement, i.e., we replaced each coordinator who did not respond with another randomly selected respondent.

Our mail-questionnaire resulted in a 53% return rate (n=178). We did not observe any significant differences between the demographic characteristics of our sample and what is believed to be known about the population of interest. The typical respondent was a 50 year old Caucasian male (see Table 5.6). The respondents ranged in age from 28 to 71, with a mean age of 50 and standard deviation 10. The overwhelming majority of respondents (85%) were male, which is typical of the gender composition of disaster coordinators. All but a few of the respondents were Caucasian (96%).

Mitigation Activity

Respondents were asked to indicate and describe what mitigation policies their county had attempted to implement during the previous ten years. Their responses comprised seven mitigation strategies: changing building codes, altering zoning laws, encouraging residents to purchase insurance, identifying and relocating stored hazardous materials, constructing physical appurtenances, educating school age children, and educating local residents about disasters.

Experience Measures

Experience was defined across several dimensions: formal education, training background, work experience, and disaster experience. Respondents were asked how much formal education they had completed (less than high school, high school graduate, some college coursework, college graduate). They were also asked if their professional (disaster) training had been primarily in military service, emergency management (EM), or neither. Respondents were asked to record the number of years they had served as LEMA coordinator and within the emergency services field generally. They were also asked to report the number of training seminars and disaster drills in which they had participated during the last two years. And, they were asked how many major emergencies and how many disasters they had responded to during their careers. They were also asked to indicate the name of the event and the year it occurred so we could ascertain if it met Fritz's (1961) definition.

Table 5.6:   Demographic Characteristics & Indicators of Experience

Age		Gender		Race	
Under 50	50%	Female	15%	Caucasian	97%
50+ Yrs	50%	Male	85%	Others	3%

Education		Background		Disasters	
High School	16%	Military	23%	0-4	49%
Some College	42%	EM	44%	5+	51%
College Grad	42%	None	33%		

Yrs Director		Yrs. EM		Training Seminars		Drills	
0-5	50%	0-14	51%	0-4	47%	0-3	46%
6+	50%	15+	49%	5+	53%	4+	54%

Experience of LEMA Coordinators

The sample was observed to include those with an array of experience (see Table 5.6). Most exhibited a great deal of experience across all eight experience indicators. Most of the respondents had completed at least some college coursework (42% had done so, while another 42% were college graduates), only one in six (16%) had less formal education. A plurality of the coordinators (44%) had obtained most of their disaster training through EM training, while only a fourth (23%) obtained it through military service, and the remaining third (33%) had no disaster training prior to becoming the coordinator. The typical coordinator reportedly had worked through five (median) major emergencies and two (median) disasters. He had served six (median) years as LEMA coordinator, worked within EM for fourteen (median) years, attended five (median) training seminars and participated in four (median) disaster drills during the past two years.

What Mitigation Activities Are Currently Favored?

Emphasis: Non-Structural (see Table 5.7).

The LEMA coordinators clearly continue to favor non-structural strategies. First, more coordinators reported implementing programs to *teach school children* (75%) about disaster response needs than any other mitigation practice. Second, television and radio *public service messages* were reportedly utilized by three-quarters (72%) of the coordinators.

A majority (59%) of the coordinators reported undertaking efforts to enact or amend *zoning laws* during the previous ten years in an attempt to prevent or limit new construction in disaster prone areas, e.g., building low income homes on floodplains. The fourth most utilized mitigation approach was the urging of residents to *purchase disaster insurance*, although less than half (43%) of the coordinators reported urging citizens to do so. Slightly more than a third (38%) reportedly worked to amend *building codes* to require new construction to be able to withstand the disaster agent(s) most likely to impact their area, e.g., requiring new homes to withstand a Category III hurricane. Only one in four coordinators (26%) reported working on a *HazMat plan* to identify and relocate hazardous materials from disaster prone locations to safer storage areas (despite SARA Title III requirements to do so--the primary reason given for not developing a plan was the lack of resources to meet the cost). And, only one in five (20%) reported having, or working to obtain, *physical appurtenances*, e.g., a flood wall. Of course, this last observation is understandable for at least two reasons. First, perhaps only a fifth of the communities are at risk of being impacted by a flood or tidal storm surge, rendering their utilization moot. Second, such devices are expensive and are often built only to sustain the last great flood or storm surge--leaving the community still somewhat exposed to a worse event. It may be less expensive in the long run to avoid the need for a flood wall by limiting (or eliminating) new construction in areas prone to such disaster agents and by requiring the construction that does occur to be able to withstand such an event.

Does Anything Impact upon Mitigation Choice?

Education Does

The amount of formal education the LEMA coordinator completed was the *only* variable which was found to have any affect on whether or not mitigation strategies were adopted. College graduates were more likely to adopt mitigation strategies (see Table 4.7). This pattern is true for five of the seven mitigation choices. The first exception was the school programs which teach school children about disaster response. The majority of coordinators adopt this strategy regardless of their educational attainment (76% of the high school graduates, 77% of those who have completed some college coursework, and 73% of the college graduates). The second exception was the building of physical appurtenances which was avoided by most coordinators regardless of education (28% of the high school graduates, 11% of those who completed some college courses, and 25% of the college graduates). A statistically significant *(or nearly so)* relationship, however, exists between education and *building code usage* (Chi-Square = 5.6, p=.06), *zoning law changes* (Chi-Square = 6.0, p=.05), disseminating information through the *media* (Chi-Square = 7.2, p=.03), urging *insurance purchasing* (Chi-Square = 4.8, p=.09), and developing a *HazMat plan* to identify and relocate materials (Chi-Square = 8.7, p=.01).

Almost No Influence: the Number of Major Emergencies Experienced, the Number of Years Served as LEMA Coordinator, and the Number of Training Sessions

The LEMA coordinator's experience, i.e., number of *major emergencies* to which he has responded during his EMS career, was found to have no influence on whether or not he adopted six of the seven mitigation policies. The only exception was insurance purchasing. A majority (54%) of the more experienced coordinators, those who responded to more than the median number of four emergencies, urged citizens to purchase disaster insurance while a majority (66%) of the less experienced coordinators did not (Chi-Square = 5.4, p=.02).

Similarly, the number of *years served as LEMA coordinator* was observed to only be associated with a higher chance of adopting building code changes. While a slight majority (54%) of the less experienced coordinators favored such adoption, almost three-fourths (71%) of the more experienced coordinators sought building code changes (Chi-Square = 1.7, p=.03). No variation was observed between the coordinator's experience and zoning changes, teaching children, media usage, insurance purchasing, HazMat planning, or building physical appurtenances.

An association was observed between the number of *training seminars* completed during the last two years and the likelihood of adopting an educational program to use in the schools (teaching children about disaster response). While two-thirds (68%) of the less experienced coordinators reportedly favor this approach, more than eight out of ten (82%) of the more experienced coordinators disseminated disaster information through the schools (Chi-Square = 3.9, p=.05). No variation was observed between the coordinator's training experience and building code changes, zoning law changes, media usage, insurance purchasing, HazMat planning, or physical appurtenances.

No Influence: Disaster Experience, EMS Experience, Disaster Drill Participation, Training Background

Disaster experience, i.e., the *number of disasters* to which the coordinator has responded, was observed to have no association with the selection of any of the seven mitigation activities. Regardless of the number of disasters the coordinator has experienced, he was unlikely to attempt building code changes (63% of the less experience and 59% of the more experienced did not), to engage in HazMat identification and relocation planning (73% of both the experienced and less experienced did not), or to engage in building physical appurtenances (79% of the less experienced and 81% of the experienced did not). Similarly, regardless of the number of disasters the coordinator has experienced, he was equally likely to attempt zoning law changes (52% of the less experienced and 66% of the experienced did) and to employ teaching strategies (75% of the less experienced and 76% of the experienced favored teaching children while at the same time 68% of the less experienced and 76% of the experienced favored media dissemination of information).

The number of *years* the coordinator has served *in EM* also had no association with mitigation choices. Regardless of the number of years served, a majority of the coordinators did not initiate building code changes (60% of the less experienced and 65% of the experienced), urge insurance purchasing (63% and 50%), engage in HazMat identification and relocation planning (74% and 73%), or initiate the building of physical appurtenances (77% and 84%). A majority of the coordinators did initiate zoning law changes (59% of the less experienced and 58% of the more experienced) and utilize the two teaching approaches regardless of their experience.

The number of *disaster drills* in which the coordinator had reportedly participated during the last two years was not observed to be associated with mitigation strategy selection. A majority of the coordinators did not initiate building code changes (67% of the less experienced and 59% of the experienced), urge insurance purchasing (63% of the less experienced and 52% of the experienced), engage in HazMat identification and relocation planning (78% of the less experienced and 71% of the experienced), or initiate the building of physical appurtenances (85% of the less experienced and 77% of the experienced) regardless of their disaster drill experience. Conversely, a majority of the coordinators did initiate zoning law changes (58% of the less experienced and 59% of the experienced) and utilize teaching strategies (75% each for teaching children and 64% of the less experienced and 78% of the experienced for media usage) regardless of the amount of their experience.

Training background was not observed to be associated with mitigation strategy selection. The majority of those who had gained their disaster experience primarily from the military, as well as a majority of those who had gained experience within EMS, and those who had no previous training, did not favor building code changes (Military: 57% against, EMS: 61% against, None: 66% against), insurance purchasing (Military: 50% against, EMS: 62% against, None: 52% against), HazMat planning (Military: 66% against, EMS: 77% against and None: 72% against), or the building of physical appurtenances (Military: 80% against, EMS: 74% against, None: 85%). Conversely, regardless of training background, a majority of the coordinators favored zoning law changes (Military: 57% favored, EMS: 57% favored, None: 60% favored) and teaching approaches (Military: 80% favored teaching children, EM: 73% favored teaching children, None: 80% favored teaching children; Military: 83%, EM: 68%, and None: 74% favored media usage).

Conclusions

Summary

The typical LEMA coordinator in our sample was a white, middle-aged male who had completed some college coursework. He has served as coordinator for approximately six years and has been involved in the emergency services field for fourteen years. During his career, he has responded to five major emergencies and two disasters. During the last two years he has attended five training seminars and participated in four disaster drills. More coordinators obtained their disaster training from EM training programs than from any other source, e.g., military service.

The most frequently utilized mitigation activity has been the dissemination of disaster information (1) through *educational* programs in the schools and (2) through the *media*. The following mitigation activities were also reportedly adopted by the LEMA coordinators in descending order of preference: *zoning* law changes, citizens purchase disaster *insurance, building code* changes, *HazMat* assessment and the building of *physical appurtenances*. Non-structural mitigation activities continue to be favored. *Mitigation* activity was found *not to vary* by seven of the eight indicators assessing LEMA coordinator experience. *Only education* impacted upon mitigation activity. College graduates were more likely than non-graduates to engage in mitigation adjustment. Training background, the number of major emergencies or disasters, the number of years of work experience (either as LEMA coordinator or within EMS generally), and the number of training seminars or disaster drills, had no (or virtually no) impact on the mitigation adjustment activity in which the LEMA coordinator engaged.

Interpretation

The lack of clarity in the literature with respect to the role experience plays in mitigation adjustment has been addressed by the current study. This representative national sample provided empirical evidence which suggests that seven separate measures of experience essentially fail to affect mitigation decisions. Only the amount of formal education, an issue not previously addressed in the literature, appears to have a major influence. These findings strongly suggest that the continued move toward a more professional LEMA workforce, i.e., college educated personnel, will bring dividends for the communities served. We argue that public policy makers should strive to facilitate the goal of professionalizing their LEMA workforce.

Table 5.7:   Does Experience Impact on Mitigation Decisions?

		Education			Background		
		High School	Some College	College Grad	Military	EM	Neither
Build	**Yes 38%**	36%	27%	48%	43%	39%	34%
Code	**No 62%**	64%	73%	52%	57%	61%	66%
		Chi-Square=5.6, p=.06			Chi-Square=0.7, p=.71		
Zone	**Yes 59%**	44%	53%	69%	57%	57%	60%
	No 41%	56%	47%	31%	43%	43%	40%
		Chi-Square=6.0, p=.05		Chi-Square=0.1, p=.94			
Teach	**Yes 75%**	76%	77%	73%	80%	73%	80%
	No 25%	24%	23%	27%	20%	27%	20%
		Chi-Square=0.3, p=.84		Chi-Square=1.1, p=.59			
Media	**Yes 72%**	52%	71%	80%	83%	68%	74%
	No 28%	48%	29%	20%	17%	32%	26%
		Chi-Square=7.2, p=.03		Chi-Square=2.5, p=.29			
Insure	**Yes 43%**	48%	33%	52%	51%	38%	48%
	No 57%	52%	67%	48%	49%	62%	52%
		Chi-Square=4.8, p=.09		Chi-Square=1.9, p=.38			
HazMat	**Yes 26%**	16%	18%	39%	34%	23%	28%
	No 74%	84%	82%	61%	66%	77%	72%
		Chi-Square=8.7, p=.01		Chi-Square=1.6, p=.46			
Phys	**Yes 20%**	28%	11%	25%	20%	26%	15%
	No 80%	72%	89%	75%	80%	74%	85%
		Chi-Square=4.8, p=.09		Chi-Square=1.9,p=.38			
Total	**0-3 56%**	56%	66%	47%	49%	54%	59%
	4+ 44%	44%	34%	53%	51%	46%	41%
		Chi-Square=4.5, p=.11		Chi-Square=0.8, p=.66			

Continued

Table 5.7, cont.

		Major Emergency		Disasters	
		0-4	5+	0-2	3+
Build	Yes	34%	44%	37%	41%
Code	No	66%	56%	63%	59%
		Chi-Square=1.4, p=.23		Chi-Square=0.3, p=.61	
Zone	Yes	50%	65%	52%	66%
	No	50%	35%	48%	34%
		Chi-Square=3.1, p=.08		Chi-Square=2.8, p=.09	
Teach	Yes	77%	76%	75%	76%
	No	23%	24%	25%	24%
		Chi-Square=0.1, p=.95		Chi-Square=0.1, p=.88	
Media	Yes	68%	79%	68%	76%
	No	32%	21%	32%	24%
		Chi-Square=2.2, p=.13		Chi-Square=0.7, p=.40	
Insure	Yes	34%	54%	37%	50%
	No	66%	46%	63%	50%
		Chi-Square=5.4, p=.02		Chi-Square=2.4, p=.12	
HazMat	Yes	21%	34%	27%	27%
	No	79%	66%	73%	73%
		Chi-Square=3.0, p=.08		Chi-Square=0.1, p=.95	
Phys	Yes	18%	20%	21%	19%
	No	82%	80%	79%	81%
		Chi-Square=0.1, p=.75		Chi-Square=0.2, p=.68	
Total	0-3	63%	48%	60%	51%
	4+	37%	52%	40%	49%
		Chi-Square=3.3, p=.07		Chi-Square=1.1, p=.29	

Continued

Table 5.7, cont.					
		Years Director		**EM Years**	
		0-5	**6+**	**0-14**	**5+**
Build Code					
	Yes	46%	29%	40%	35%
	No	54%	71%	60%	65%
		CSq=1.7, p=.03		CSq=0.3, p=.56	
Zone					
	Yes	55%	62%	59%	58%
	No	45%	38%	41%	42%
		CSq=0.7, p=.41		CSq=0.1, p=.91	
Teach					
	Yes	75%	75%	80%	70%
	No	25%	25%	20%	30%
		CSq=0.1, p=.93		CSq=1.7, p=.19	
Media					
	Yes	70%	73%	67%	77%
	No	30%	27%	33%	23%
		CSq=0.2, p=.66		CSq=2.0, p=.16	
Insure					
	Yes	38%	49%	37%	50%
	No	62%	51%	63%	50%
		CSq=2.1, p=.15		CSq=2.5, p=.11	
HazMat					
	Yes	22%	30%	26%	27%
	No	78%	70%	74%	73%
		CSq=1.2, p=.27		CSq=0.1, p=.86	
Phys					
	Yes	24%	16%	23%	16%
	No	76%	84%	77%	84%
		CSq=1.5, p=.22		CSq=1.1, p=.29	
Total					
	0-3	60%	52%	55%	57%
	4+	40%	48%	45%	43%
		CSq=0.9, p=.37		CSq=0.1, p=.84	

Continued

Table 5.7, cont.

		Training		Drills	
		0-4	5+	0-3	4+
Build Code					
	Yes	35%	40%	33%	41%
	No	65%	60%	67%	59%
		CSq=0.3, p=.59		CSq=1.1,p=.29	
Zone					
	Yes	61%	57%	58%	59%
	No	39%	43%	42%	41%
		CSq=0.2, p=.64		CSq=0.1, p=.94	
Teach					
	Yes	68%	82%	75%	75%
	No	32%	18%	25%	25%
		CSq=3.9, p=.05		CSq=0.1, p=.92	
Media					
	Yes	59%	83%	64%	78%
	No	41%	17%	36%	22%
		CSq=9.2, p=.001		CSq=3.6, p=.07	
Insure					
	Yes	41%	46%	37%	48%
	No	59%	54%	63%	52%
		CSq=0.4, p=.54		CSq=1.8, p=.18	
HazMat					
	Yes	23%	30%	22%	29%
	No	77%	70%	78%	71%
		CSq=1.0, p=.32		CSq=1.0, p=.33	
Phys					
	Yes	17%	22%	15%	23%
	No	83%	78%	85%	77%
		CSq=0.7, p=.41		CSq=1.7, p=.19	
Total					
	0-3	62%	51%	66%	48%
	4+	38%	49%	34%	52%
		CSq=1.9, p=.16		CSq=4.6, p=.03	

FOURTH CASE STUDY: Earthquake Hazard Risk Reduction
& Seismic Vulnerability: Low Risk + No Experience with An
Agent = No Mitigation

The lack of experience with a particular disaster agent, when coupled with a low
risk of impact from such an agent, often leads to ignoring preparation for such a
disaster. Mitigation and response planning activities may be totally ignored in areas
where the infrequently occur. While it is wise to devote limited time and other resources to those events which have the highest likelihood of occurring, other disaster agents should not be totally ignored. An all-hazards approach may provide the
greatest mitigation and response service to the community one is serving. The
blame-fixing process may be somewhat alleviated as well. Fischer, Scharberger,
Geiger and their student research assistants conducted an assessment of Pennsylvania's earthquake preparedness in 1995. The next case study shares their findings.

Abstract

Pursuant to assessing Pennsylvania's earthquake (EQ) preparedness, the 67 LEMA
coordinators were surveyed via a mail-questionnaire. A response rate of 87% was
achieved. EQ experience, risk assessment activity, mitigation activity, and planning
for EQ response and recovery were all found to be very low and did not vary by
level of vulnerability (high versus low risk counties). Findings were consistent with
research literature outlining circumstances under which hazard reduction is likely to
occur. The typical coordinator was found to be a middle-aged male who had completed some college course work and had a wide range of experience in emergency
services. This project was funded entirely by FEMA Comprehensive Cooperatve
Agreement No. E-1 EMP-94-K-0301. The contents do not necessarily reflect the
views or policies of FEMA (Fischer, Scharnberger and Geiger, 1995).

Earthquake Hazard Reduction

The National Earthquake Conference was convened in 1993 as an activity of the
International Decade for Natural Disaster Reduction. The conference goal was to
share and disseminate information to disaster researchers and practitioners which
might facilitate earthquake hazard reduction. Pursuant to effecting earthquake hazard reduction in the Commonwealth of Pennsylvania, an assessment of the current
level of preparedness among Pennsylvania's local emergency management agencies
(LEMA) was conducted during 1994-95. This paper compares the research literature on preparedness and mitigation effectiveness with the LEMA assessment findings.

Local Emergency Preparedness

After passage of the 1974 Federal Disaster Act, the fifty states received grants to facilitate further disaster planning. "Most states mandated local governments to meet minimal disaster planning criteria" (Drabek, 1986). What has been the outcome? The organization designated as having the responsibility to coordinate the community response is the local emergency management agency (Gillespie and Mileti, 1993). To effectively respond, this organization must have a well developed and well rehearsed disaster plan. Planning is more likely to occur when a particular hazard frequently threatens a community (Drabek, 1986). The perceived likelihood of a threat from a particular hazard tends to govern whether that particular hazard will be addressed in any planning (Quarantelli and Tierney, 1979). For example, if an earthquake is perceived as very unlikely to occur, planning for one is not likely to be addressed in the community's overall disaster planning. The goals of an effective response plan include meeting immediate victim needs and initiating a process that will facilitate recovery (Gillespie and Mileti, 1993). Effective emergency response plans have been found to follow certain basic principles which are outlined below.

Planning

Planning has a greater chance of being effective if it is viewed as a continuous process (Gillespie and Mileti, 1993). Plans need to be updated regularly. The act of creating the written document serves to function as an on-going educational or training process for those involved in the planning. It informs those who must implement the plan. Continuous planning results in reducing the unknown. It increases the likelihood of anticipating problems and developing solutions. Since all problems cannot be anticipated, the plan must be flexible enough to allow for accommodation of the unanticipated. While plans must provide enough detail to articulate needs and responses to those needs, plans should emphasize the general principles to be followed over specific detail. The effective plan is one which is based upon real disaster problems, not imagined or mythical ones. Those involved in the planning process must, therefore, also be involved in a continual educational process which differentiates fact from fiction.

Disaster plans should contain the following specific elements (Gillespie and Mileti, 1993). First, the plan should identify the basic emergency functions and tasks to be undertaken, e.g., hazard detection such as conducting risk assessments, implementing mitigation protection alternatives for both normal and emergency time periods, and developing necessary emergency response and recovery procedures (alerting and notification procedures, emergency relief activities, medical services, search and rescue, shelter, health and sanitation, debris removal). Second, the plan should identify the roles of key organizations in risk assessment, mitigation and planning for response and recovery. Task definition reduces the conflict commonly resulting from "turf battles" and minimizes duplication of effort. Third, the plan should outline the steps for completing the tasks. And fourth, the plan should provide for resource allocation, e.g., provide for specialized equipment, necessary facilities, communication equipment, and personnel needs.

A major impediment to planning, and preparedness generally, is the constant assault on the limited community resources. While a damaging earthquake may impact a community sometime within the next century, most communities face pressing social problems such as street crime on a daily basis. These more obvious problems usually garner both the community's attention and resources. When the earthquake does impact, however, it will be readily apparent if the planning has been effective. The blame assignation process commences when planning does not result in an effective response. While the public, the media, and emergency personnel were very critical of FEMA's performance after Hurricane Andrew and the North Ridge earthquake, state emergency management agencies and LEMA's are certainly not immune to receiving the very same treatment. Pursuant to maintaining effective planning, emergency officials must work during normal time to maintain the interest in preparedness of community decision-makers and average citizens. Emergency personnel must receive regular training and exercise the plan in order to maintain effectiveness.

Mitigation Activity

During the 1960s and 1970s there was a major shift in mitigation activity emphasis in the United States. While the construction of physical appurtenances continued to be a worthwhile strategy under appropriate circumstances, e.g., flood walls, policy makers increasingly emphasized the adoption of various non-structural techniques. The Federal Emergency Management Agency (FEMA) accelerated the trend towards non-structural approaches in 1979. The philosophy changed from attempting to control the ravages of nature, to creating policies which reduce the likelihood of victimization (Drabek, 1986).

Mitigation activities tend to fall into one of four categories: those which limit access to disaster prone areas; those which create physical appurtenances to protect the community; those which educate the populace to take action which will reduce the likelihood of their victimization; and those which seek to replace property lost during a disaster (Drabek, 1986; Fischer, 1993). For example, governments have enacted zoning laws which limit habitation in areas frequented by disasters and building codes which require new construction to be able to withstand the stipulated hazard. Some communities seek to enhance their evacuation response by educating elementary school children on evacuation techniques in an attempt to get this information home to their parents. And, many communities actively encourage their residents to purchase disaster insurance to protect themselves against possible financial loss (Drabek, 1986).

Local governments play a critical role in mitigation activity. They have the authority to regulate land use and building design. Communities should develop a comprehensive plan to guide land use and development over a 20-30 year time frame (Gillespie and Mileti, 1993). Such a plan should include land use regulation, building regulations, policing power, mapping of hazardous land areas, and maintaining a building inventory. Considerations that impact upon which mitigation activities are implemented include effectiveness of reducing seismic vulnerability, political acceptability, public cost, private cost, administrative cost and complexity, as well as ease of enforcement (Gillespie and Mileti, 1993).

Factors Affecting Adoption of Mitigation Strategies

Under what circumstances are communities more, versus less, likely to engage in mitigation adjustment? Some communities devote relatively few resources to mitigation activity. Most communities are affected by many other problems, such as drugs and crime, which demand their attention and scarce resources on a daily basis. The possibility of a disaster may seem remote. Consequently, funds are allocated to disaster mitigation policies which are viewed as cost-effective and relevant to their community (Fischer, 1994). Several factors have been previously identified (Drabek, 1986) which impact upon the likelihood of mitigation policy adoption. These include tax base affluence, level of political activism, and extent of urbanization. An affluent, urbanized, politically active community is more likely to engage in mitigation adjustment.

Disaster experience also plays a role in mitigation adjustment (Fischer, 1994). Some communities fail to benefit from their encounter with a hazard, i.e., they fail to adopt mitigation strategies to reduce the effect of any future encounter. Other communities will act to mitigate against a repeat of the past experience during the window of opportunity that apparently exists during the post-impact and early recovery periods. A decay curve works against mitigation adjustment, however (Drabek, 1986). Over time, the effects of the recent event are no longer as salient and individuals become less concerned with the possibility of a disaster striking their community again. While "disaster events do open up the constraint structures that typically restrain the adoption of mitigative adjustments, such effects are temporary. Available evidence suggests that a feeling of enhanced invulnerability emerges as the fresh memories of the horror are replaced with a sense that past hazards were more or less weathered after all" (Drabek, 1986). "Soon codes for improved building standards are questioned on the grounds of additional costs" (Oliver, 1975). People have been found to be more likely to undertake mitigative action if they perceive the risk as real, if they have previous experience with the hazard, and if such measures are undertaken by others they know such as friends, neighbors, or relatives (Gillespie and Mileti, 1993).

The Role of the State

The state can play a key role in promoting earthquake preparedness on the local level (Olshansky, 1992a and 1992b). States should take an active role in encouraging local action. Traditionally many states tend to follow the lead of federal policy initiatives and federal funding. The current national political climate encourages states to assume the leadership role for developing planning and mitigation strategies appropriate to their needs.

Earthquake awareness studies (Gillespie and Mileti, 1993) show that high levels of awareness and concern by key state officials do not easily translate into action on the local level. Why not? Areas of risk are not often well known to local decision-makers or average citizens. The benefit is not always apparent when the cost-benefit equation is computed. The cost is immediate and obvious, the benefit is uncertain--especially when the risk of the seismic hazard is unknown or perceived as low. Elected officials often perceive the risk to be unrealized during their brief term in office, yet the cost must be born during their service. Other public issues presently demand their attention and the community's limited resources.

Case studies of local implementation suggest a role for state government in promoting local preparedness (Gillespie and Mileti, 1993). Seismic safety policies are adopted by local governments when: earthquake awareness is developed among local decision-makers and community members, preparedness advocates are credible and persistent, windows of opportunity are utilized, politically acceptable and feasible solutions are developed, linkage is established with other key issues, and communication between key participants is maintained to coordinate their efforts. The state can assume a leadership position in seeking to increase awareness on the local level, provide support and encouragement for maintaining a credible presence pursuant to preparedness needs, seizing windows of opportunity to promote preparedness, and coordinate efforts to develop workable and politically feasible planning and mitigation strategies. One strategy for promoting awareness in state agencies and for promoting activity on the local level is through earthquake advisory councils. They can be very effective in assembling expertise and promoting interorganizational coordination (Gillespie and Meliti, 1993). Seismic hazard maps are very useful in facilitating earthquake hazard reduction. Such mapping provides information which helps risk assessment and planning for response and recovery needs (Gillespie and Meliti, 1993). The diffuse nature of the seismic hazard often results in high risk zones traversing political boundaries. Perhaps as a direct result, local decision-makers often fail to employ land use regulation as a mitigation strategy. Local planning agencies are often unaware of earthquake hazards and do not see an earthquake mitigation role for themselves. The state has a leadership role to play. Leadership should come from the state level to encourage and support seismic hazard mapping in at-risk counties. Increased awareness frequently fails to translate into action without such support and encouragement.

The state also has a role to play in the adoption of appropriate building codes to make new building in high risk areas earthquake resistant and to retrofit existing buildings, where economically prudent and politically feasible. Various states have adopted either the BOCA code, the Uniform Building Code, or Standard Building Code to make new construction earthquake resistant (Gillespie and Meliti, 1993). Pursuant to retrofitting existing buildings, the Unreinforced Masonry Building Law was adopted by California, but this may be politically unacceptable to some state governments as it might not be viewed as cost-effective. While retrofitting is preferable, some states at least identify hazardous structures in order to determine which are most vulnerable to seismic activity and to facilitate an appropriate EQ response strategy. Regardless of the strategy that a state develops, state-wide adoption of a risk-appropriate plan is deemed the most effective approach.

LEMA Survey Assessment Issues: Risk Assessment, Mitigation Activity, Earthquake Response & Recovery Planning

Pursuant to assessing Pennsylvania's earthquake (EQ) preparedness, the 67 LEMA coordinators were surveyed (mail-questionnaire). Those who did not respond at first were telephoned at three week intervals. Each coordinator was contacted by telephone at least twice. A good response rate of 87% was attained (Babbie, 2004). We sought to ascertain their degree of earthquake experience, the extent to which EQ risk assessments have been undertaken, their level of mitigation activity, and the extent to which they engage in EQ response and recovery planning. Hazard experience was measured in terms of their history with the various types of disaster agents as well as their specific experience with the earthquake hazard. Coordinators reported their current degree of satisfaction with their agency's level of EQ preparedness and their budgetary ability to address perceived EQ needs. They compared their level of EQ preparedness with that for other types of hazards.

Risk Assessment & Mitigation Activity Issues

Risk assessment was examined by ascertaining the extent to which plans have been considered, initiated, and completed pursuant to structural assessment, structural rehabilitation, non-structural assessment, contents protection, vacating of facilities, identification of hazardous materials stored within the community and initiating an earthquake insurance program. Respondents indicated whether the following had been completed: an inventory of buildings likely to be susceptible to the earthquake hazard, mapping of areas within the county which may be at risk to the earthquake hazard (e.g., landslide, subsidence), or made government buildings more earthquake resistant. Level of mitigation activity was assessed in terms of whether the following had occurred: building codes which would require new structures to be earthquake resistant, retrofitting existing buildings to withstand EQ damage, and adoption of land use zoning ordinances to limit building in areas where seismic activity is likely.

Earthquake Response & Recovery Planning Issues

Planning for earthquake response and recovery was assessed by ascertaining if a written disaster plan existed specifically including an earthquake component, if mutual aid agreements were in place, if interagency interaction occurred addressing earthquake preparedness, if there is participation in EQ drills and training programs, if EQ supplies are stockpiled, and if EQ preparedness information is regularly shared with the community.

Demographic Characteristics of LEMA Coordinators

The typical LEMA coordinator in the Commonwealth of Pennsylvania is currently a middle-aged (average age is 49) Caucasian (100%) male (86%) who has completed some college course work (68%). His prior work experience before becoming the LEMA coordinator was in the emergency services field (85%) and he is a Certified Emergency Coordinator (94%). While there is a wide range of experience as a LEMA coordinator, ranging from less than a year to twenty years on the job, the average coordinator has been serving for eight years (please refer to Table 5.8).

Prior Earthquake Experience

Earthquakes were the least frequently experienced hazard among the various hazards which have reportedly occurred within Pennsylvania during the last ten years. Only three LEMA coordinators (5%) reported experiencing an earthquake. All three were from high risk counties, i.e., those found to be within the most active seismic areas in Pennsylvania.

Table 5.8:	LEMA Coordinator Demographic Characteristics N = 55		
Gender		**Years as LEMA Director**	
Male	86%	1 - 4	34%
Female	14%	5 - 10	36%
		11 - 20	30%
Age (in years)		**Work Experience in Emergency Management**	
30 - 42	34%	Military	9%
43 - 54	32%	Emergency Services	85%
55 - 77	34%	Other	6%
[average age = 49]			
Race		**Attained CEM?**	
Caucasian	100%	No	6%
None-Caucasian	0%	Yes	94%
Education			
High School	11%		
Some College	68%		
College Grad	13%		
Graduate Work	8%		

The most commonly experienced hazards during the last ten years were reportedly HazMat transportation accidents (91%, of the LEMA coordinators reported having to response to them), floods (88%), tornadoes (74%), and fixed-facility HazMat accidents (62%). The second tier of most frequently experienced hazards included mass transportation accidents (38%), major fires (33%), and hurricanes (21%). Even nuclear power plant incidents (14% of the LEMA coordinators reported having to respond to this hazard) were reportedly encountered more frequently than earthquakes (please refer to Table 5.9).

LEMA Satisfaction with Current Level of Earthquake Preparedness

Given the low level of risk for most Pennsylvania counties, it is not surprising to find that the majority (60%) of LEMA coordinators consider earthquake preparedness to be rather unimportant in comparison to the other hazards they more

Table 5.9: Counties Reportedly Experiencing the Following Hazards at a Level Requiring a LEMA Response (1985-1995)

Hazard	%	(n)
Hurricane	21%	(12)
Tornado	74%	(43)
Flood	88%	(51)
Earthquake	**5%**	(3)
Mass Transportation Accident	38%	(22)
Conflagration	33%	(19)
Nuclear Power Plant Incident	14%	(8)
HazMat: Fixed Facility	62%	(36)
HazMat: Transportation	91%	(53)

frequently encounter. They report that their level of concern for earthquake preparedness has not changed during the last two years (88% report the level of concern has remained the same). Furthermore, less than a third of the coordinators (29%) believe an earthquake will impact their counties during the next ten years. However, a majority (58%) consider the portion of their budget allocated specifically for earthquake mitigation and planning to be inadequate (please refer to Table 5.10).

High Risk County LEMAs' Rate Preparedness Importance Higher

High risk county LEMAs are more likely to consider EQ preparedness important (a majority did, 58%, while only a third of the medium risk (31%) or low risk (37%) county LEMA's did). They were also somewhat more likely to have viewed such preparedness as increasing in importance over the last several years (25% reported an increase in the level of importance given to earthquake preparedness) than medium risk (6% reported an increase) or low risk counties (10% reported an increase). A majority (52%) of low risk counties reported that their budgets gave adequate attention to earthquake preparedness, while approximately two-thirds of the medium risk (69%) and high risk (67%) counties reported their budgets were inadequate in providing for earthquake preparedness needs (again, please refer to Table 5.10).

Table 5.10:	Changes in Earthquake Preparedness (Total 100% Down Column)			

EQ Preparedness Importance		County EQ Risk Level		
		Low	Medium	High
Important	40%	37%	31%	58%
Not	60%	63%	69%	42%
Level of Importance Changed During the Last 2 Years?				
Increased	12%	10%	6%	25%
Same	88%	90%	94%	75%
Decreased	0%	0%	0%	0%
Available Financial Resources to Support Earthquake Preparedness				
Adequate	42%	52%	31%	33%
Inadequate	58%	48%	69%	67%
Do You Expect an Earthquake to Impact Your County within the Next 10 Years?				
No	29%	24%	27%	42%
Unsure	50%	48%	60%	42%
Yes	21%	28%	13%	16%

LEMA View of Overall Preparedness

Rating Preparedness for All Hazards

The hazards for which the most mitigation activity has occurred are, in descending order, floods (79% rated their activities to mitigate against the flood hazard as their best mitigation effort), fixed facility HazMat accidents (76%), transportation HazMat accidents (62%), major fires (53%), tornadoes (48%), mass transportation accidents (45%), hurricanes (41%), and nuclear power plant accidents (33%). The coordinators rated their agency as being best able to respond to floods (91%), transportation HazMat accidents (88%), mass transportation accidents (83%), fixed facility HazMat accidents (81%), tornadoes (81%), hurricanes (61%), major fires (62%), and nuclear power plant accidents (47%). And, the coordinators rated their agency as being best able to recover from floods (81%), transportation HazMat accidents (79%), fixed facility HazMat accidents (74%), tornadoes (72%), mass transportation accidents (67%), major fires (55%), hurricanes (53%), and nuclear power plant accidents (43%, please refer to Table 5.11).

Table 5.11:	Hazards LEMA Believes it is well prepared for [Percentages Are of Counties Reporting They Are Well Prepared For Hazard Indicated]		
	Mitigation	Response	Recovery
Hurricane	41% (24)	62% (36)	53% (31)
Tornado	48% (28)	81% (47)	72% (42)
Flood	79% (46)	91% (53)	81% (47)
Earthquake	**3% (2)**	**21% (12)**	**14% (8)**
Mass Trans Accident	45% (26)	83% (48)	67% (39)
Conflagration	53% (31)	62% (36)	55% (32)
Nuclear Plant	33% (19)	47% (27)	43% (25)
HazMat: Fixed Site	76% (44)	81% (47)	74% (43)
HazMat: Transport	62% (36)	88% (51)	79% (46)

LEMA's Indicate Earthquakes Are the Least Prepared for Hazard

The coordinators rated their earthquake mitigation efforts and ability to respond to and recover from an earthquake as the hazard they are least prepared to confront. They are presumably not concerned by this circumstance given the low risk of encountering an earthquake during last ten years and their accompanying expectation that this low risk level will extend into the future. Only two coordinators (3%) rated their mitigation efforts to be better for earthquakes than for other hazards. Less than one in five coordinators (21%) rated their ability to respond to an earthquake as being better than their ability to respond to any other hazard. And, less than one in seven (14%) rated their ability to recover from an earthquake to be better than that of any other hazard (please refer to Table 5.9).

Earthquake Hazard Risk Assessment

LEMA coordinators report engaging in little earthquake risk assessment

One in five coordinators (21%) had reportedly considered initiating a structural risk assessment in their county, but almost no one (4%) had initiated or completed (4%) one. Fewer (14%) have considered structural rehabilitation; no one has begun the process and only one has completed it. Few have considered (9%) or initiated (2%) a none-structural risk assessment; no one has completed one. A few have considered the possible need for a contents protection assessment (16%); a few have either begun to take steps (5%) or have completed it (2%). Very few (12%) have considered the need for vacating facilities and only one (2%) has done so. Similarly, few have considered (21%), initiated (5%) or completed (5%) a HazMat storage assessment. Development of a program to encourage the purchase of earthquake insurance has been considered by a few coordinators (16%), some (5%) have begun to take such steps, and one (2%) has done so (please refer to Table 5.12). Risk assessment activity did not vary by a county's level of earthquake risk, i.e., high risk counties were found to be no more likely than medium or low risk counties to conduct any of these assessments.

Table 5.12: Perception of Earthquake Preparedness by County EQ Risk Level			
	Low Risk	Medium Risk	High Risk
Mitigation	7% (2)	0% (0)	0% (0)
Response	23% (7)	6% (1)	33% (4)
Recovery	13% (4)	6% (1)	25% (3)

Earthquake Hazard Mitigation Activity

Building Codes

LEMA coordinators reported that most counties (84%) do not have building codes which require earthquake resistent design for new construction. Only nine counties reportedly have such a building code. The BOCA National Building Code is the type of building code reportedly adopted by six counties, one follows the Uniform Building Code, and two were not sure what type of code is in place in their county. Approximately two-thirds (67%) of those with a building code, indicated it is fully enforced-- the others felt it is only enforced to some extent (please refer to Table 5.13). High risk counties were found to be only slightly more likely to have a building code than the others.

Retrofitting, Zoning, Building Inventory, Mapping

Only one county reportedly has a building code in effect which addresses the retrofitting of existing buildings to enhance resistance to EQ damage (it is a high risk county). Only one county has taken steps to retrofit any government buildings. No counties reportedly have a zoning ordinance in effect which regulates the development or sale of land in areas vulnerable to seismic activity. Most (98%) report they have not conducted an inventory of buildings that would likely be severely damaged by an earthquake. And, most (97%) have not identified or mapped specific areas within their county that could be especially hazardous in the event of an earthquake, e.g., areas prone to liquefaction, landslides, land subsidence, or fault rupture.

Table 5.13:	Earthquake Risk Assessment & Mitigation Activity [Percentage Engaged in Each Activity Indicated]			
	Nothing	**Considered**	**Begun**	**Completed**
Structural Assess	71% (42)	21% (12)	4% (2)	4% (2)
Structural Rehab	84% (49)	14% (8)	0% (0)	2% (1)
None-Structural	89% (52)	9% (5)	2% (1)	0% (0)
Contents Protection	77% (45)	16% (9)	5% (3)	2% (1)
Vacate Facilities	86% (50)	12% (7)	0% (0)	2% (1)
HazMat Storage	69% (40)	21% (12)	5% (3)	5% (3)
EQ Insurance	82% (48)	16% (9)	2% (1)	0% (0)

Earthquake Response & Recovery Planning

Some Written Plans & Mutual Aid Agreements, But Little Training, Drills, Stockpiling or Information Distribution

The coordinators reported that while many do have a written disaster plan (75%), it does not include a specific component outlining their planned response to the earthquake hazard (only 16% have an earthquake component). Almost all LEMA's (98%) report having mutual aid agreements with other organizations to provide reciprocal assistance in event of an earthquake. Most coordinators (98%) do not conduct disaster drills to practice their response to an earthquake. Most (93%) do not attend training programs with an earthquake component. A majority (62%) do not stockpile supplies in anticipation of an earthquake. And, more than two-thirds (71%) do not provide earthquake response information to their communities (please refer to Table 5.14).

Level of EQ Risk Does Not Affect Level of Planning

High risk counties were found to be no more likely than others to develop a written disaster plan (with or without a specific earthquake component), to establish mutual aid agreements, to engage in earthquake disaster drills, to engage in earthquake training programs, or to stockpile earthquake supplies. They were somewhat more likely to provide their communities with earthquake response information (half of the high risk counties do, while 69% of the medium risk counties and 80% of the low risk counties do not--please refer to Table 5.14).

Table 5.14:	Earthquake Mitigation Activity

Does Your County Have a Building Code Which Requires EQ Resistant Design on New Construction?

	No	84%	(48)
	Yes	16%	(9)

    If Yes, What Type of Building Code is in Effect?

	BOCA	86%	(6)
	Uniform	15%	(1)

    If Yes, Is Building Code Enforced?

	No	0%	(0)
	Some	33%	(2)
	Yes	67%	(4)

Does Your County Have a Building Code in Effect to Require Existing Structures to be Retrofited to Resist EQ Damage?

	No	98%	(55)
	Yes	2%	(1)

Does Your County Have a Zoning Ordinance in Place Limiting Land Use in EQ Active Areas?

	No	100%	(56)
	Yes	0%	(0)

Has Your County Completed a Building Inventory?

	No	98%	(56)
	Yes	2%	(1)

Has Your County Mapped Areas At-Risk to the EQ Hazard?

	No	97%	(55)
	Yes	3%	(2)

Have Government Buildings in Your County Been Made More EQ Resistant?

	No	98%	(56)
	Yes	2%	(1)

Inter-Agency Interaction

Little interaction has occurred with other agencies within the county to effect earthquake preparedness. The primary contact with respect to earthquake planning activity was with PEMA. One in five (22%) reported such interaction within the last two years. Some have had contact with other emergency coordinators (14%), the Red Cross (14%), school districts (12%), county planning commissions (12%), emergency medical services (10%), and FEMA (10%). Negligible contact has occurred with police departments, building departments, city/county managers, mayors, administrators and supervisors. Little or no contact occurred with city/county financial departments, fire departments, hospitals, airports, public works departments, colleges, businesses, or the USGS (please refer to Tables 5.15 and 5.16).

Table 5.15:	Earthquake Planning for Response & Recovery			
		County EQ Risk Level		
		Low	Medium	High
Have a Written Disaster Plan				
Yes, Include EQ	16% (9)	17%	20%	8%
Yes, No EQ	75% (42)		76%	73%	75%
No	9% (5)		7%	7%	17%
Have Mutual Aid Agreements With Other Organizations				
No	2% (1)		3%	0%	0%
Yes	98% (57)		97%	100%	100%
Participate in Earthquake Disaster Drills				
No	98% (57)		100%	94%	100%
Yes	2% (1)		0%	6%	0%
Participate in Earthquake Training Programs				
No	93% (54)		90%	94%	100%
Yes	7% (4)		10%	6%	0%
Stockpile Supplies in Preparation for Earthquake				
No	62% (36)		57%	56%	83%
Yes	38% (22)		43%	44%	17%
Provide Earthquake Response Information to Public				
No	71% (41)		80%	69%	50%
Yes	29% (17)		20%	31%	50%

Table 5.16: Percentage of LEMA's Having Interaction with These Agencies for EQ Preparedness Activity - During Last 2 Years	
City Police Department	2% (1)
County LEMA's	14% (8)
County Police Department	7% (4)
Hospitals	5% (3)
City Planning Commission	0% (0)
City Health Department	0% (0)
County Planning Commission	12% (7)
County Health Department	2% (1)
City Building Office	0% (0)
City Public Works	0% (0)
County Building Office	2% (1)
County Public Works	3% (2)
Mayor	2% (1)
School Districts	12% (7)
City Manager	0% (0)
Colleges	0% (0)
County Administrator	0% (0)
Red Cross	14% (8)
County Commissioners	5% (3)
Emergency Medical Services	10% (6)
City Finance Office	0% (0)
Businesses	3% (2)
County Finance Office	0% (0)
Airports	3% (2)
City Fire Department	3% (2)
PEMA	22% (13)
County Fire Marshall	7% (4)
FEMA	10% (6)
City LEMA's	5% (3)
USGS	3% (2)

Summary

What is the state of EQ preparedness in the Commonwealth of Pennsylvania? It does not exist. In fact, this outcome is predicted by the literature reviewed earlier in this paper. The EQ hazard has not been widely experienced in the Commonwealth during the recent past (those which have occurred have been relatively minor in impact), leading to a complacent view that preparedness is unnecessary this far east of California. As a direct result, it is the hazard which has been least likely to have resources devoted to risk assessment, mitigation, or response and recovery planning. However, when we consider the potential seismic vulnerability to the populations of the high and medium risk counties within the Commonwealth (for example, an earthquake impacting southeastern Pennsylvania at a 6.5 level would have a devastating impact on communities such as Philadelphia), one realizes that continued complacency is unacceptable.

The level of EQ preparedness in Pennsylvania was assessed in terms of risk assessment, mitigation activity, and planning for response and recovery. The level of EQ preparedness across each of these three dimensions was found to be extremely low. For example, very little planning for EQ response and recovery has occurred. Written disaster plans usually fail to include an EQ component. Participation in EQ drills and training programs is essentially non-existent. EQ specific stockpiling of necessary post-impact supplies is rare--which would render an impacted community vulnerable to an unnecessarily long recovery period. The misery and complaints following Hurricane Andrew in Homestead, Florida, provide an image of what the outcome of the lack of such supplies in Pennsylvania may be. Dissemination of information to the public, including community decision-makers, is also virtually non-existent, which helps explain the lack of awareness of the need for increased EQ preparedness within the Commonwealth. Only mutual aid agreements (which are in existence as of a result of planning for other hazards) are widely in place. There has been very little interagency interaction addressing earthquake planning and mitigation.

Almost no earthquake hazard risk assessment or mitigation activity has been conducted. There has been a paucity of hazard mapping, structural assessment, HazMat identification, building code implementation, retrofitting of identified vulnerable existing buildings, zoning to control access to seismically vulnerable areas, implementation of EQ insurance programs, and vacating of seismically vulnerable buildings. Earthquake preparedness appears to be so lacking that there is no real, meaningful variation by risk category, i.e., counties identified as being at-risk of experiencing an earthquake appear to be only marginally better prepared than those who have little risk of experiencing this hazard. Almost half of the Commonwealth's counties (28) face a great enough risk of experiencing a damaging earthquake to render EQ preparedness prudent, responsible, and necessary.

Hazard Reduction Recommendations

Since public and private resources are always limited, recommendations suggesting risk assessments, earthquake mitigation activity, and emergency response planning will be viewed critically by decision-makers. Imposing a state-of-the-art program would be naive and ultimately counterproductive, as it would be ignored. It will be necessary to work for consensus among relevant constituencies within the Commonwealth. Clearly, awareness of the EQ hazard and the need for EQ risk assessment, mitigation and planning does not exist among LEMA coordinators. The first necessary task is to redress this problem. Steps should be taken to:

1. Increase EQ awareness and need for EQ risk assessment, mitigation, and planning among local decision-makers.

Action needs to be taken to not only increase such awareness among the Commonwealth's LEMA coordinators, but also among those they report to, as well as local opinion leaders of relevant constituencies, and at least a critical mass of the general public. Target populations should include, but not be limited to, business and community leaders, local political leaders, emergency personnel (LEMA's as well as other emergency organizations), and related organizations (for example, county planning commissions, building associations, engineering organizations, colleges/universities, school districts). Strategies for increasing awareness (for example, see Nigg, Mushkatel, and Moore, 1992) could include dissemination of materials to educate the relevant constituencies on the EQ hazard in the Commonwealth and the need for preparedness--and what constitutes preparedness. The mass media could be used as a means for disseminating awareness information to the general public as well as key decision-makers. For, example both public service announcements and interview format programming could be broadcast on commercial and public television and radio. Similarly, such videotaped productions could be directly mailed to the organizational heads of targeted constituencies. Awareness enhancement workshops and conferences could be periodically held for targeted constituencies. Both onsite and teleconferencing could be utilized. Without designing and implementing strategies for increasing awareness of the hazard and the need for preparedness, support for risk assessment, mitigation, and planning will fail to be realized.

As awareness of EQ vulnerability and the need for preparedness increases, provision should be made to:

2. Provide training on how to conduct AND support to facilitate completion of:
     EQ risk assessments,
     EQ mitigation, and
     EQ response and recovery planning.

EQ preparedness should be especially undertaken in the high and medium risk counties; however, an all-hazards approach has been found to be effective and cost efficient. Hence, relevant constituencies in every county should undergo training and support pursuant to risk assessment, mitigation and planning applicable to all hazards which include relevant hazard-specific components, e.g., an EQ component for high and medium EQ risk counties.

EQ risk assessment and mitigation should include mapping of risk areas, structural and non-structural assessments, identification of rehabilitation needs, contents protection needs, HazMat identification and relocation needs, vacating of necessary facilities, and initiation of an EQ insurance program. An appropriate building code, e.g., BOCA, should be developed (through consensus with relevant constituencies), adopted, and implemented state-wide. A state-wide program for retrofitting existing vulnerable buildings should be developed, funded, and implemented. And, an appropriate state-wide program should be developed for implementing zoning to control access to and use of hazardous areas. The latter three issues have not been resolved in the experience of other states (see Nigg, Mushkatel, and Moore, 1992) by simply imposing such; success has been previously found to be more attainable through consensus building. The following recommendation is, therefore, made.

2. (a) A conference or workshop should be held to engage the relevant constituencies in the process of reaching consensus on appropriate building code, retrofitting, and zoning needs to enhance EQ preparedness.

Pursuant to fostering effective planning for EQ response and recovery, strategies should be developed which result in the following being in place as well as regularly maintained and updated. As part of an all-hazards approach relevant organizations should develop and maintain written plans which include hazard specific components, e.g., EQ component.

2. (b) On-going EQ response and recovery planning should occur which interactively involves all relevant organizations.

On-going interaction with relevant organizations should occur which facilitates mutual aid agreements, mutual planning, hazard specific drills and training, stockpiling of needed supplies, and a community education effort. To facilitate necessary on-going interaction, the following recommendation is made.

2. (c) Develop and implement mechanisms for on-going normal time AND disaster time communication with relevant constituencies.

These mechanisms could include, but are not limited to, a series of advisory boards which would include and be representative of relevant constituencies, a cellular phone system which would link representatives of relevant organizations and constituencies, and computer access via the Internet which would link relevant organizations and constituencies. The most effective way to utilize limited resources as well as to build a consensus on prioritizing action is to link hazard specific needs to the larger preparedness goals common to the mitigation and planning needs of any community. For example, supplies which need to be stockpiled will often be similar for floods as well as earthquakes. Some supplies are hazard specific, many are not. The recommendation is made to link hazard specific needs to an all-hazards approach.

3. The recommendations to facilitate EQ preparedness should be implemented as part of an all-hazards approach to improving preparedness.

The present study was conducted to not only assess the current state of EQ preparedness within the Commonwealth, but to also provide a baseline of information against which future progress could be measured. Longitudinal studies should be periodically undertaken to also assess the success of future efforts to enhance EQ preparedness as the Commonwealth moves into the next century. An all-hazards assessment of preparedness should be conducted as well. Codes representing level of preparedness could be incorporated into the GIS mapping of the Commonwealth. Such mapping would enable PEMA to ascertain the preparedness needs and vulnerability issues on an on-going basis during both normal time and disaster time. Hence, the following recommendations are made.

4. Longitudinal research should be conducted to measure changes in preparedness (for EQs and other hazards) AND these changes should be incorporated into the PEMA EOC GIS for access during both normal and emergency time periods.

4. (a) Interview relevant organizations in high and medium EQ risk counties to specifically determine their needs re preparedness awareness, training, and implementation of an all-hazards approach with an EQ component.

4. (b) Survey all relevant organizations within the Commonwealth to complete an all-hazards preparedness assessment re risk assessment, mitigation, and planning.

4. (c) Develop a coding system for identifying level of preparedness (EQs as well as other hazards) on a county and/or organizational level. Incorporate the coding into the PEMA EOC GIS for access during both normal and emergency time periods.

While risk can never be fully mitigated and response and recovery planning can never eliminate all problems during the post-impact period of any hazard, the previous recommendations should help the Commonwealth better serve the citizens of Pennsylvania. Increased preparedness will increase the saving of lives, property, and tax revenue. The Commonwealth has been lucky that it has not recently experienced a major earthquake event. While previous research has clearly demonstrated that Pennsylvania's emergency organizations and general population are quite typical in ignoring potential vulnerability to hazards until one is experienced, we do not recommend that the Commonwealth await a major earthquake experience before seriously enhancing EQ preparedness.

FIFTH CASE STUDY: THE 2004 BOXING DAY SOUTH ASIAN TSUNAMI: MASS FATALITIES MANAGEMENT—OBSERVATIONS OF THE FIELD TEAM IN THAILAND

(This work was made possible by a grant from the National Science Foundation, NSF HSD SGER Award #0522362.)

Abstract

The death toll after the Boxing Day 2004 tsunami was terribly high. How did the impacted communities respond to their mass casualties? How were dead bodies recovered, identified, and disposed? How were relatives of deceased victims notified and how were foreign victims repatriated? Did ethnicity, socioeconomic status, nationality or international assistance affect how bodies were handled? These questions formed the nexus of the research focus when three field teams gathered data (e.g., face-to-face and telephone interviews, photographs, GPS readings) in the impacted communities within India, Sri Lanka, and Thailand while another team did the same in the European nations most involved in the post-tsunami disaster victim identification (DVI) process (see Fischer, et al, 2005).

Why? Little prior research had been completed enumerating the challenges encountered in mass casualty disasters with the exception of Blanshan and Quarantelli's work enumerating the steps followed in handling dead bodies after September 11, 2001. The question then becomes: to what extent is their work culturally transferable? The current project findings build upon the paucity of basic knowledge on this issue. In 1999 Mileti suggested "catastrophic events may become more prevalent with mass deaths in natural events and terrorist attacks." Hurricane Katrina provides a salient example. The findings should help emergency planners enhance their response planning for such events.

Project participants include nineteen researchers drawn from five nationalities and seven disciplines—emergency management, engineering, journalism, geography, language studies, medicine, and sociology. This was both an international and interdisciplinary team which is directly responsible for a number of outcomes. First, we are working with two universities, one in India and one in Thailand, to develop future interdisciplinary education programs in emergency response. Second, we are sharing the findings with key responders, planners and public policy decision-makers in the impacted nations. Third, we are sharing the research findings with scholarly audiences outside the normal disciplinary boundaries, e.g., a sociologist is presenting a paper at a medical conference while another sociologist has had a paper accepted for publication in a geography journal. Fourth, non-geographers are involved in GPS data gathering and sharing with supercomputer geographers.

The project findings provide basic knowledge on organizations under stress in mass casualty disasters. Findings also identify challenges that necessitate the implementation of new procedures. It will also contribute to the record of this major event via the University of California-San Diego supercomputer project—resulting in enhancing further education efforts. Presentations at professional conferences, papers published in scholarly journals, web site dissemination of findings, and several books have either been completed or are under development.

Key findings include, but are not limited to, the following. First, detailed, specific enumeration of answers to the research questions noted above have been developed for the mass casualty response and challenges in the three impacted nations visited by the field teams. These findings will be disseminated as noted earlier and are too numerous for inclusion in this abstract. Second, cross-cultural observations drawn from the combined data bases, are summarized below.

In the early response phase, emergency organizations quickly realize their prior preparation is inadequate to the task of responding to a mass casualty disaster (in contrast to the everyday emergencies for which they trained).

Emergency organizations undergo social-structural changes during the early response phase as emergent organization structure develops to address the limitations of the institutionalized, normal time emergency organizations. When emergency organizations become overwhelmed by the number of dead to be identified and processed, volunteers, survivors and those converging to the site provide the primary assistance for body handling and removal.

When international assistance for disaster victim identification (DVI) is provided, emergency organizations in impacted nations transfer their response efforts to domestic DVI while international or foreign organizations focus on DVI and repatriation of their deceased compatriots.

Prior to international assistance in disaster victim identification (DVI), local DVI custom is followed.

When international assistance for disaster victim identification (DVI) is provided, Interpol DVI standards are implemented as the standard applying to all victims.

Mass burial is more likely to be the chosen response when the deceased are local population and cultural prohibitions do not prohibit the practice. Mass burial is less likely to be chosen when foreign visitors, e.g., tourists, are among the deceased. Mass burial is less likely to be chosen when cultural custom prohibits the option. Communication breaks down and remains a difficult challenge throughout the response phase; responders improvise, i.e., make their own decisions on how to proceed in the absence of a chain of command with the effectiveness of their decision-making dependent upon the quality and completeness of their prior training.

Misinformation emerges quickly and is communicated all too quickly through informal human networks when normal communication processes are disrupted.

Where turf battles existed prior to the disaster, they are exacerbated during the stress of a disaster response.

Response and recovery decisions vary by the socio-economic circumstances of the impacted populations, e.g., the lower the socio-economic status, the longer it takes for their recovery to be effected.

Restoring the functionality of the local economy is a priority after survivors are rescued.

Mass media accuracy suffers when editorial gate-keeping declines in the rush to publish. Inaccuracies emerge in both domestic and foreign media outlets, e.g., while mass burials were used in India and Sri Lanka, they were not in Thailand, contrary to print and broadcast media reporting.

NGO's provide valuable assets and expertise in disaster response and recovery.

Field Team Observations – Thailand Team

After the tsunami impacted the coastal provinces, the Community Foundations, i.e., emergency search and rescue organizations (Thailand system for search and rescue is based upon private foundations), local police, and survivors converged to the beaches to begin search and rescue operations. Surprise at the total devastation and the number of dead was reported to be a common initial reaction.

After the tsunami impacted the coast provinces, medical teams, etc., from Bangkok converged to the impacted areas to provide medical assistance to survivors and to assist in DVI.

Responders from all organizations indicated they quickly realized the disaster had overwhelmed their ability to respond (e.g., search and rescue, medical assistance, DVI).

Responders indicated they realized early in the response phase that their prior training had prepared them for emergencies, but not for a disaster of this magnitude.

Emergence occurred during the first hours and days of the response phase as survivors joined with the emergency response organizations to assist in search and rescue, temporary burial for later removal (to preserve the bodies), temporary trench creation as well as icing to preserve the bodies for later removal, body removal, and so forth. The emergency organizations emerged into a structure where responders became leaders and on site instructors of the volunteer staff of workers that emerged from on site survivors.

Within the first two or three days volunteers converged from outside provinces to augment the previous noted work.

Bodies were handled initially in one of three ways: (1) temporarily buried under two feet of sand (or less) and marked with a stick and flag (small piece of cloth) in order to find and remove the body later (this "burial" was designed to keep the body cool to retard decomposition and make it easier for later DVI; (2) temporarily moved to trenches for "mass storage" (i.e., many bodies lined up next to one another) and covered with bocks of ice when it was available in order to retard decomposition and aid in later DVI; or (3) removed and released to family when if identified at that point—family then proceeded with funeral arrangements.

Families were able to make identification visual identification or viewing a photo that had been taken and attached to the body—before deterioration.

In the early response phase, DVI work was complicated by the large number of casualties, Thai customs were followed (no moving of deceased until death investigated by police, description of body completed for reporting, release to family for funeral). With the magnitude of the mass casualties, the normal thoroughness of local customs was rendered impossible and only cursory body descriptions were possible—resulting in later international criticism for bodies being released to the wrong families when deceased vacationers were repatriated.

The early DVI process was further complicated by three issues: (1) large number of western vacationers with no family on site to identify them, (2) the hot summer temperatures led to rapid decomposition making it difficult to differentiate between Thai versus non-Thai victims, (3) presence of undocumented deceased workers illegally living in the area.

During early response phase, conflict emerged between two power sectors within the national government. One sector sought to adhere to local DVI custom while the other sought to adhere to Interpol standards. The two sectors had a prior history of turf battles and this disaster event appeared to exacerbate that prior history into a full blown inter-governmental conflict.

Interpol standards were eventually adhered to during the middle part of the response phase. This came about primarily as a result of the Thai government's decision to accept outside DVI assistance from other nations. Australia was the lead nation to emerge in this process.

When international DVI assistance arrived, bodies were relocated from their temporary burial sites to DVI Centers. Over time the number of DVI Centers were reduced to three (when we were in the field) and were expected to be further reduced over time as victims were further identified and released to family.

After international DVI assistance arrived, cooling units were brought to the DVI Centers where the remaining bodies (at that point well over 2,000) were stored at -15 degrees Celsius. The bodies were now "so blackened" that only DNA testing would enable successful DVI. DNA testing was initiated by sending a DNA sample outside of the country where such work could be completed.

When the team was in the field, the DVI teams indicated 40% of the bodies in Thailand had been identified and released at that point. They estimated that it would take an additional two years to complete the task with many probably never being identified.

Before, during and since the Thailand Field Team's field work, mass media outside of Thailand reports mass graves were the method of body disposal in Thailand. There is no evidence of this. In every impacted province, every government interviewee, response organization interviewee, DVI center interviewee, and survivor we meet indicated this to be false. Religious and cultural values prohibit this. It is believed that the individual soul must be properly "sent off" or be doomed to haunt the area in which the person died. Custom dictates that the deceased must be properly cleaned, wrapped, and taken to the Temple for a funeral and cremation. The ashes then sent out to see to release the soul. One impacted area, had great difficulty obtained workers to clear the debris and rebuild as many souls were lost there and feared to be haunting the area.

During the later response and early recovery phases, the foundations (emergency response organizations) and government (local, provincial, and national) worked closely with NGO's to obtain needed equipment, etc., for debris removal, the building of temporary housing, as well as initiated the rebuilding process.

In Phuket, the military was used to aid in the recovery. They were used to clear the beach and tourist sites of debris. Rebuilding was initiated and nearly completed within four months in order to help the town resume its primary industry: tourism. The explanation was given that this would put people back to work and aid in the recovery generally. Other communities within the impacted provinces did not receive rapid assistance and the recovery phase had only begun when the team was in the field. There were noted socio-economic differences observed in where resources were deployed first, second, and so forth.

GPS data collection was conducted for every site visited, e.g., impacted beaches, towns, DVI Centers.

Summary

Research Focus

- How did the impacted communities respond to their mass casualties?
- How were dead bodies recovered, identified, and disposed?
- How were relatives of deceased victims notified and how were foreign victims repatriated?
- Did ethnicity, socioeconomic status, nationality or international assistance affect how bodies were handled?
- How do the answers to these questions vary cross-culturally?

Methodology

- Field Teams
    o Europe: Scanlon
    o India: Phillips, Neal, Wikle, Subanthdre, Hyrapiet
    o Sri Lanka: Oyola-Yemaiel, Wilson, Freir, Gupta
    o Thailand: Fischer, Falkiner, Buchanan, Jankaew
- Interviews & Site Visits
    o Face-to-Face & Telephone
    o Respondents were from Emergency Organizations, Forensics Personnel and Government Officials

Preliminary Findings Cross-Cultural Overview

- Emergency organizations quickly realize their preparation was inadequate
- & they are overwhelmed by the magnitude of the disaster
- Emergent social structure develops to provide assistance in body handling and removal

- Prior to international assistance in disaster victim identification (DVI), local DVI custom is followed
- After international DVI assistance provided, the Int'l organizations assume DVI responsibilities and Interpol standards applied
- Mass burial more likely when the deceased are local population and there are no cultural prohibitions
- Mass burial unlikely when foreign visitors, e.g., tourists, are among the deceased
- Mass burial is unlikely when cultural custom prohibits the option
- When communication capacity breaks down, survivors and responders improvise--emergent norms
- Mass media accuracy suffers when editorial gate-keeping declines in the rush to publish
- Misinformation is quickly communicated through informal human networks
- Prior turf battles are exacerbated during the stress of disaster response
- Response and recovery decisions vary by the socio-economic circumstances of the impacted populations, e.g., the lower the socio-economic status, the longer it takes for their recovery to be effected
- Restoring the functionality of the local economy is a priority after survivors are rescued
- NGO's provide valuable assets and expertise in disaster response and recovery

Normal Procedures for Handling Deceased

- Law requires that the dead are reported to local police
- Medical examiner conducts a post mortem exam and issues a death certificate
- Body is preserved at morgue located in the local medical facility (hospital)
- After the body is identified by family members, it is released from the hospital into their custody for funeral, etc.

Procedures Implemented for Handling Deceased

- Initially no systematic method
  o   Visual ID
  o   Photos
  o   Written and tagged to body
  o   Jewelry or other personal items
- Eventually Interpol standards adopted
- Facilities quickly overwhelmed (hospital morgue)

- Decomposition was rapid:
  - o Bodies in water long time
  - o Very hot 100 degrees
  - o Lacked cold storage for days or more
- Bodies identified by relatives or others, were released
- ID locations varied:
  - o In situ
  - o Moved to central outdoor/indoor location
- Sri Lanka: mass burials for unidentified bodies
- India: unidentified
  - o individual burial in situ
  - o mass burials
  - o cremations
- Thailand: no mass burials (custom is cremation)
  - o Attempts to slow decomposition
    - ▪ temporary burial on beach
    - ▪ trenches dug and ice use
  - o Unidentified and foreign tourists moved several times
    - ▪ temporary morgues
    - ▪ series of DVI Centers
    - ▪ 60% identified via DNA … 2+ more years to complete

Mass Fatality Management Stages Observed

- Bodies taken to central location
- Temporary morgue established
- Identification
- Photos, Forensics were cost prohibitive in India;
- attempted in Sri Lanka & Thailand
  - o Release to family
  - o Individual or mass burial (India, Sri Lanka)
  - o Funeral, Cremation (Thailand)
- Non-Identification
  - o Mass Burial
  - o In Situ Burial
  - o Cremation
  - o Cooling Units - DNA

Conditions Influence Management Options

- Magnitude, scope and distance of the event
- Prior experience including emergency management training and disasters
- Number of deaths

- o   decomposition, stench, dismemberment, debris problems
- Cultural, Religious Beliefs
- Availability of key resources
- Pressing need to take care of the living

SIXTH CASE STUDY: THE EMERGENCY MANAGEMENT RESPONSE TO HURRICANE KATRINA: AS TOLD BY THE FIRST RESPONDERS—A CASE STUDY OF WHAT WENT WRONG & RECOMMENDATIONS FOR THE FUTURE

(A Quick Response Grant from the Natural Hazards Center at the University of Colorado, Boulder, made this field work possible.)

The United States suffered an attack on September 11, 2001 that resulted in publications articulated (re)learned[1] lessons on how to better prepare to respond to such major disastrous events. During the ensuing years after "9.11" billions of dollars have been spent in the quest to address and redress these lessons, e.g., communication failure, pre-positioning supplies, inter-government and agency cooperation enhancement. The Department of Homeland Security was created which rearranged the federal bureaucracy including the repositioning, or demoting, of the Federal Emergency Management Agency (FEMA), again, pursuant to addressing the lessons of 9.11. On the state and local levels, new emergency training centers, training regimens, organizational structures, and a vast array of equipment have been built, developed or acquired. The attack of 9.11 was also the basis for the U.S. military being used to invade Afghanistan and Iraq. Given the post-9.11 reactions of the U.S. government, one would conclude it took the need for better disaster response seriously. On the other hand, the question often heard around the nation in the post-Katrina era is, what have we gained as a result of this investment to date? This paper shares one answer to this question based upon the interviews of first responders in the immediate aftermath of Hurricane Katrina.

On his first visit to the Katrina-impacted Gulf Coast President George W. Bush appeared to summarize his view that the lessons had been learned when he said to FEMA Secretary Michael Brown on national television, "Brownie, you're doing a heck of a job." Within days Secretary Brown resigned his position. The following sampling of news headlines are closer to the reality observed in the field. "When the cops turn into the bad guys—the New Orleans Police Department hits its nadir" (Mulrine 2005), "no evidence shots fired at helicopters—post-Katrina rumor

---

[1] We suggest (re)learned because a reading of the research literature on disaster response challenges suggests that the "lessons learned" that are inevitably published after virtually every disaster now, are not new lessons. They tend to read the same—we just need to learn them and implement accordingly. For a popular media example see "April 18, 1906: Lessons from the Earthquake that Shook the World," by J. Madeleine Nash in the April 10, 2006 issue of Time magazine, pages 57-63. For a research literature resource, one example is Fischer, 1998, Response to Disaster, Lanham, MD: University Press of America.

delayed rescue actions in New Orleans" (Hill and Spangler 2005), "exposed: Katrina urban legends—rumors of murder, mayhem debunked" (Gillin 2005), "now the real looting begins: purging the poor" (Klein 2005), "hurricanes come and go, but coastal (real estate) markets only go up—just look at Biloxi" (Max 2006), "on life support—New Orleans's against-the-odds struggle to care for the infirm" (Shute 2006), "the social fabric is stretched thin, if not shredded altogether" (Mulrine 2006), "a post-Katrina public flaying: the first reviews are in on Washington's response to the storm and they're scathing" (Marek 2006).

Stark Questions

Thousands of illustrations could be provided, the above, however, provide an adequate summary. In short, lessons continue to go unlearned. The stark questions researchers and practitioners are left with at this juncture are: if we keep producing the same observations, yet the problems go unaddressed in subsequent disasters, does this mean research provides more historical record than applied outcomes? And, are practitioners simply the janitors of disaster history—left to clean up afterwards as adequate resources and real authority (political power) will continue to elude their grasp?

Katrina's March into the Gulf Coast

August 27. After a long, slow progression across the Atlantic and into the Gulf of Mexico, on August 27, the National Weather Service issued an advisory at 7:00 a.m. which concluded with the statement that Katrina would make a "gradual turn toward the west-northwest . . . during the next 24 hours" making New Orleans – Biloxi the target when the storm reached landfall (Duffy, 2005:26). The warm water fed Katrina's strength.

FEMA's emergency watch center was already operating at Level 1 which is its highest alert status. The Louisiana State University's Hurricane Center communicated with emergency planners that their data suggested "levee overtopping for west New Orleans and perhaps in New Orleans East as well and St. Bernard Parish" (Duffy, 2005:26). At 9:00 p.m. Max Mayfield, National Hurricane Center – Miami, called Louisiana Gov. Kathleen Blanco. After briefing her on the path and severity of Katrina, he kept repeating "I'm sorry" offering his sympathy even before impact as he knew what was coming.

August 28. At 4:00 a.m., Maj. Rich Henning was part of a weather reconnaissance team that had taken off from Mississippi's Keesler Air Force Base to fly into the eye of the storm in order to determine its current strength. Henning's eyes locked on the computers on the aircraft and yelled "Holy s- - - ! The pressure is 915 millibars" (Duffy, 2005:29). The storm had been at 935 earlier, a Category IV hurricane. Now, with a pressure of 915 millibars, it had continued to strengthen into a Category V storm. At 7:00 a.m. the National Weather Service issued a new bulletin: "Now a potentially catastrophic Category V Hurricane . . . headed for . . . New Orleans and Lake Pontchartrain . . . preparations to protect life and property should be rushed to completion." At 10:00 a.m. on Sunday, August 28, New Orleans Mayor Ray Nagin ordered a mandatory evacuation. State officials ordered contraflow on all roads leading away from New Orleans and the coast. An estimated 1.4 million people did evacuate which is an excellent outcome. Police and fire personnel used loudspeakers to plea for the remaining (up to) 150,000 people to leave. Many could not, some would not. The Superdome began to fill up with those who could not leave town, but could move to the dome.

August 29. At 5:00 a.m. the Harrison County Emergency Management Coordinator, Joe Spraggins, was on Coastal Highway 90 examining the waves preceding the storm surge. They were cresting at 10 feet or so. Suddenly the waves and wind speed were rapidly rising even further. When the waves began surging across the macadam, Spraggins and his colleagues headed back toward the county courthouse in Gulfport where the EOC was located.

By 7:00 a.m. Katrina was making landfall along the coast—from the borders of Alabama to Texas. In one EOC emergency personnel found themselves prisoners to Katrina. The generator did not work when the electricity went out. The doors and window coverings were controlled electrically. When the storm surge water began to flow under the doors, the emergency workers could not flee the EOC, they were locked in. The water rose rapidly in the one story building. Soon the emergency personnel were using indelible ink to write the social security numbers on theirs bodies, tied themselves to each other, and prepared to drown. Fortunately the water stopped rising.

At noon FEMA Director Michael Brown reportedly sent a memo to Homeland Security Secretary Michael Chertoff making a request for 1,000 employee volunteers to be dispatched to the impacted areas within the next two days. It was recommended that volunteers should bring insect repellent and plenty of cash as "ATMs may not be working" (Duffy, 2005:32). At the Superdome, the evacuees swelled to 20,000. By 2:00 p.m. the Times-Picayune reported in its online edition that at least one levee, the 17th Street Canal, had been breached. The levees had been built to withstand up to a Category III storm, not a Category IV-V Hurricane.

August 30. President Bush, on vacation, was briefed on the situation and was reportedly assured all appropriate steps were being taken. While television images showed a starkly different picture, the President rarely watches TV news and practices a management style delegating vast responsibilities.

Misery was widespread across the Gulf Coast: Mississippi and Louisiana. Survivors emerged from the rubble to find it difficult to recognize their community; they could not even be sure where the roads were, making it impossible to move around to help others. Electricity and communications were gone. It was very difficult for assistance from the state level to begin to move in since devastation was so widespread and severe. The federal response is designed to be the third line of response anyway and the scope and magnitude of this event was appearing to be beyond any of the prior federal planning. In the view of those who survived and responded in those early days, it seemed to continue to get worse and worse, before it got better.

Interviewed First Responders: What Worked, What Did Not, & Recommendations

The research literature on preparedness clearly articulates what has been previously learned as necessary for disaster preparation. "The purpose of preparedness is to anticipate problems in disasters so that ways can be devised to address the problems effectively and so that the resources needed for an effective response are in place beforehand" (Mileti 1999:215). Activities to be included in planning and preparing for hurricanes such as Katrina, include but are not limited to the following: "formulating, testing, and exercising disaster plans; providing training for disaster responders and the general public: and communicating with the public and others about disaster vulnerability and what to do to reduce it . . . Preparedness activities can be analyzed at various levels: families households, organizations, communities, states and nations" (Mileti 1999:215).

Beginning with the immediate post-impact period, anecdotal evidence indicated that disaster researchers, responders, the mass media and the general public perceived the organizational response to Katrina as inadequate on a number of levels. This research project was designed to contribute to the assessment of what did and what did not succeed in the response to Katrina, from the perspective of those responding to the event, i.e., first responders. The research contribution envisioned was a testing of the efficacy of previous research findings reflected, for example, in the both first and second assessments. The specific focus was on determining the continued efficacy of the literature on preparedness and response (e.g., Mileti and Fitzpatrick 1993, Wenger et al. 1986, Wenger et al. 1989, Quarantelli 1982, Fischer 1998).

The Center for Disaster Research and Education (CDRE) monitored the progress of Hurricane Katrina and its aftermath. Contact information, logistical planning, and field preparations were ongoing in anticipation of conducting post-impact research. Three CDRE faculty members and three CDRE student research assistants flew to the Gulf Coast to begin field work in Mississippi and Louisiana. They worked as three two-person interview teams (one faculty member and one student). These teams interviewed emergency responders from the local, state and national levels in Mississippi and Louisiana. Our approach was to implement a detailed interview guide in which we stressed with the respondents that our primary objective was to identify, from their perspective, (1) what worked, (2) what did not work as anticipated, (3) what they did differently (from what was planned or anticipated) to deal with the situation, and (4) what recommendations they have for their colleagues who may find themselves in a similar situation. A wealth of data was gathered. The interviews ranged in length of time from one to three-and-a-half hours. The respondents were far more forthcoming than we expected. The interview experience was, in the view of the field team, a cathartic experience for the respondents who appeared to just be waiting for someone to come along and ask our research question. While most of the interviews were completed face-to-face while in the field, some were conducted as telephone interviews while the teams were in the field as well as after returning to the CDRE. Two additional field visits were completed in the first year after impact (funded from other sources). A total of 58 interviews were conducted.

The actual words of those responding to Katrina will be interspersed as we identify the patterns that emerged from the interviews themselves. The field experience was sobering. It has left an indelible imprint upon those of us who spent those eight days in the field and hours on the telephone. Reviewing our own photographs as well as those of others served to reinforce the vivid images that have written themselves into our collective memories. The suffering of those who experienced the disaster is something this field team will long remember. Our hope in the society's ability to learn from the experience has, admittedly, been shaken. We fear the current social structure guarantees repeated failure going forward.

Confusing Emergency Preparedness with Disaster Preparedness; then Viewing the Federal Government as Savior.

"We kept asking, 'where is the federal government?'" A common remark made by citizen and responder alike in the days after Katrina paid an unwanted visit to the Gulf Coast. One by one, many responders in key positions of responsibility confessed, "we thought we were prepared, but early on we knew we were not prepared for something like this! We also thought that the feds would save us if something of this magnitude would befall us. We didn't realize they wouldn't be able to get to us."

After Hurricane Andrew, for example, FEMA received a great deal of criticism for not responding as quickly as Florida would have liked. While FEMA was less than perfect in its Andrew response, it was never designed to be the cavalry to arrive in the nick of time to save those from their lack of preparedness. FEMA has since made a point of trying to teach the nation that individuals and communities must prepare to be on their own for the first 72 hours as it will take at least that long for help to even begin to arrive. And, in a catastrophic event it may take weeks.

After Katrina we kept hearing that the emergency organizations believed they were well prepared for everyday emergencies and even lower grade disasters. Some indicated they believed a major event like Katrina would be a problem, but they felt, Hurricane Andrew aside, the FEMA and others from the federal level would "bail them out." They had not anticipated a disaster that destroyed the coast from the Alabama border to the Texas border, making convergence of assistance impossible. In the words of one local responder, "when we emerged after the storm passed, we could not see any roads . . . anywhere . . . that is when I knew we were really in for it. I then knew we would be on our own for a very long time."

Exhausted Before Impact. Many responders indicated they had plans in place, had practiced and were ready for much of what occurs in emergencies and disasters, in their view. However, in an effort to help their comrades going forward, they were quite open about what they felt they overlooked or had not anticipated. For example, "to make matters worse, we were already exhausted before impact even occurred. When it became more and more obvious that this storm was going to hit us for real and that it was a monster, we went into full alert for several days before impact. Instead of creating shifts so we could get rest, we stayed up preparing 24x7. Then it hit and after the terrifying event we emerged in the rubble and then had to begin search and rescue—but we were already exhausted. We were burned out within the next 48 hours, with no replacements in sight. We really screwed up. I would recommend that others in the future plan for down time no matter how bad things look or get, without some rest you are ultimately worthless."

Emergencies vs. Disasters. "We could handle anything . . . as long as we could drive to it." Katrina reminded the responders that being well rehearsed and well prepared for an emergency is not the same as being well prepared for a major disaster. "When we came out after the wind stopped, we had no vehicles to begin search and rescue—they were all destroyed. And, even if they weren't there were no roads to drive on, the debris was everywhere. And, there was no electricity, so even if we had cars and roads, we would soon run out of gasoline since we couldn't pump anymore." For many responders their generators failed as well. The responders were victims as much as the others in their communities. The only thing they did not know at the time, was that it was not just their community that was in such a state of affairs. Why? Communication, of course, was out.

The Loss of Communication, Equipment & Ability to Respond

One of the most common lessons learned in virtually every disaster is that communication is lost early in the impact stage. Perhaps the most frequent statement we heard during our post-Katrina interviews was that "communication was lost early on. Electricity, telephone, cell phone, everything was gone! It didn't come back in some cases for weeks." The lack of communication destroyed much of the inter-agency, inter-organizational coordinator for an extended period of time in the early days, weeks. Ironic in a hi-tech communications age, the most reliable and helpful communication equipment was reported to be the ham radio.

The most heartbreaking event reported to us involved a young responder who was home with his family (did not evacuate) during impact, when he called for assistance to save his family he indicated that he had "tied his family members to the roof of his house, begged us to come and get them, but we could not as the rescuers, at that point, because we would have perished trying to do so. The phone died as this strong man was crying. When we were able to find our way eventually through the debris, only the foundation pad of his house remained. Not even their bodies were ever found. Between the wind and the storm surge, they never made it."

Exacerbating the situation, the loss of emergency equipment, e.g., police and fire cars, trucks, ambulances, made it impossible for search and rescue to begin in the immediate post-impact period in those areas impacted by the hurricane winds and storm surge. With the loss of equipment, even when roads begin to be cleared, responders were reduced to "acquiring what was needed. If a private car was found usable, we appropriated it for the time being in order to help find and transport those needing care to an appropriate location, we siphoned gas from cars that were destroyed and unusable. Sometimes we appropriated gasoline being brought in; we even appropriated the vehicles of others converging to the site. We did what we had to do; we prioritized needs. Some people will think we were stealing or wrong, but we were trying to save lives here and this is what we were reduced to. It looked like a third world country around here, I'm afraid we had to act like it too."

Inter-agency & Inter-organization Cooperation

A pattern of responder perception was observed for local, state and federal governmental cooperation. Local responders reported feeling that cooperation was very good, "all things considered," between all of the locals. "The problem was between levels, it was impossible to get anything going with the state or the feds." On the other hand, those working from the state perspective suggested "the problem was at both the local and the federal levels. We did fine working with each other, but getting the locals to act in concert with us was mission impossible—ditto for the feds." Those working from the federal perspective conformed to this pattern: "we are fine, they are not."

Disorganization and turf conflicts were evident at every level we interacted with. Conflicting reports were the norm among those working at EOCs. Some claim "fabulous coordination and cooperation among knowledgeable responders." Others suggest a "disorganized mess among those who know nothing."

Medical workers and medical volunteers reported "breaking into a local closed pharmacy in order to acquire needed basic medical supplies since we had no other recourse. Even after we could communicate with officials, they still did not deliver what they promised. We had patients continually coming in and we needed the basics to help them. But no one will tell you the truth on this."

FEMA within Homeland Security Viewed as Problematic. A prevalently articulated assessment was the "failure of the HSD to focus on an all-hazards approach before Katrina. While terrorism may occur again, we know hurricanes and other types of disasters will." Furthermore, "the loss of FEMA personnel and budgetary support as a result of being swallowed up by HSD" was noted to be a problem which was perceived as contributing to the "problematic response to Katrina which was systemic and far more than just the incompetence of Director Brown."

While an enhanced role for the U.S. military was frequently recommended "as long as it is in conjunction with and under civilian control and leadership," not a single respondent was in favor of the U.S. military becoming the disaster manager of choice. Instead, the greatest value of the military was seen as being the trans-porter-in-chief. The military was favored for the purpose of transporting personnel and supplies into a disaster zone, for transporting out evacuees who have no other means of leaving, and for providing support (food, shelter, transportation, road clearance of debris) for other needed disaster personnel, e.g., medical, logistical, temporary housing and some types of construction and repair work to facilitate rapid restoration of basic services.

Reported Deviance and the Behavior of Survivors: Acquiring vs. Looting

The usual research literature pattern was observed. Conflicting reports were constant. "There was little or no looting." "There was some looting, but mostly for survival needs that were not being met in any other way . . . so I guess I wouldn't really call that looting." "The crazies were out of control. Looting was everywhere, no excuse for it at a time like this. Just stealing cigarettes, booze, fishing rods, a TV . . . my god, there still isn't electricity to watch the damn thing."

The research team is convinced looting did occur in this event. It is also con-vinced that much of it was not looting as much as acquiring the means for survival. Notice that it is labeled acquiring by officials when they need supplies to support their survival and mission, but it is labeled looting when citizens need resources to support their own survival. However, there was also looting in both Mississippi and in Louisiana. The question then arises, why does it occur and when will it occur? Prior research has repeatedly found that it is rare. And, the crime reports from New Orleans demonstrate that even in Katrina the overall crime rate was much lower than in normal time. Never the less, looting occurred for non-survival reasons. Why? Is it media socialization, i.e., looting is normal, so follow the norm? Is it akin to civil disturbances for disasters of the magnitude (in scale and scope) of a Katrina, i.e., the disenfranchised attacking the perceived oppressors? Is it anomic loss of social control, i.e., police unable to fulfill social control function of normal time in a disaster of this magnitude?

The prior research literature on this issue may be skewed: based on small west-ern populations experiencing more limited disasters in scale and scope. We will return to this issue in the discussion section of this paper, taking up an application of Fischer's disaster scale (2003). Hurricane Katrina demonstrates, it will be ar-gued, that it is time to think in terms of a disaster scale for which all previous and future research findings will need to be qualified.

The issue of behavior is not merely something that inquiring minds want to know. In Katrina it had a major impact on the actions of responders and the pro-longed misery of victims. The continual media reports of looting, marauding street gangs, shooting at rescue helicopters, and so forth, had a paralyzing affect on many responders. For example, responders on their way to help those trapped at the Super Dome ceased their advance on the other side of the bridge and decided not to pro-ceed for fear of encountering bodily harm by those allegedly exhibiting deviant behavior. Those trapped at the Super Dome without food, water, and other necessities, continued to suffer until the entertainer Harry Conneck, Jr. drove over the bridge and participated in a live Today Show interview on NBC wondering aloud "what the problem is?" Articulating he could drive over without incident and did not understand why the responders could not. They eventually did venture forth. Unfortunately, the NBC program continued to fan the flames of exaggeration, i.e., disaster myths, even though their news people were present and should have known better, myth was still reported as fact.

Conditions that Contribute to Acquiring & Looting Behavior. "So, you are in the evacuation center you were told to go to, the food runs out as does everything else. People are frustrated, scared, becoming angry at their situation which they view as being left to die. The look at the locked store next door where they see food through the windows going to waste as there is no electricity. Eventually they decide this is crazy, so they break the windows and go in to get the food, water and diapers they need and don't have. Meanwhile, no one seems to be able to get to these people to provide help, except the reporters manage to get there to cover the story of their misery. The 'stealing' is shown on national TV. The tongues begin to wag and the fingers are pointed at these 'looters.' What the hell does anyone expect to happen? We created the situation to guarantee 'looting' would occur, and then we blame them (the victims) for their desire to survive. Is this nation nuts or simply incapable of overcoming racism and classism?"

Over time the altruism of survivors was seen in Katrina as being replaced by anger among those (victims and sometimes the first responders too) who felt abandoned and betrayed by a social system that was supposedly designed to help them. As the anger increased to rage, the conditions appear to have been increasingly similar to those in civil disturbances more than disasters. In time the disaster victims felt "more victimized by 'society' than by Katrina, we were treated like animals, in fact many times pets received more help; racism was responsible for our plight."[2]

Reducing the Likelihood. Many responders we interviewed kept returning to the idea that while help was beyond slow, the media was always there first and showed what was not being accomplished. "How come emergency organizations could not get there but media organizations could? If nothing else, perhaps we should turn over meeting immediate needs via rapid response to the media. While this idea was rather tongue-in-cheek, one that was not was, "Wal-Mart is good at tracking and moving supplies, perhaps the government should pre-contract with them to bring in the basics needed before, during and after an event like this."

Another idea articulated by first responders was "instead of owners locking their stores and evacuating, they should either leave them unlocked or give the keys to the police so that an orderly distribution of needed supplies can be easily organ-

---

[2] We interviewed first responders, not citizen victims. However, a composite was created here to illustrate the sentiment we frequently observed in television and newspaper coverage and accounts.

ized after something like Katrina—that would be a lot better than starving people to the point of their having to break in and feel like thieves, be called thieves, and be shot at."

Mass Media: Part of the Solution and Part of the Problem

Media as Helper. Without the television broadcast media calling attention to the plight of those stranded at the Super Dome and the Convention Center, the misery of these evacuees would undoubtedly have been unnecessarily lengthened even further. The media was characteristically extremely helpful in calling attention to problems that needed to be redressed, in providing information to evacuees and survivors, and in providing information of responders as well—in some cases the media was the only source of information for an extended time (radio and then television for those who could obtain electricity via generator or service restoration). A typical responder comment indicated their dependency on the media in the absence of communications when he said, "I had a ten gallon can I filled with gasoline before impact that enabled me to run my home generator and that gave me access to radio and some television I could capture off the antennae that was on one of my small televisions. This is all the communication (one way at that) I had for the first six or seven days. It was impossible to travel with all the debris. I could not do anything except help survivors in my own immediate area. For all I knew the world ended. All I knew was from the mass media when I turned it on, which I did sparingly in order to preserve my gasoline as long as I could. That is how I eventually knew how big the event was and how long it was taking, and going to take, to get help to all of us."

Media as Part of the Problem. There was also the usual problematic aspect to the mass media reporting, exhibited by the following responder's experience. "I saw (TV) how people were really acting out in New Orleans—it scared me. I knew we were going to need police and military help to get control." Another responder indicated, "it was through television that we knew about the looting, raping and killings in NOLA; we had some of the looting here (Mississippi), but nothing like those crazies."

A volunteer medical responder in New Orleans shared, "we drove over the infamous bridge one evening to go to see who may need some medical attention and we were immediately surrounded by scary people pounding on the ambulance, we locked our doors, they had a crazed look in their eyes. We didn't get out, we just slowly back up until they stopped, then we turned around and left. The next day we went in with some support (National Guard) and then helped them. We then realized what was going on. Those pounding on our vehicle the night before were going through drug withdrawals. They saw the ambulance and assumed we would have something they could shoot themselves up with to get high and stop the withdrawal symptoms. They weren't intending to harm us, they were desperate for the drugs they could not now buy since they were cut off from their dealers. Everything here is just one hell of a mess. Reporters see some things, make assumptions and come to the wrong conclusions about what is really going on which only makes it worse."

Rumor, as is noted in the research literature, was often reported as fact. "We kept hearing (from media reports) about the shootings at helicopters by marauders in the city, we were afraid to go in because we didn't want to get shot trying to help these damn ungrateful people." Later, it was determined that these alleged shootings never occurred: rumor reported as fact suppressed responder action which prolonged misery. Others indicated they "were afraid to go in because we felt uncomfortable, I'm not prejudiced, but in this situation we were only a few whites surrounded by many blacks. We had to be prudent." Fear of what deviance may occur had a restraining effect on how quickly help was provided. The desire for police or National Guard protection was frequently articulated as a precondition for feeling comfortable to provide assistance to the victims. The nature of the mass media reporting was the primary source of perceptions of the dangers of advancing into large populated areas with minority populations.

Media Convergence. Responders indicated they "need more training in how to deal with the mass media when they converge in such large numbers, are pushy and rude. The media was in sooner than anyone else. We would have liked to have had some control on the media's ability to move around in such large numbers. Perhaps a media pool would be less bothersome when we are trying to complete our mission. Prevent them from wandering around the city; instead, give them information periodically from press meetings."

The Convergence of Volunteers Who Are Not Self-Sufficient

The Problem. "We were overwhelmed with our own needs—inadequate water, food, shelter, transportation, medical care, and so on—and the 'doc-in-a-box' (doctor living out of his car with his own supplies in the back of his car) arrives, then a group of fire fighters arrive, then . . . in each case they come up to me and say 'we are here to serve.' They have this angelic look on their face and want to be of help, but the first thing they ask is 'where can we eat, sleep . . . .' and I say, 'you know we are in the middle of a major disaster, right?' I mean, I wanted to appreciate their offer, but they only added to my problems. I needed people and supplies, not people to take care of, as I already had that."

The Solution. The Governor of Mississippi telephoned his counterpart in Indiana activating a prior reciprocal agreement that enabled the Indiana National Guard to transport the Indiana medical team to Mississippi, set up their encampment, and feed them for the duration of their service in the Biloxi area. Self-sufficiency resulted in providing service to the victims without adding to the local burden.

One responder expressed appreciation for those who arrived self-sufficiently, "I could have kissed them. In they came one day and told me what they came prepared to do, I was expecting another housing and feeding burden, but they told me not to worry about that, they came prepared to take care of themselves as well as care for those who were in need of medical treatment. I thought, finally something that works. God bless them!"

Pre-Positioning of Personnel and Materials

As one responder put it, "pre-positioning supplies in Atlanta and Houston is sure better than leaving them in D.C., but it still doesn't cut it. It is a long way to here (Mississippi and Louisiana) from Atlanta even if the roads along the entire coast weren't impassable. I don't know what they are thinking." Another said, "we can't go without water for a few weeks, maybe a few days but not a few weeks. We're the only remaining super power and we can't even transport basic disaster needs for our own population, even position them close enough for use. I thought this country was supposedly better prepared after September 11th. My god, what are we going to do if we ever really have a terrorism attack?"

Recommendation. "We should build hardened buildings where pre-positioned materials can be safely warehoused, something like during the Cold War days when we had those air raid shelters and all that. Build them in Mississippi and in Louisiana in buildings that can withstand flood water and high wind. Then make sure the personnel and supplies are there before impact, ready to go immediately afterwards. This is pitiful." Another responder noted that "the logistics just weren't there. We didn't stockpile locally for something of this magnitude, the state was good, but not good enough for something like this, and the feds, oh man, they just weren't there. We all thought a disaster was like an emergency, except that you just raise the level a bit, you know, a disaster is like a big emergency, you just do what you normally do but do it on a bigger scale. We now know it ain't that way. You need real planning by those in the know; you can't run these things with just volunteers, part-timers, and those whose only experience is everyday emergencies. What is this country thinking? They way we do it now is like sending Mom and Pop to run a Corporation!"

Corporate Citizenship

The Problem. "Ok, we all believe in profit, the free market and all that. But at the same time we are all in this together. Corporations are made up of people. Those people need to remember they make a living off of us and they are just like us. They need to have more of a service (ethic) . . . rather than leach off of victims. They offer a service we pay for and then do everything they can to avoid providing what they led us to believe we were buying." Insurance companies were highly criticized by responders and victims for not paying what was anticipated for rebuilding. Insurance claims were reportedly turned down by companies claiming the storm surge was a flood and the victim needed FEMA flood insurance.

Responders were distraught over property insurance problems for several reasons. First, they were seeing their fellow citizens suffer through the disaster and now they were seeing them suffer economically. And second, some of the victims were also responders which impacted on the responders' ability to do their job. "I have a man who is burying some of his family, other family members evacuated out of state, and he lost his car, his part time job (as a result of the disaster, the work does not exist now), and his house. And, his insurance company won't pay. He can't concentrate. He can't do his job. I fear he might even be a suicide risk."

Recommendation. One responder's words represent a viewpoint we frequently encountered. "There should be a fund created that is especially earmarked for responders. One that takes care of them so that they can do their job for the community . . . not help everyone else and then eventually go home and have no one to help them. Their house should be rebuilt, their car payment covered. Some of these people lost more than half their incomes due to the loss of their spouse's job and their own part-time work. How are these people expected to work as responders and survive?"

Failure of Emergency Personnel to Stay or Report for Work

Confusion is the operative word on this issue. In some instances emergency personnel evacuated their families and were unable to return as Katrina impacted making it impossible for these workers to travel. NOLA first reported many police officers had not reported for work, later reports suggested many of these alleged officers actually did not exist. Their positions were reported to be falsely created as part of a corruption scheme. In other cases, some workers did fail to stay on the job. In those instances the research team was able to track, workers had left their post due to exhaustion after days of none stop work. These individuals had apparently not left for selfish reasons. The number and percentage of workers who failed to report for work or stay on the job as well as the reasons for their actions, is still unclear. However, it does appear that a higher percentage did so than the research literature on this subject would have predicted.

Police Protection. Responders would have liked to have felt they had police protection rather than feeling like everyone had left and they were own their own. Even if some deviance during a disaster is more illusion than reality, the responder's comfort level would have been enhanced, during an already highly stressful first few weeks, if protection had been more evident. A common recommendation by responders was the desire for police and perhaps a National Guard presence to assist them in their work, particularly in urban areas.

The Lack of Planning for Pets

As with most disasters, plans for dealing with pets were described by responders as insufficient. Many animals were left on their own when their owners evacuated as they were not allowed to bring pets to shelters. This resulted in the responders using limited human resources to rescue animals in the weeks after Katrina's impact. In some cases this provided additional risk to these responders who had encountered hungry, thirst, fearful pets, e.g., dogs.

Some victims did not evacuate because they knew they were not permitted to bring their pet to a shelter. In some communities animal shelter personnel engaged in heroic efforts to move their housed animals before and after impact. Responders frequently noted a plan would be needed going forward to better serve the community as human beings are often in greater risk when their pets, which are viewed as family members, are at risk.

Summary of First Responder Recommendations

The following list of recommendations reflects the compilation of what the research team gathered through our interviews. This list summarizes what was presented above. The first responders we interviewed were, in our view, very forthcoming and spoke freely in an effort to draw from their experiences in order that others might benefit in the future. They were assured confidentiality, which we have protected, even though they almost unanimously indicated it was not necessary.

Macro & Micro Issue Summary List

- Create a National Disaster Plan that shares the economic impact of a community issuing an evacuation order, so that they don't go bankrupt if an evacuation was not necessary; also to interface more effectively when various levels of government and various agencies become active in responding
- Re-establish FEMA as a separate agency, (remove from Homeland Security), Director as Cabinet level position
- Increase funding and number of full time professionals in FEMA in order to meet the needs of the nation during disaster events—continues to be understaffed
- Provide direct assistance to first responders who are also victims: who lose homes and cars yet still have mortgages and car payments, and lose their job, their spouse's job, or either lost their part-time job(s)
- One communication system for all—and workable despite disaster, e.g., satellite cellular communication
- FEMA, Government, should give contracts before impact, during normal time, so everything can be quickly activated—not wait to let contracts after impact, too slow
- Consider involving companies like Wal-Mart directly in a disaster response: (a) they have and can move supplies quickly and (b) to leave stores "unlocked" in impacted areas so community can access needed items

- Better interfacing needed for local, state, federal need identification and provisions allocation
- Develop Disaster Check Lists for Responders to use for their jobs
- Develop standardized forms, e.g., DMORT forms, consistent across the nation, available electronically, saved on jump drives, to go into field for use onsite
- Create ethics guidelines to help responders know difference between acquiring necessary supplies from impacted environment versus stealing
- Need additional training on crisis management to differentiate between normal time habits that, if repeated in disaster, become counter productive, dangerous
- Need for all-hazards approach to be taken seriously
- Need for planning to be taken seriously
- Need to prepare for disasters differently than how we prepare for everyday emergencies
- Volunteers must be self-sufficient when they arrive in a disaster zone
- Educate the nation on what is needed (self-sufficient help, financial donations) versus what is not needed (random convergence of volunteers who are not self-sufficient, material donations trucked in randomly)
- Educate the nation on disaster mythology versus disaster reality with respect to behavioral response patterns and organizational response challenges
- Educate disaster planners and first responders that a disaster is not just a large emergency
- Develop disaster planning in concert with different levels of disasters; the scale and scope of a disaster requires different responses (localized disaster responded to by local and state resources, perhaps some federal support long-term; Katrina sized disaster requires immediate federal involvement partnering with localities and states)
- Pre-locate supplies closer to potential impact areas—permanently located within or near communities in hardened buildings
- Organizations need to develop plans for responders having time on and time off even during disaster, otherwise, they burn out and become worthless
- Organizations institutionalized debriefing sessions between rotating shifts of workers in order to transfer information
- Create a media pool, provide regular news conferences rather than allowing reporters to go wherever they want to go within the disaster area—responders have a job to do first and foremost
- Change insurance system so that victims really are fully covered; too many policy holders were told the storm surge was not weather related, but flooding and they needed flood insurance to be covered for the loss of their home

- Create procedures for organizing and implementing effective large scale evacuations, e.g., National Guard trucks to move evacuees who do not have personal means of transportation
- Create plan for providing means of support into hands of evacuees, e.g., emergency money card held by every citizen, activated during disasters ($2,000) which can be used for gasoline, lodging, food, and other relevant materials
- Standardize Protocols in the U.S. so that doctors, etc., can automatically practice in another state during a disaster
- Develop evacuation plans that include family pets

Chapter 6

Future Research Needs

DISASTER HISTORIANS & DISASTER JANITORS

My three post-Katrina trips to the Gulf Coast during 2005-2006 really depressed me. I have not been the same since. We had productive research, interviews, etc, but the totality of the event haunts me. Since my graduate school days I had believed, perhaps naively, if we just continue to do the research, publish the results, teach the findings, and so forth, we will turn the corner and make a difference.

I want to still believe. The problem is the lesson I learned in the field this time is not only do we relearn the same old "lessons" after every major disaster, I learned we really do not! I now fear research provides more historical record than change in applied outcomes and practitioners simply function as the janitors of disaster history—left to clean up afterwards as adequate resources and real authority (political power) to effect change eludes their grasp. The social structure guarantees this perpetual outcome.

The social construction of disaster outcomes derives from elitist domination, labeling and prioritization. For example, former first lady Barbara Bush blamed the victims in Katrina when she said of those evacuated to places like Houston "they're getting a pretty good deal, they're better off now than before." Wow! And President George W. Bush, on a trip to the Gulf Coast, said "we (federal government) write the checks, but it is the responsibility of state and local government to see that the money gets to the people who need it." The President is not only blaming the victimized state and local governments, but is also providing an inaccurate portrayal of how the federal structure works (Whether his inaccuracy is the result of being a misinformed President or a Machiavellian gambit, the socially constructed failed outcome is the same for the victims further down the socio-economic ladder.). This is the same President who appointed a man as FEMA Director who had absolutely no experience in emergency management. One would think that those in the USA might draw some inference from the President's seriousness of purpose in so doing.

While large numbers of middle, working and lower class Katrina victims continue to be displaced, we observe examples of how the socially constructed post-Katrina recovery was able to be expedited for the more advantaged. Mississippi gambling casinos have returned bigger and better than before—perhaps Barbara Bush was partially correct, but had the wrong social class in her sights. Limited resources, builders, plumbers, electricians, etc, were diverted from rebuilding housing for individual citizens and directed toward restoring such enterprises. The socially constructed recovery outcome was, somehow, able to function effectively for part of the socio-economic spectrum, but not the other. We observe everyday norms returning very quickly in the usual disproportionate manner conforming to how the social structure has been created. The Katrina recovery is certainly conforming to the normal power-elite's domination of limited wealth and power.

Meanwhile, many altruistic individuals and organizations continue to volunteer their time and resources in an attempt to fill the socially constructed void. Unfortunately, as noble and helpful as these efforts are, they are drops in the flooded waters that surged ashore or poured through the levies. No serious observer can claim that "putting people first" is socially constructed into the post-Katrina recovery—or any disaster of even lower categories on the disaster scale.

A paradigm shift will be needed that results in the social reconstruction of disaster mitigation, planning, response and recovery. It is no accident that emergency management is only now in the 21st century attempting to become a profession. It had been socially constructed to be at the mercy of the power-elite. It will be a very long time before it, if ever, becomes more than the janitorial service for the privileged. Perhaps disaster researchers can help foment the reconstruction and cease being mere disaster historians?

NECESSARY RESEARCH ADVANCES

Great progress has been made in disaster research during the last five-plus decades. As Professor Quarantelli noted in the foreword to this book, social scientists in the 1940s were beginning to suspect that behavioral response problems were not correctly understood. Anecdotal evidence gathered by disaster researchers during post-impact studies conducted over the past fifty-some years continually suggest that myths pervade the public's perception of human response to disaster. Subsequent research has suggested that the media plays a role in the perpetuation of the mythology. It has even been found that those trained to respond to disasters subscribed to the myths. This book sought to contribute to the literature by sharing empirical evidence which tested these anecdotal field observations. This work has provided an empirical link between the media portrayal of the over-generalized behavioral response to disaster or mythology. It also demonstrated the consequences which may result when local emergency managers become preoccupied with the media's portrayal. Professor Quarantelli noted the work found in this volume exemplifies "the kinds of semi-replication and cumulative studies that should be more widely undertaken" in order to advance a scientific field of study.

Many issues continue to demand the attention of disaster researchers. There is little practitioner-researcher interaction, i.e., the practitioner is usually ignored by the researcher when the research agenda is being developed. Determining and assessing effective mitigation continues to require the assistance and direction provided by research findings. The relationship between training, formal education, experience and an effective organizational response needs further exploration. The opportunities the new information technologies, e.g., the Internet, provide for enhancing mitigation and planning continue to evolve. The field continues to suffer from a lack of an integration of the applied findings with theoretical explanations and models—though some progress has been made during the past decade. New disaster agents continue to emerge. And, a disaster scale is needed to not only help researchers assess the limitations and applications of the research literature, but to also assist responders in their ever challenging need to anticipate what and how to mitigate, plan and respond. Each of these needs will be discussed in this final chapter.

Increased Practitioner-Researcher Interaction

While progress has been made since September 11th in particular (and despite the best efforts of research centers such as the University of Colorado's Natural Hazards Application and Information Center), researchers continue to be too isolated from emergency personnel. Communication from the researcher to the practitioner is necessary to facilitate the dissemination of new knowledge. Communication is also necessary from the practitioner to the researcher to facilitate an understanding of what type of new knowledge the practitioner needs. At the 1993 annual Natural Hazards Workshop, practitioners *urged* the researchers present to ask them what information they feel they need, i.e., what research *they* would like to have conducted. The practitioners are, of course, absolutely correct.

Most disaster researchers work directly with their funding agencies, e.g., FEMA and the National Science Foundation, when setting research agendas. The researcher closely ties his or her research focus to the desires of the funding agency. In order to get funded one obviously needs to adhere to the articulated needs of the agency providing the research support. The perceived needs of the agency, of course, sometimes result from prior research. This funding process does result in overlooking the research needs of state and local emergency personnel. Since the state and local emergency managers are normally not the source of research funding, their input is not readily sought by the researcher. The outcome: state and local emergency managers are only involved in the research process when their area is impacted by a disaster agent. The researchers converge to study the event--and *now* the state and local managers become important to the researcher. Perhaps third generation disaster researchers could help to redress this limitation. Many projects of interest to state and local managers may not require a major funding source. Under these circumstances, applied research could be conducted which not only contributes to the research literature and the vitae of the researcher, but also contributes to the community and region seeking the assistance of the researcher. Often the reward system of major research institutions is not geared to responding to such smaller research projects. The result: a second reason for reduced interest on the part of the researcher for initiating these smaller projects. Researchers who work in a less myopic research environment may find it advantageous to make a contribution at this level.

Training, Certification, Education of a Professional Workforce

Fischer and Drain (1993), as well as Fischer and McCullough (1993), have demonstrated the value of developing a professional, educated workforce of emergency managers. The probability of developing an effective mitigation plan and of conducting an effective disaster response appears to be correlated with the trend toward creating a professional workforce. LEMA coordinators who were college educated were found to be more likely to implement a multitude of the more effective mitigation strategies and to coordinate an appropriate disaster response. Further research is needed to test the dynamics of this relationship. Federal, state and local decision-makers, e.g., governors, county commissioners, and mayors, need to be continually educated on this point. Once again, increased researcher-practitioner interaction may help achieve this goal.

It is encouraging to note that the federal government (U.S.) has been increasingly seeking to enhance the mitigation and preparedness levels of the country through increased attention to training and education. The Federal Emergency Management Training Center in Emmitsburg, Maryland, for example, offers regular training sessions for various emergency responders. Another illustration is provided by the U.S. Department of Defense which has sought to take steps to prepare the nation for possible chemical and biological terrorist attacks through new training activities. Research Planning, Inc., of Church Falls, Virginia, is one company which has contracted with the Department of Defense to conduct such training exercises in various U.S. cities.

Increased Public Education

Two case studies (Fischer & Bischoff, 1988; Fischer, Schaeffer, and Trowbridge, 1992) presented in this volume have demonstrated how the public and the media continue to subscribe to the disaster mythology. This trend continues to place communities at greater risk than would otherwise occur during a major emergency or disaster. A population educated in the actual problems normally encountered before, during and after a disaster would be more likely to respond to warnings in an effective manner. For example, they would be more likely to evacuate when it is appropriate to do so. Fischer and McCullough (1993) found that most LEMA coordinators currently emphasize two educational approaches. (1) They attempt to educate their communities through *reverse socialization* programs. Elementary school children are taught basic information about disasters likely to occur in their area. The goal is to teach the children who are encouraged to go home and socialize their parents. (2) Public service messages are periodically printed and broadcast by the local media. These messages also contain basic emergency response information.

Research should continue to obtain a better understanding of the conditions associated with an effective disaster warning and response. At present the extent of the public's understanding of how to effectively prepare for and respond to a disaster is minimal. Greater effort on the part of researchers, community decision-makers, and practitioners is mandatory to enhance public safety to even the minimally acceptable level. In Chapter 1 you read about the likelihood of greater victimization from disasters in the future. This projected trend is expected to result from the national population growth and especially the population expansion into disaster-prone areas. It is incumbent upon us to improve public education to enhance mitigation.

Recent trends in higher education, as a direct result of the FEMA Higher Education Project (directed by Dr. Wayne Blanchard), provide encouragement. Various colleges and universities in the United States have developed an emergency management minor, an undergraduate major, certification programs, master's degree programs, and even PhD programs in emergency management. Many of the programs are classroom based, however, a few are offered totally online as distance education programs.

The New Information Technologies May Serve as a Bridge to Increased Practitioner-Researcher Interaction, Training, and Education

The technological advances of the last few decades have resulted in a communications explosion and a leveling of information hierarchies. Some (Burstein & Kline, 1995; Davis & Botkin, 1994) argue these technologies sound the death knell of academic institutions as they are currently structured. They are increasingly viewed as having become information and communication dinosaurs. The revolution that these emerging technologies are creating continues to transform how we work, live, communicate and learn (Drucker, 1993; Gates, 1995; Jones, 1995). Workers can communicate with the company CEO by e-mail without having to traverse the chain of command. Students are able to access a wealth of information on-line as well as communicate directly with professors at any institution in the world. Any citizen who has access to a computer connected to the Internet can quite easily access holdings of libraries around the world, publications lists at university research centers, academic articles as well as "how to" fact sheets outlining how to prepare for and respond to hurricanes (and other disaster agents), and explanations on how hurricanes form--complete with pictures, sound, and video vignettes. Disaster victims in the United States can directly access the Federal Emergency Management Agency (FEMA) and complete on-line applications for assistance.

As impressive and helpful as this information revolution appears to be, there have been some, and possibly will be more, problems encountered on the way to the new information forum. Quarantelli (1997:96-104, for a thorough discussion of these issues please see the original article) has insightfully identified ten issues which may be problematic with the advent of these technologies:

1. The probability that the 'rich will become richer' in dealing with disasters.
2. The possibility that technology that is a 'means' will be turned into an 'end' in itself.
3. The inevitable information overload problem.
4. The loss of, or outdated, information.
5. The greater likelihood of the diffusion of inappropriate disaster relevant information.
6. The implications of even further diminution of non-verbal communication.
7. Intra- and inter-level group communication will be made even more difficult.
8. The negative consequences of the probable acceleration of fads and fashions associated with computer use.
9. The kinds of general social infrastructures and cultures necessary for the adequate functioning of disaster relevant technology.
10. The certainty of computer system-related disasters.

Quarantelli admonishes us to be careful, "if we do a good job, the actual future will be different from the [problematic] projected future" he outlines. The question presenting itself is: how can we use the new information technologies yet assuage at least some of Quarantelli's concerns?

The New Technologies Considered

First let's identify the new technologies we are talking about harnessing for our future. The first is the multi-media capabilities resulting from the creation of the DVD (One of Quarantelli's concerns is that the technology may become an end in itself instead of a means, the constantly changing "gadgetry" he notes, may make it more difficult to actually respond to the overflow of information that already exists *during* a disaster. The technological *advances* come so quickly it is difficult to keep up to date with hardware, software, skills, and compatibility between agencies. This, of course, also illustrates another of Quarantelli's concerns, i.e., that wealthier communities may gain some benefit from the new technologies, but those which are not wealthy will be at an even greater disadvantage.) The second is the utility of Web Sites on the Internet and, third, the use of e-mail as a means of disseminating information and enhancing communication during real time with knowledgeable sources located anywhere in the world. The fourth application is that known as distance learning, an increasingly used form of *face-to-face* interaction (connectivity achieved via cyberspace and/or satellite) for conferencing and training of participants who are in geographically diverse locations.

Web Sites, E-Mail and the Forum. The world of online communications continues its exponential growth. In many ways we are still in the early stages of what will continue to lead to readily accessible information and real time communication. Hundreds, perhaps thousands, of new web pages appear daily. Businesses, with many being entrepreneurs, government and service agencies, as well as the academy currently proliferate this medium.

The information found on websites can be very useful to both researcher and practitioner. A few examples include contact information, publications lists, actual real time publication access, training and instructional materials, links to relevant government agencies and disaster organizations.

Most of us have a love-hate relationship with e-mail. It is a wonderful means by which individuals can communicate with one another by electronically mailing text through cyberspace to and from anyone anywhere in the world anytime. Of course, that means many of us are inundated by hundreds of emails per day—which means the word "convenience" is no longer as applicable a term for email.

Increasingly a forum, or chat room-type of environment, is being used by specialized groups of users to train, educate, decision-make and brainstorm. This is also useful for disaster researchers and emergency managers.

Distance Learning. "Distance learning" simply refers to the concept that the instructor is in one location while the students are in another--and *each* student may be in a different location. While distance learning is being increasingly used for training and education, there are many who continue to embrace the "old school" belief in face-to-face instruction. The same was true during the change over from typewriters to word processing (stage coach to railway travel, etc). Some of us will blaze the new trail and the others, or their replacements, will follow along later. Every format has its advantages and disadvantages. The distinct advantages of distance learning, e.g. elimination of travel of site, flexible meeting times or no meeting times, are particularly desirable for those in emergency management seeking advanced degrees or further training.

Many of us have been using distance learning for a number of years and find it quite useful. Many of our students report the advantages as including flexible meeting, reduced travel, more focused on the student and active rather than passive. It is true that eye contact is currently lacking, however, there are advantages and disadvantages to both distance education and bricks-and-mortar. The use of the internet for such purposes will undoubtedly continue to advance. Those who resist will simply retire at some point and be replaced by those who embrace it. The stage coach was replaced by the iron horse which was replaced by the automobile. What else can be said?

Integration with Theory

Disaster researchers have noted the paucity of theory in the disaster literature. This challenge continues to be addressed, as noted in chapter 1. Over the next fifty years disaster researchers will, I am confident—and encourage, the mitigation of this paucity. Traditional sociological theories are salient, new theory will emerge, and both the theory of emergency management as well as emergency management theory will mature.

Disaster Scale & Findings in the Literature

A disaster scale is needed. An appropriate scale would provide practitioners with some guidance in mitigation, planning, and response that is currently lacking. An appropriate scale would also enable researchers to assess the literature. Much of what is currently known will likely have caveats applied when an appropriate scale is used. The Fischer Scale (chapter 1) has been offered as an example. It may or may not stand the test of time. However, the primary argument is for a scale.

Expanded List of Disaster Agents

The natural and technological disaster agents examined in chapter one have traditionally completed the list considered by disaster researchers. Increasingly the question is being asked: what about other disastrous events which severely disrupt the normal time activities of a significant portion, or entire, population (Drabek, 1996)? Should political or economic dislocation and disorganization be conceptualized as a disaster? Should conflict events such as war or terrorism be included? Why not include famines and epidemics such as AIDS? If we do expand the list of what constitutes a disaster, how will this impact the current research literature? Will the findings of the past forty years be applicable to these new areas of possible inquiry? Research is needed to determine the answer to these questions. Let's consider the implications of applying the behavioral and organizational response literature to a terrorist event--one which is increasingly possible in the United States. First we will consider some background information, apply the literature to understanding possible response challenges, and be mindful of the fact that research is needed to determine the applicability of the case considered below.

New Danger from Weapons of Mass Destruction

A foreign or domestic group which is angry with the United States government for allegedly blocking its legitimate aspirations, who seeks to coerce U.S. policy change or wishes to avenge prior U.S. military intervention, may unleash a weapon of mass destruction (WMD) on a major U.S. city. In 1995 the Japanese Aum Shinrikyo cult released Sarin nerve gas in Tokyo--several people died. Some analysts believe that the 1993 World Trade Center bomb as laced with cyanide, but failed when it burned up in the explosion (cyanide use is unconfirmed, but a large amount was found in the perpetrators' possession). Future terrorist attempts may prove to be less incompetent (Betts, 1998).

Cold War Legacy

With the end of the Cold War, the fear of mutual nuclear destruction through the unleashing of the nuclear arsenals of two superpowers has largely dissipated among the citizenry at large (Betts, 1998; Christopher, et al., 1997). While concern remains for the "loose nuke" problem, the U.S. has been actively trying to mitigate against it. Nuclear arms, however, are no longer the only concern. Chemical and biological weapons are probably more likely to be used as WMD (Betts, 1998). These are increasingly seen as more viable choices for weaker states or terrorist groups which find themselves as decidedly disadvantaged in contrast to U.S. conventional weapons capability. U.S. strategy during the Cold War era emphasized deterrence via conventional and nuclear capability. Chemical and biological WMD pose an increasingly more serious deterrence challenge. This is especially true when WMD are in the hands of terrorists (Betts, 1998).

It is Time to Focus on the Domestic Threat

During the last 30 years administrations of both political parties have taken steps to make it increasingly difficult for terrorists to attack U.S. personnel and facilities overseas (Tucker, 1998; Simon, 1997). Terrorists launched 177 attacks on U.S. diplomats, military personnel, and other U.S. government officials in 1980. In 1995 10 such acts occurred. Americans have not ceased to be targeted by terrorists, greater overseas security measures have simply been implemented by the U.S. government. Unfortunately, this success has probably been somewhat offset by the likelihood that disrupted terrorist attacks have probably deflected some attacks onto easier targets, such as American businesspeople or other civilians. What about the U.S. domestic population? How safe from terrorist attack are citizens living within U.S. borders? The 1993 World Trade Center bombing, the 1995 release of Sarin nerve gas in Tokyo, the Oklahoma City bombing, and the September 11th 2001 attack have all contributed to the heightened U.S. awareness and mitigation activity. In June 1995, the White House issued Presidential Decision Directive 39 (PDD-39), "United States Policy on Counterterrorism." PDD-39 stipulated measures be taken to reduce the nation's vulnerability to terrorism, to deter and respond to terrorist acts, and to strengthen capabilities to prevent and manage the consequences of terrorist use of nuclear, biological, and chemical (NBC) weapons including weapons of mass destruction.

Since the Cold War has ended, the likely future weapon of choice for domestic terrorism is expected to shift from conventional explosives to NBC agents of mass destruction (Betts, 1998; Steinbruner, 1997; Zilinskas, 1997). While nuclear and chemical WMD continue to be of great concern, it is the menu of biological agents that may be more attractive to terrorists. How has this come to pass? *During* the Cold War, WMD were the centerpiece of U.S. foreign policy. Nuclear deterrence theory suggested that aggression was deterred through the mutually assured destruction of the superpowers. With the breakup of the former Soviet Union and the reduction of nuclear stockpiles by both the U.S. and the former Soviet states, the risk of nuclear miscalculation has shifted from superpower nuclear warfare to the use of nuclear weapons by rogue governments or terrorist groups. The difficulty (and expense) of delivering nuclear WMD to a target, along with the likelihood that the perpetrator would have access to few such weapons, makes the use of this terrorist option possible, but less likely than other options.

Chemical Terrorism

Chemical weapons were employed by Iraq against Iranian troops in the1980-88 Iran-Iraq War and against Kurdish civilians in 1988. Chemical weapons are far more widely available than nuclear weapons. The technology to produce them is simpler. Chemical weapons, however, are not as capable of inflicting a huge number of civilian casualties in a single strike as a nuclear weapon. This is not to say that attempts to eradicate chemical weapons are misguided. It is merely argued that nuclear weapons are probably preferred to chemical by those seeking to inflict huge casualties quickly. However, there is another alternative likely to be preferable to both of these options.

Biological Terrorism

Biological WMD have the advantage of combining maximum destructiveness with easy availability. While nuclear arms have great killing capacity, they are difficult to obtain; while chemical weapons are easy to obtain, they lack great killing capacity. A 1993 Office of Technology Assessment study concluded that 100 kilograms of anthrax spores distributed by aerosol on a clear, calm night over Washington, D.C., by an airplane could *kill between 1 and 3 million people* (Betts, 1998). Anthrax spores constitute the dormant phase of a bacillus that multiplies rapidly in the body, producing toxins and rapid hemorrhaging within days of exposure.

Bacteria, viruses, or toxins may be used as biological agents. Examples of likely biological agents include anthrax (*B anthracis*), botulinum toxin, plague (*Yersinia pestis*), staphylococcal enterotoxin B, viral encephalitis virus, brucellosis, Q fever, tularemia, smallpox, and viral hemorrhagic fevers (Franz, et al., 1997). They can be dispersed in aerosols which may remain suspended for hours for inhalation by numerous potential victims. The aerosols may be delivered by simple industrial sprayers from an airplane or boat upwind of the potential target. Diseases produced by such agents could be disabling or lethal for many civilians. Some biological agents (e.g., anthrax) produce diseases *not* communicable between individuals, while other agents produce those which are.

Illustration. Anthrax is caused by *B anthracis*, a sporulating bacillus. Found naturally in the soil, the organism is found worldwide. Anthrax spores can remain viable for decades in adverse environmental conditions. Aerosol delivery would most likely be employed in a terrorist attack using this biological agent, resulting in inhalational anthrax. After being inhaled, the spores would be deposited in the lower respiratory tract, germinate into vegetative bacilli, and produce necrotizing hemorrhagic mediastinitis. Symptoms begin with fever, malaise, and fatigue. They may include a nonproductive cough and vague chest pains. There may appear to be improvement for 2 or 3 days, or the victim may progress directly into severe respiratory distress, meningitis, and death within 24 to 36 hours (Franz, et al., 1997).

The medical response will vary depending on whether measures are initiated before exposure, after exposure but before symptoms appear, or after symptoms are present. Active immunization with antibiotics may prevent illness if administered before exposure--an unlikely possibility among the civilian population at large. After exposure, but before symptoms are present, active or passive immunization, as well as pretreatment with therapeutic antibiotics or antiviral drugs, may ameliorate disease symptoms--a viable medical response *if* the terrorist announces what was done, where and when *and if* medical supplies are available in sufficient quantities for a sufficient number of medical personnel to administer to a sufficiently responsive population (all this seems problematic). Once symptoms of inhalational anthrax appear, treatment is likely to be ineffective. Diagnosis of the disease and general supportive care remain the only viable options for health care providers (Franz, et al., 1997).

If future exposure is expected, the vaccine, an aluminum hydroxide, may be administered in doses at 0, 2, and 4 weeks, then again at 6, 12, 18 months, followed by annual boosters. After exposure, penicillin has been the usual treatment for inhalational anthrax: two million units given intravenously every 2 hours. Streptomycin has been found to provide additional benefit. It is apparent that in addition to the detrimental health effects on the target population, the health care system would be significantly impacted as unprecedented numbers of patients would inundate providers. Large quantities of medications and vaccines, which are not generally available in standard pharmaceutical stocks, would be needed. Health care and lab personnel may be exposed to biological hazards pursuant to interring the remains (Franz, et al., 1997).

So, what can we expect if a terrorist act employing a biological agent occurs? Protective equipment and vaccines are not currently readily available to civilian populations at large. If there is nor prior knowledge of an attack, human victims will likely be the first detectors of a biological attack (Franz, et al., 1997). Most diseases caused by biological agents will present nonspecific symptoms, easily misinterpreted as natural occurrences. Epidemiological investigations of such a disease outbreak are not likely to occur rapidly enough to avoid undesirable results. While a compressed epidemic curve with a peak in a matter of days or hours would be a good indicator (in naturally occurring epidemics disease incidence gradually increases as people are progressively exposed; those exposed to a biological attack would come into contact with the agent at approximately the same time), a large number of fatalities would already be likely by the time an attack could be verified and the pathogen identified (Franz, et al., 1997).

Need for Mitigation & Response Planning

A serious program to blunt the effects of WMD should now be given the highest priority (Betts, 1998). Attempts during the Cold War to implement a civil defense program were ultimately ignored by many and even opposed or ridiculed by some. Hindsight yields a clear understanding of the inadequacy of the "duck and cover" approach of the 1950s. Subsequent attempts at civil defense were often viewed as providing a false sense of security which may even contribute to miscalculation in the use of nuclear weapons. It should be easier to appreciate the value of effective contemporary measures which could be taken in the face of more limited attacks. A host of measures, which are actually far more inexpensive than attempts to provide a defensive umbrella to missile attack, are available to mitigate greater death and suffering than need occur in a chemical or biological attack. Examples include stockpiling or distribution of masks, the distribution of equipment for decontamination, implementation of training programs, the mass inoculation of vaccinations (or at least a standby program to do so), creation of standby programs for emergency treatment with antibiotics, and the implementation of public education efforts to enhance cooperation in evacuation, sheltering, and health care provision (Betts, 1998). Such attempts should limit death and injury, but probably not even approach eliminating them. It is better, however, to act in the face of the limitations of defense than fail to try. Our humanity demands it. Furthermore, the blame-fixing process that follows disaster events clearly makes it evident that long-term political interests are better served by such attempts as well (Fischer, 1994).

Need to Prepare for Behavioral & Organizational Response Challenges

Mitigation and response planning must also consider the behavioral and organization response problems likely to be encountered in such a catastrophic event (Holloway, et al., 1997). How will individual citizens respond? How will organizations function? All too often there is a tendency in American society to overlook the sociological outcomes likely to confound responders. A discussion of the likely behavioral challenges must be undertaken in order to enhance mitigation and response planning for these WMD.

Is a Domestic Incident in Our Near Future? An apparent outbreak of flu has impacted a major metropolitan area in the United States. Family medical practitioners are inundated with patient phone calls for appointments; medical centers and hospital emergency rooms are suddenly besieged with those experiencing severe symptoms. Initial diagnoses are made based upon the general flu-like symptoms and apparent appropriate remedies are prescribed. Within 24-36 hours at least half of these patients are dead. Serious testing has begun to determine the precise medical culprit. Local political leaders and the media, almost simultaneously, become aware of what the medical practitioners are encountering. It is determined that perhaps tens of thousands have developed these symptoms in this metropolitan area alone. The local health care delivery system has become completely overwhelmed.

Rumor is rapidly spreading throughout not only the city, but the nation and the world as television networks pickup the story. Reporters speculate that there is either a problem in the food distribution system, or there has been an accident at a laboratory that has been covered up, or we may be under attack from a foreign or domestic enemy. Political leaders at various levels indicate that an investigation has begun, the Centers for Disease Control have begun their work, and all appropriate steps are being taken to control the problem--there is no need to panic. They admit, however, all they really know at this point is what they themselves are getting from the media.

Emergency response organizations begin to take steps to determine what they should do. Political leaders, law enforcement, and others discuss what steps they should take to prevent further exposure to whatever is causing the illness. The idea to quarantine emerges. The question is asked, "Who and how large an area should we quarantine?" Others suggest an evacuation of the healthy to prevent further exposure to the causal agent. It is also noted that the point of release has yet to be identified. Attempts are made to project an air of confidence to the public. In the absence of hard information on what is occurring, leaders are actually freelancing what the appropriate action should be (much like federal and state leaders and agencies found themselves doing during the Three Mile Island incident).

It is eventually determined that the city has been exposed to anthrax spores. An act of terrorism is assumed. All appropriate federal agencies have become involved. Fear is widespread throughout the nation. Is this the first of numerous cities to be attacked? Will the country fall? A media feeding frenzy has ensued. Reporters demand to know from the President what is being done to prevent further deaths, who is responsible for this despicable act, and what retaliatory steps are to be taken? Broadcast media is giving constant coverage to the crisis. Some are suggesting retaliatory military strikes on those suspected of responsibility. Estimates indicate a million people have died from the disease in the last 3 days.

1 Year Later. The city's final death toll was 2.5 million. Several rogue governments and terrorist groups are suspect, but the actual perpetrator is still not known. There is increasingly the realization that no one (individuals, cities, states or the nation) was prepared to mitigate or respond to something like this. Since biological agents are invisible, odorless, and tasteless, no one knew an attack was under way until it was too late for the victims (Simon, 1997). Political careers are in ruin. The civil rights of certain ethnic groups have been abridged as a direct result of suspicion that their compatriots are guilty. A crash program is underway to stockpile protective masks and decontamination equipment. Widespread training in decontamination procedures has begun. Mass vaccinations have been initiated as well as standby programs for mass emergency treatment with antibiotics. Planning for appropriate emergency response procedures has been initiated. Public education programs are being created to teach citizens what to do should such an attack ever occur again.

Response to Terrorism?

If a biological or chemical agent were to be deployed against a U.S. urban population, what would the behavioral response be? What do political-decision makers,
medical personnel, and emergency organization coordinators need to know about
likely behavioral responses to enhance mitigation and to organize an *effective* response? The sociological findings describing the behavioral response to other disaster agents will be applied to answer these two questions. We will apply them to outline the likely behavioral response to a chemical or biological terrorist act.

*Applying the Current Literature to Anticipate the Likely Response to Bio-
Terrorism.* More than fifty years of research into the behavioral and organizational
response to disaster has resulted in a rather clear understanding of how victims and
survivors, organizations, and the media respond during the various time periods of a
natural or technological disaster. If we extrapolate from these sociological research
findings, the implications of the likely behavioral response to incidents of domestic
terrorism come into focus. Anecdotal information from previous terrorist acts, e.g.,
the World Trade Center bombing and the Oklahoma City bombing, suggests the
validity of such an application. The reader should note, however, the writer is nevertheless making the assumption that findings in natural and technological disasters
parallel likely responses to biological and chemical terrorist events. Researchers
have fortunately not had the opportunity to conduct exhaustive research to absolutely confirm the accuracy of this assumption. In the absence of any reason to suggest the contrary, we will assume the veracity of such an application.

Pre-Impact & Impact Time Periods. If a biological or chemical agent is released
without prior warning, the first victims will provide the first indication that an attack
is underway. Of course, without prior warning the first victims to fall ill will not
know they had been exposed to a biological or chemical agent. Disease symptoms
appear several days after exposure to the agent. Victims will assume they are "coming down with something" such as the flu. Many will simply take steps to treat
themselves, others will contact their family physician, and still others will go to the
emergency room of a hospital or medical center. Medical personnel are likely to
initially view the symptoms as indicators of a common illness as well. Medical practitioners will suddenly suspect something is amiss when they are inundated with
telephone calls and emergency room patients. The media will become aware of the
rash of patients overwhelming the health care system long before the outbreak of
disease is confirmed to be the result of a terrorist attack. Normal programming will
be interrupted to report on the sudden outbreak of disease. Not only the impacted
area, but the world will quickly learn of the existence of a severe medical problem.
[If the terrorists decide to announce that an attack is about to be or has been
unleashed, then the initial confusion over whether or not the symptoms are a result
of natural events, a hazmat accident, or a terrorist attack will be eliminated. Hys-

teria, i.e., false belief among many that they have contracted such an illness, may overload the health care system even more quickly than if the attack had not been announced. Other behavioral response patterns would be expected to commence earlier as well--these will be outlined below. On the other hand, medical practitioners and emergency organizations may be able to initiate their response more quickly thereby effecting greater mitigation.]

Immediate Post-Impact Period: Initial Behavioral Response. The media will initially focus on reporting hard news related to the dramatic convergence of the ill to health care providers in the impacted metropolitan area. In the absence of more details as well as media attempts to get at the story, rumor will increasingly be reported as fact. Media personnel, concerned relatives, and the curious will converge to the area. Many of those already there will converge to the medical centers. Telephone and electronic communications will converge to the area overwhelming the communications system. If the agent is still viable, more potential victims run the risk of being exposed. If the disease developed by those previously exposed is communicable, more potential victims will result. Political decision-makers will be scrambling for answers.

Confusion will be a common experience for citizens, medical practitioners, media personnel, political leaders, and emergency organizations alike. Massive death rates can be expected. Political decision-makers and emergency personnel struggle to determine the appropriate organizational response to an event they do not yet fully understand. Is it a massive hazmat accident of some kind? Is it a terrorist attack? What is the exact causal agent? Their mitigation and response efforts are tied to the answers generated by these questions. Of course, the initial answers may or may not be correct; hence, the initial mitigation and response decisions may or may not be effective ones.

Evacuation Behavior. If an evacuation is deemed appropriate to mitigate further exposure, how will those who are apparently healthy respond? Families will not want to leave as individuals, they will seek to determine where each family member is located (adding to the already overloaded local communications system) and to arrange a meeting time and place. They will not want to leave until they can leave together. Unfortunately, many (perhaps most) healthy citizens will not become aware of the evacuation order at first. Some will be sleeping others will simply not be accessing media outlets when the order is given. In fact, many will not even know the emergency exists. Many will refuse to evacuate for fear that they may actually become exposed to the agent by doing so. Many will refuse to leave for fear that their property may be looted. They will need to be convinced that their property will be safe or at least be convinced that their lives are more important than any property. For all these reasons, a large percentage of the population to be evacuated will not evacuate when told to do so. The percentage that does evacuate (perhaps a third to a half of the affected population) will be larger than when a natural disaster event is pending (which is normally only 10% of the affected population), but many will remain in the metropolitan area.

Some of those who do evacuate will follow the instructions provided, i.e., use of designated roads; many, however, will not. There is, of course, the expected grid lock as traffic converges along the exit routes. Those who decide to evacuate will not leave immediately, they will tend to straggle out over a period of hours. Those who have the ability to relocate to relatives or friends will do so. Those without other options will go to a designated evacuation center. While panic will be the outcome most feared and assumed by citizens, media personnel, and officials, there will be far less of it than the stereo-typed image suggests. What will be characterized as panic will more likely be a hurried, but purposeful, evacuation. Indeed, if the perception among those in the process of evacuating is that their opportunity for survival is diminishing rapidly, a panic response may then ensue. But only under such a circumstance would such a response be likely to occur. Too much attention will probably be given to the fear of a panic response by decision-makers. In fact, decision-makers may indeed make poor response decisions due to their exaggerated fear of panic. They may hesitate to order an evacuation for fear of causing panic. They may question whether they should even try to evacuate in fear of creating panic--not only an unethical and cynical response, but one not justified by previous disaster research findings (Fischer, 1994). Failing to call for an evacuation if one is justified would likely result in greater victimization rather than mitigating further exposure. The greatest challenge will actually be how to convince the healthy population to evacuate and to do so in a timely manner. Repeated efforts will be necessary to increase the percentage of those who will do so.

Those with critically ill family members will not want to leave. They will want to stay to provide aid and comfort. The challenge of getting these people to evacuate will be even more difficult. A convergence of an increasing number of telephone calls from outside and within the area will strain the communications system as relatives seek to determine the whereabouts and safety of their loved ones. Emergency responders and health care providers will seek to determine that their families are safe. Most will stay on the job but will be distracted until they know their loved ones are safe.

Quarantine Behavior. If quarantine is determined to be the appropriate mitigation step, several challenges will present themselves. First, many of the exposed may work in the city but live in the suburbs. By the time symptoms appear, they will already be outside of the city. Second, some will have spontaneously evacuated before decision-makers announce the quarantine. Third, some will successfully avoid attempts to keep them within the quarantined area. Most will probably cooperate without incident. Most will accept their fate with resignation, but there will be those who will feel and openly express resentment at such treatment.

Many will expect deviant behavior to emerge, e.g., looting, price gouging, even though such fears are not justified. Many will also fear that victims and their loved ones will become emotionally incapacitated and unable to cope. This behavior, however, is also unlikely to occur. During the first days of the crisis citizens will be very altruistic. They will help one another. They will rise to the occasion emotionally as well. As the crisis continues over time, it will become increasingly difficult for victims, survivors, and care-givers to meet all the challenges they face. If it becomes difficult to meet basic human needs during the crisis, citizens will take whatever action they deem appropriate to address those needs. For example, those in need of food and medical supplies may decide to take what they need from available sources. This will not be an incident of looting, but rather the operation of the collective will to meet basic needs by procuring necessities from available resources. Individuals will generally not go hungry while perishable food lies rotting in the grocery store. Emergent norms will develop to guide behavior to foster survival in the new circumstance within which the healthy and critically ill find themselves.

If residents are able to obtain food through the normal distribution process, the food supplies in these stores will rapidly be depleted--primarily because there will be a mass convergence of shoppers who fear additional supplies will not be available for some time to come (especially milk, bread, and other staples). Telephone calls into, out of, and within the area will continue to exceed the capacity of the communications system. Similarly, gasoline stations are likely to experience a convergence of such customers. And, the health care system will continue to be overwhelmed.

Media Response. An audience rivaling any preceding it will turn to the print and broadcast media for information. The various talking heads will result in a conflicting view of what is occurring and what is to be done. It is imperative that political decision-makers and emergency organizations seek to distribute information through a highly trained spokesperson. Information, instructions, and so forth, should be given repeatedly, clearly, specifying precisely what is being suggested to the audience. There will be a tendency to distrust political decision-makers as rumor is reported as fact.

Local broadcasters will tend to relay information on evacuation or quarantine plans, medical distribution centers, and other helpful news for the victims and survivors. National broadcasters will tend to focus on broader issues of what happened, who did it, how people are responding (or believed to be responding as the network reporting will be heavily laden with myth). Local and national news organizations will look to decision-makers as the primary source of information. Failure to provide a steady diet of information will result in the feeding frenzy turning on decision-makers, consuming them in the process.

Print and broadcast news personnel will converge from throughout the country and the world. The EOC, the site command post and the perimeter of the affected area will be the locations most targeted by the media. Again, the role of the press demands a steady diet of information. Information and answers must be provided--the alternative will be to find them turned loose to find their own story which will undoubtedly not be helpful to the community or to the decision-makers trying to cope with the crisis. The press tends to function as pack animals seeking to avoid being scooped rather then seeking a scoop. One need only look to the experience of O.J. Simpson, Princess Diana, and Monica Lewinsky for illustrations.

Altruism and acting to help the victims will gradually give rise to the inevitable blame-fixing. Voices will increasingly be asking why more had not been done to prevent the attack. Some will charge that those responsible for mitigating further exposure to the biological agent and for responding with aid were slow to meet their responsibilities. A desire for vengeance will emerge as attention turns to wanting to capture, prosecute or retaliate against those believed responsible for unleashing the attack. Domestic ethnic populations who share a heritage with the perceived perpetrators will be in danger of citizen (or even official) retaliation akin to that experienced by Japanese-Americans after the bombing of Pearl Harbor.

Decision-makers and Emergency Organizations. A number of challenges face political decision-makers and emergency organizations. If the attack was not suspected or announced in advance, they will not even know one has occurred until mass symptoms and deaths become apparent. Even then they will not know if it is a local hazmat accident, terrorism, or something else. It will take time to determine the location and type of agent that victims were exposed to and how to best respond, i.e., evacuate, quarantine, or what? Medical supplies and medical personnel will not be adequate in number to meet the need (not too dissimilar to the Hiroshima and Nagasaki experiences). The community will be unable to tend to its dead in any kind of normal fashion. The crisis will place demands on all organizations, e.g., health care providers, law enforcement, political decision-makers, that far exceed their ability to effectively respond. An incidence of biological terrorism will obviously not be a normal emergency. Federal support, such as military transport and dissemination of needed medical and subsistence supplies, will take longer than what the public would imagine for reasons obvious to most planners. A large percentage of the exposed will likely be dead before it is totally understood what has occurred and long before additional personnel and supplies are able to be brought onsite. Expectations will always be unrealistic and blame-fixing will begin early in the post-impact period. Training and stockpiling of relevant supplies within metropolitan areas is, of course, very important; it is also important to educate the public to the reality of the challenges facing victims and survivors, emergency organizations, and governments. Citizens need to be armed with accurate, factual information to enhance their chance of effectively responding at the individual and family level thereby enhancing mitigation. Without an honest dialogue with the public, potential victims will have unrealistic expectations of their (local, state, and federal) officials. Greater death and injury are likely to occur. Decision-makers and emergency personnel need to use their expertise to act in partnership with the less knowledgeable public. We must put aside the fear of scaring the public. Such a fear insults those who should be served, increases the likelihood of harm to potential victims, and casts such officials in the role of the all-knowing, yet ineffective Big Brother.

Slow Citizen Response. During an emergency event citizens slowly respond to information and instructions. Instructions for obtaining medical assistance and subsistence supplies as well as instructions for an evacuation or quarantine are more likely to be responded to if they are frequently repeated, articulated clearly and with specificity. All too often emergency personnel assume that because the information was disseminated, the intended recipients have received it, understood it, and responded to it in the desired fashion. Nothing could be further from the truth. Many will not receive the information the first, and perhaps even the second or third, time it is provided. Many of those who do will not have a clear understanding of what is being communicated and will fail to respond. Many will interact with others to determine what is to be done. Rumor and fact will blur in the process. Even when the information is clearly understood, the recipient may still not follow the instructions for any number of reasons (e.g., disbelief, distrust, refusal to leave home at least while awaiting other family members). As with natural disaster agents, the best time to begin educating citizens on how to respond to a biological or chemical terrorist attack is during normal time. They will be in a much better position to respond effectively if they have prior training. Decision-makers may hesitate to engage the public in such a dialogue prior to an actual terrorist event for fear of upsetting the public or contributing to a panic. Anecdotal evidence consistently supports the argument that the public can be trusted far more than decision-makers think it can. Such decision-makers should perhaps be reminded that they are, after all, public servants; it is their role to provide such information to the public so that citizens can then be armed to be better able to act on their own behalf.

Conclusions about Behavioral Response to a Biological or Chemical Terrorist Attack

What can we conclude about the likely behavioral and organizational response to an act of biological or chemical terrorism? Victims and survivors are likely to act in ways that many in the media and emergency organizations will not expect. Individual citizens are likely to be altruistic, initiate search and rescue activities, offer whatever medical assistance they can, and generally behave very rationally. They will not behave in ways many of the untrained believe is typical. For example, almost no one will panic, almost no one will steal from another (though they may appropriate property collectively defined as necessary for response to the event) they will not become emotionally incapable of responding. Many will hesitate or even fail to evacuate even after being told to do so. Some will resist attempts to enforce quarantine.

The media will be both a help and a hindrance. Local media will assist in disseminating needed information to the public to facilitate an effective response to the attack. National media will be less helpful in that their self-perceived role will be to describe the unfolding story which will often be largely fiction. Their reporting will be governed by their belief in the disaster mythology. They will actually increase concern for panic, looting, price gouging, and an incapacitating emotional shock. Rather than covering the story in such a way as to help ameliorate misplaced concern for these behavioral myths, they will facilitate their growth. Both the local and national media will converge to the area. Curious non-residents will also converge to the area creating traffic control problems over the life cycle of the event.

Officials will also fear panic and believe in the likelihood of the largely mythical deviant behavior. As a result many will hesitate to announce that an attack is underway. The greater concern should be with how to accurately, clearly and convincing inform the public what is happening, what they need to do, how to do it, and when. For example, who, when, how, and where should people evacuate? Who, when, and where should they seek medical assistance? Chaos will most typify the initial organizational response. The lack of good information will drive the confusion. Medical and emergency organizations will find themselves outpaced by the scope of the event.

The best hope of garnering an effective mitigation response lies in the following: educating the public about the scope of the likely medical outcome and response problems, educate the public about how to prepare themselves for such an event, inoculate citizens when appropriate and possible to do so, stockpile equipment and medical supplies in a manner which will lead to their effective use during the pre-impact and immediate post-impact time periods, train decision-makers and emergency personnel in the actual rather than mythical behavioral and organizational response problems. After doing our best we can still expect to experience a large number of casualties; this likely outcome does not deter the necessity of planning and acting in a manner likely to reduce that number. Appropriate national political and economic policies remain very important ingredients in mitigating a terrorist attack. The United States will reduce its chances of being attacked by reducing terrorist motivation to launch a biological or chemical attack on a U.S. city . . . or on several cities simultaneously.

All-Hazards Approach & the Usual Suspects

The reader should keep in mind, on the other hand, that floods, hurricanes, tornadoes, all the usual suspects, occur continually. Another terrorist attack may or may not occur. The rational approach to planning is to continue with the all-hazards planning. The biological, chemical, nuclear and radiological hazards are very dramatic to read about and are capable of conjuring up an array of nightmare scenarios. All of which can also be found in the movies. We can essentially look out our windows or turn on the news on any given day and find plenty of the usual suspects. Planners please keep this in mind!

New Disaster Agents—Old Socio-Political Challenges

Edward R. Murrow is a distinguished figure in U.S. journalism for his critical analysis of the communist witch-hunt hysteria among political decision makers of the 1950s. Since our perception of reality drives our behavioral response on many levels, the combination of fear of terrorism and perceived behavioral response is a volatile combination borne out in the post September 11th world. What follows (drawn from Fischer, 2005) addresses this challenge.

The Danger in Over-reacting to Terrorism: Has the U.S. Embarked Upon a Road that Should Have Remained Less Traveled?

From a post-September 2001 vantage point, the organizational response to terrorism is examined. The argument is made that in addition to the previously observed realization that the behavioral and organizational response to disaster model is applicable to terrorist events as well, the U.S. government, as a disaster response organization, displayed its own version of the common chaos that accompanies disasters generally. The argument is also made that the political decision-makers were driven more by fear than by rational decision-making based upon knowledge. In so doing, it is argued that Al Qaeda was helped to achieve the first goal of terrorists, i.e., instill fear. The question remains is the second goal now more achievable as a direct result? The second goal of a terrorist: the target of terror accedes to terrorist demands in return for ceasing the terror campaign.

Those who systematically study terrorism from a social and political science perspective, note that the first goal of terrorists is to instill fear in their victims. Why? In order to achieve the second goal: get the fearful to agree to their demands. How does that work? Thinking like a terrorist, if we do not have the power to force the opponent to meet our demands or if we do not have something to offer our opponent to achieve a negotiated outcome (e.g., trade money for votes), we can employ techniques that instill fear—so much fear that he will meet our demands in return for our removing the threat. The U.S. response to 11 September 2001 demonstrates the success achieved by Al Qaeda with respect to the first goal.

Citizens of the U.S. were understandably afraid in the hours and days after the World Trade Center collapsed. It was evident that political decision-makers (PDM) were also fearful as well as unusually quick to reflect their constituent's views. Prudent action to close the USA airspace, borders, and so forth, as well as enhancing security in the aftermath was quite rational and very responsible. At some point, however, the words of Franklin D. Roosevelt would have proved quite instructive for all living within the U.S., "we have nothing to fear but fear itself." Nothing to fear, but fear itself is on target with the goal of not allowing terrorists to achieve their first goal. To live in the face of fear, to be undaunted, and to refuse to be traumatized by fear is denying the terrorist the opportunity to achieve his goals.

The road that should have remained less traveled

What did the PDM in the USA do? They rewarded Al Qaeda. They helped it achieve its first goal. When PDMs change legal statutes that have the potential to undermine the very values they portend to be protecting, it can be argued that a threshold has been crossed demonstrating how fear has been successfully instilled in the intended victims.

The U.S. government formed the Northern Command and reversed a policy that had been in existence since the end of the U.S. Civil War—a policy that had prohibited the use of military troops within U.S. borders. The overturning of *posse comitatus* was sought to gain legal authority to deploy troops in support of domestic police action during any future terrorist attack. The *Patriot Act* was enacted to save "our way of life," however it arguably threatens some of the Constitutional protections of the Bill of Rights. The Department of Homeland Security (DHS), by its very name, connotes, in the minds of some, brown shirt goose stepping. Why not the Department of Domestic Security? An un-precipitated war on Iraq in apparent violation of international law followed by the handling of detainees in Cuba and Iraq in apparent violation of international norms, demonstrate how *fear* results in a very unholy outcome. We *should fear, fear itself* as it has moved the U.S. to go where many had thought it should not. Depending upon one's level of cynicism, the U.S. simply acted out its true nature while others believe it became something other than its high ideals would allow.

Over-reaction?

Between 12 September 2001 and 12 September 2005, a massive proliferation of federal government contracts were let to provide consulting services on homeland security, develop sensing devices (human, bio-agents, eye and face recognition devices, etc.), inoculations against bio-agents, and so forth. While the tax cuts and the military actions in Afghanistan and Iraq are often viewed as the primary causes of the budget deficit, the opening of the anti-terrorism purse strings are high on the list of actual causes as well.

The DHS, from its inception, embraced the crime model. It does not appear to view terrorism as an outcome of those who perceive disempowerment (political model and collective behavior model). Most of those currently employed by the DHS do not appear to champion the all-hazards approach either—despite the wisdom of the Federal Emergency Management Agency (FEMA) which has essentially been castrated by DHS. Since its birth in 1979, FEMA has had an erratic emergence, sometimes performing, in the view of some, in a less than stellar fashion. Particularly under the leadership of James Lee Witt, FEMA became increasingly adept at meeting its actual mission and educating the various publics as to the nature of the mission. FEMA took steps to reduce false expectations and to enhance the service it was designed to provide as well as initiate advances in disaster reduction through mitigation strategies. Much of the FEMA gains came to a screeching halt after 11 September 2001. Fighting terrorism from a crime fighting mode, rather than viewing terrorism as another disaster agent, has resulted in a collapse of morale at FEMA and a diminished role. While the U.S. has not suffered a repeat of 11 September, everyday disasters continue, e.g., four hurricanes impacted the state of Florida during the summer of 2004, mudslides in California during 2004-2005, and so forth. Perhaps DHS should have been part of FEMA rather than the reverse? Has the U.S. over-reacted? After the terrorist attack, I was fearful. Was this the beginning of . . . well, what? The unknown was perhaps the largest fear generator. The imperative under such circumstances is to remember, what we should fear is fear itself. The alternative is likely to be a series of poor decisions, based upon fear, rather than rational, thoughtful decisions directed by knowledge.

Example of Disaster Mythology

While PDMs may have been doing their best, in their view, to make the right decisions to defend the U.S., they fell prey to the disaster mythology. When I participated in the TOPOFF 2 planning session in Washington, D.C., during the summer of 2002, it became readily apparent that rather senior cabinet personnel completely subscribed to what is known in the disaster research community as the disaster mythology. In an earlier article (Fischer, 2002), I noted that the terrorist attack provided an unfortunate opportunity to test the previously argued (Fischer, 1998) hypothesis that lacking a better model, the body of knowledge previously developed on how citizens and emergency organizations respond to disaster, was found applicable in terrorism events such as the 11 September attack. Those in attendance at the aforementioned Washington meeting articulated or considered the need for policy and plans to control (in a terrorist event) mass panic flight, looting, and other deviant behaviors they believed were likely to occur. To enhance local police, alternative state and federal options were thought to be necessary. Were these PDMs on target? We are currently in a race between the forces of knowledge and the forces of misperception. Let's review the previous findings.

Most people in the U.S. believe in the *disaster mythology* (for example, see Wenger, et al, 1975; Fischer, 1998). Most of us assume that *individuals* cease to act in a predictable, orderly, normative fashion. Sociologically speaking, most people expect the everyday behavior governing norms to collapse into Durkheim's anomie. Conversely, most of us assume that *emergency organizations* will be well prepared to immediately respond to and help us recover from the event.

The common perception, which is myth more than reality (for example, see Fischer, 1998), is that people will flee in panic (necessitating, it is believed by many emergency personnel, holding off as long as possible on calling for evacuations), suffer from psychological dependency (will be unable to think for themselves), and disaster shock (will be unable to act on their on). It is often believed that evacuations must not be called too soon, for fear of encountering massive, uncontrollable flight behavior. It is also commonly believed that shelters normally overflow beyond capacity and organizers will be unable to deal with a mob mentality they will invariably confront. Both survivors and those converging to the scene are viewed as being driven by base, depraved instincts. These individuals are commonly perceived as likely to loot property, price gouge one another, and generally behave in other selfish ways—most of which are imagined to spread from individual to individual in a contagious fashion. Martial law is assumed to be necessary to quell such behavior—at the very least, a patrolling by the National Guard is expected. Death, injury, and damage are often estimated to be quite high. More than 40 years of research into the behavioral response to natural and technological disasters has resulted in a consistent and clear understanding of the above, though common, perceptions to be far more myth than real. It is often difficult for lay people to believe that the *disaster mythology* is really myth. Why? There are several sociological reasons. First, we are commonly socialized from an early age by significant others and mass media (print, broadcast, and film) to believe in the depraved nature of behavioral response to disaster events—because such has been assumed for eons of time. And second, our experience with civil disturbances where looting, for example does commonly occur, is thought to be applicable to disaster response when, in fact, it is not. And third, so-called common sense seems to dictate that one would be panic stricken, and so-forth, in such events. [Again, please refer to Fischer, 1998, for a detailed discussion of the mythology and reasons for belief in the common perception of myth as reality.]

Actual Behavior

This perception that a disaster results in the display of human depravity, is not supported by the evidence (for a diverse examination of social science perspectives on the nature of disaster, see Quarantelli, 1998). The community of human beings does not break down. There is, instead, an emergent norm process that occurs resulting in the adoption of those behavioral guides that subscribe to the belief, or value, that humans in trouble must be helped. Actually the best within us is usually exhibited as we become much more altruistic. Survivors share their tools, their food, equipment and especially their time. Groups of survivors tend to emerge to begin automatically responding to the needs of one another. They search for the injured, the dead, and they begin cleanup activities. Police and fire personnel stay on the job, putting the needs of victims and the duty they have sworn to uphold before their own personal needs, concerns and safety. In sharp contrast to the image commonly perceived, survivors are not apathetic or panic stricken. Looting behavior and price gouging are exceedingly rare following a disaster. Survivors act on their own and respond to help that is eventually provided, i.e., they do not become psychologically dependent or go into disaster shock. Martial law is almost never declared. Evacuations are often called much later than they should be, affording potential evacuees too little time—and, decision makers are too quick to assume that their call for evacuation will be heeded rather than implement a follow-up plan designed to enhance the evacuation response. And those who do evacuate are least likely to go to shelters; they tend to, instead, go to the homes of relatives and friends or to motels. Damage, injury and death estimates are normally revised *downward* as we move from impact through the recovery period.

Okay, so we find that reality and popular perception diverge—so what? Well, emergency personnel tend to plan for and respond to those events they anticipate facing before, during and after a disaster (or terrorist) event. *If,* as is commonly found, they plan to respond to myth, they will *not* be prepared to respond to reality. The result? Unnecessary suffering will likely be added to that already experienced by the victims. For example, if we plan to focus on controlling deviant behavior, which we then do not find, we are unprepared to effect a successful evacuation.

Disaster Response Literature Found Applicable to Terrorist Events

The short answer to this question is as follows. We learn that the argument advanced in 1998, i.e., the disaster research model of behavioral response to disaster as applicable to terrorism events as well, is salient. While a plethora of empirical research findings are expected to emerge from the NYC terrorism experience, preliminary findings (some based upon preliminary content analyses of broadcast media live behavioral response footage and others based upon anecdotal evidence from a variety of sources) suggest that the previously reviewed findings are supported by behavioral responses observed in the aftermath of September 11. Illustrations will be shared below.

Panic. Even though the word was often used by mass media personnel and laypeople to describe the escape of many running from the twin towers as they collapsed, a careful examination (via content analysis of the live video footage) of the behavior of these survivors indicates that they were rationally moving away from the obvious danger. Did they experience grave fear? Undoubtedly. Were they in a state of panic? No! They were rationally moving from point "a" to point "b" or from danger to a safe place. Furthermore, conversations (while not a random sample) with survivors who descended the stairways in the twin towers prior to their collapse, unanimously indicate that these individuals behaved in a very orderly, altruistic fashion. They helped one another down the steps, they proceeded as according to previous evacuation plans. They were calm and followed directions.

Altruism. The Fire Department of New York (FDNY) lost many brave members when the towers collapsed. Automatically responding to the call, these firefighters ascended the stairwells in the towers—and died doing their job. Others kept coming. Fire departments from around the country sent personnel too numerous to even be used at "ground zero" (convergence behavior of an altruistic nature). Other FDNY members did not want to leave the impact area and resisted efforts to give them relief—they stayed on the job often to their own detriment.

Individual citizens throughout the United States donated financial resources to help the victims. Citizens from varied backgrounds converged to offer their help, e.g., medical personnel, counselors and therapists, average people seeking to help in any way they could. Altruism was extremely evident in the immediate post-impact period and the recovery period.

Disaster Shock and Psychological Dependency. Anecdotal evidence suggests that numerous cases illustrate that survivors assessed the information they were able to obtain as they obtained it and sought to take charge of their individual situations, not waiting for others to direct their behavior—except where it became necessary to do so. For example, one teaching assistant in a local elementary school received a cell phone call from her husband, who worked at the trade center, shortly after impact. He indicated that two planes had hit the Twin Towers and he had evacuated to a safe site "down the street." As she was talking to him the towers collapsed and their phone line went dead. She was not certain of her husband's fate (he survived), but refused to go home to wait for word about her husband preferring, as she said, to "stay on the job where she is needed—with the children."

Media. The major network news reporters based in NYC, e.g., NBC Today Show personnel and the NBC Evening News personnel, functioned very much as local media do generally during disaster events—suspending normal programming and focusing on providing information on local people and organizations for local citizens and organizations (live programming broadcasting from NYC were the local stations on this occasion as well as national). Accuracy was greater as long as the focus remained on live broadcasting of local responders and needs. Later broadcasting increasingly focused on reporting on behavioral issues as they, media personnel, anticipated they would be (disaster mythology), e.g., asking about panic, looting.

Martial Law. Even in this tragic event involving a WMD martial law was not declared. While the military offered to relieve the city of the burden of responding to the event, NYC officials declined the offer and continued to coordinate the organizational response. The original EOC no longer existed as it had been in one of the towers and the city had to established a new, emergent EOC. Despite all the challenges NYC faced, its response was heroic in proportions.

Local Decision Makers. Local decision makers, e.g., the mayor's office, sought to establish a command center (and, as noted above, they had to reestablish their EOC), designate a spokesperson to interact with the media, and update the community and nation at regular intervals. Perhaps benefiting from prior training sessions and drills, the mayor's office in particular mastered the ideal model of providing regular briefings to the press (feeding them) during which they delineated what they currently knew and what they currently did not know. It would appear that the mayor became a role model for future decision makers in his information gathering and disseminating.

Looting and Price Gouging. While some reports eventually appeared declaring the existence of some looting at ground zero and some price gouging by outsiders, the final data are not yet in to ascertain how accurate (versus rumor reporting which is typical of disaster events generally) these reports were. It can be concluded, however, that even if the few reported instances turn out to be true, the mayor's office has already reported that crime in general was dramatically down during the aftermath of the terrorist event. This is a pattern commonly found in the literature on behavioral response to natural and technological disasters as citizens become very altruistic in meeting the needs of others.

Estimates of Damage, Injury and Death. Happily the usual pattern of overestimating the death toll is in tack in the NYC twin tower collapse. We will have to await final tabulations for all three of these categories to know the extent of these aspects of the tragedy. But we do now know that the actual death toll appears to be less than half of the initial estimate which is consistent with research findings for natural and technological disasters generally.

Emergency Organizations

While the public often believes the behavioral response to disaster is deviant and chaotic, it tends to believe emergency organizations are prepared to respond fairly effectively (Fischer, 1998). The behavioral response, as previously noted, is actually very altruistic. Ironically, the organizational response is often quite chaotic. The effectiveness of the organizational response may depend upon the level of prior planning, the extent to which emergency plans are rehearsed, and the degree of prior disaster experience. For example, in 1988 a small mid-western city ordered an evacuation for about 800 people who lived near a burning warehouse which housed toxic substances. Evacuees were not found to panic, engage in looting, or exhibit any of the other behaviors which constitute the disaster mythology. However, when I called the local emergency manager's office I was told that they "think he is at the fire." They had been unable to reach him and were not sure where he was. I found him at the temporary command post about a half mile from the burning building. Then when I called the mayor's office, he said that he had been sitting there for "the last hour and a half answering the phone, I cannot call out and find out what is going on because every time I finish an incoming call another one comes before I can call out." It is typically difficult for those attempting to respond to a disaster to quickly communicate with one another and obtain accurate information. For this reason many emergency personnel resort to the media, just as the average citizen does. When asked how many were asked to evacuate, the mayor replied: "I really don't know, our best source of information has been the local radio which has people on the scene." If the media is the best source, then one hopes that the media is a very accurate source of information during the disaster.

Emergency organizations often strive to convey the image "that everything is under control." What occurs in most post-impact communities is closer to organized disorganization. Accurate information is difficult to obtain; decision-makers often have a hard time communicating with one another; the written disaster plan (if one exists) is often ignored during a real emergency; the pre-impact designated disaster coordinator may not emerge as the actual post-impact leader; individual organizations are likely to carry out their self-defined mission without coordination with the other emergency organizations; decisions are often made based upon disaster myths and inaccurate media information, and turf battles often result in less than complete cooperation between the various emergency organizations (Fischer, 1989). The aftermath of a disaster is usually nothing like that which the organizations had anticipated (Fischer, Schaeffer & Trowbridge, 1992). Its massive disruption of normal time activities requires much more organizational flexibility and inter-organizational cooperation than had been previously expected.

For example, in the aftermath of Three Mile Island (TMI), local leaders, the Governor's office, the Nuclear Regulatory Agency (NRA) and the (U.S.) President's office all sought to learn what had happened, why, and what to do about it. They were interested in managing the damaged reactor and protecting the affected population. Emergency managers and political leaders, as well as the populace, had a very difficult time trying to obtain accurate information about what had happened at the power plant, what to do about it, and how to best protect people in the area. The national media reported everything from a meltdown to a leak of a small radioactive cloud into the atmosphere. The implications of these two events vary greatly. A complete meltdown would be a catastrophe for at least hundreds of thousands of people, while a radioactive leak may possibly become a problem for a few hundred or few thousand people. "Nearly a quarter of the reporters had a single expert on tap . . . the rest of the reporters made *themselves* into experts--fast" (see Fischer, 1998a). "Many reporters had no scientific background. . . and had difficulty presenting this information to the public in a form that would be understandable" (Fischer, 1998a).

Political decision-makers

In the aftermath of 11 September 2001, U.S. PDMs exhibited the disorganized behavior commonly observed among lower level emergency responders—the result was going down a road that should be less traveled. No PDM wants to be accused of not taking their responsibility to defend and protect the population seriously. Every PDM should also seek to not over-react to such an extent that they unwittingly help the terrorists succeed. The terrorist seeks to instill fear and to cause disruption, the ultimate goal being to use the fear to make the target accede to his demands in return for withdrawing the threat. Then fear will cease. As noted earlier, U.S. PDMs did not fear fear itself, they embraced it and made decisions based upon it. The U.S. response to 11 September 2001 helped Al Qaeda achieve its first goal.

The decision to form the Northern Command and overturn *posse comitatus*, the enacting of the *Patriot Act*, the creation of the Department of Homeland Security and the devolution of the Federal Emergency Management Agency, massive spending of tax dollars for anything imagined to be related to enhancing security, the war on Iraq, the placing and treatment of detainees in Cuba, all serve to demonstrate the wisdom in those words uttered by FDR, "we have nothing to fear, but fear itself." Indeed, PDM fear drove policy decisions. PMDs scrambled to respond to an unimagined event. PMDs generated chaos. What we observe is once again the reverse of popular perception. The disaster mythology suggests victims and survivors are chaotic, even deviant; but organizations are not, they are seen as being organized.

The U.S. federal government, in this disastrous event, exhibited the chaos, disorganization, and maybe more. The attack on 11 September 2001 provided the unfortunate opportunity to observe the organizational damage that can occur when mitigation, planning, and response are not based upon a body of knowledge. Whether it is swaggering or just walking, we really do need to fear, fear itself. The alternative is really not very functional.

Final Question

What remains is the question as to whether or not the second goal of the terrorist is now more attainable. If the U.S. PDMs unwittingly helped Al Qaeda achieve its first goal, does that guarantee the second? Let's consider the war on Iraq in an attempt to seek insight into a possible answer. It is now generally agreed that terrorists did not have a hold on any part of Iraq before the U.S. invasion. It is also now generally agreed that Iraq contains quite a few terrorists and terrorist organizations. That would suggest a step back rather than forward. The resulting insurgence is believed to be a challenge that the U.S. military may not be large enough to combat, given the troop strength devoted to it. With parallels being increasingly drawn between the war in Iraq and the Vietnam War, how long will it be until the outcome is the same? Will one last helicopter hover above one of Saddam's former palaces to pick up one last group of evacuees from Baghdad before the fall of Iraq into undemocratic hands? Did Al Qaeda leaders read history while U.S. PDMs did not? Do they understand the U.S. better than the U.S. understands terrorism and its roots? Do I really need to provide you with the answers to these questions?

Author's Final Note

Disaster research is an exciting field. It challenges the researcher to employ field research techniques as well as quantitative methods. It also provides the researcher with the opportunity to make a contribution to the literature which may result in influencing both practitioners and public policy makers. A more rewarding field is difficult to find. Thank you for caring enough to read this book and for putting up with my writing style.

Bibliography

Aga Khan, P.S. 1983. "Disasters: Myth and Reality." *Undro News.* November/December.

Anderson, P.S. 1995. "The Biggest Mutual Aid System on Earth: The Internet in Emergency Management." *NCCEM Bulletin*, pp. 7-9.

Anderson, William A. 1969. *Local Civil Defense in Natural Disaster: From Office to Organization.* Columbus. Ohio: Disaster Research Center, The Ohio State University.

Babbie, Earl. 1997. *The Practice of Social Research.* Belmont, CA: Wadsworth Publishing Company. Eighth Edition.

Bartlett, G.S., P.S. Houts, L.K. Byrnes, and R.W. Miller. 1983. "The Near Disaster of Three Mile Island," *International Journal of Mass Emergencies and Disasters*, Vol. 1, March, pp. 19-42.

Barton, Allen H. 1969. *Communities in Disaster: A Sociological Analysis of Collective Stress Situations.* Garden City, New York: Doubleday and Company, Inc.

Baumann, Duane D., and John H. Sims. 1978. "Flood Insurance: Some Determinants of Adoption." *Economic Geography* 54 (July):189-196.

Beres, L.S. 1997. "Preventing the Ultimate Nightmare: Nuclear Terrorism Against the United States." *International Journal Of Intelligence and Counter-Intelligence.* 10-3:333-342.

Betts, R.K. 1998. "The New Threat of Mass Destruction." *Foreign Affairs.* 77-1:26-41.

Birkerts, S. 1994. *Gutenberg Elegies: The Fate of Reading in an Electronic Age.* Boston: Faber and Faber.

Botterell. A. 1996. "The Emergency Information Infrastructure." http://www.incident.com/papers/eii.htm.

Britton, Neil, G.E. Kearney, and K.A. Britton 1983. "Disaster Response: The Perception of the Threat and Its Influence On Community Decision on Insurance. Pp. 260-332 in *Insurance and Natural Disaster Management.* Paper presented at a seminar, Townsville, July 1983, John Oliver (ed.). Townsville, Queensland, Australia: Centre For Disaster Studies, James

Cook University of North Queensland.

Bryan, J.L. 1982. "Human Behavior in the MGM Grand Hotel Fire." *Fire Journal* 76, (1982): March 2.

Burstein, D. and D. Kline. 1995. *Road Warriors, Dreams and Nightmares Along the Information Highway*. New York: Dutton.

Butler, David. 1994. "The Information Revolution and Disaster Management." *The CUSEC Journal*, Volume 2, pp. 4-10.

Butler, David. 1995. "Information Systems and Knowledge Transfer. Prospects for Better Understanding, Opportunities for Increased Hazard Mitigation." Unpublished paper, Boulder, Colorado: Natural Hazards Research and Application Information Center, The University of Colorado.

Chandessais, Charles A. 1966. *La Catastrophe de Feyzin* (The Feyzin Catastrophe). Paris: Centre d'Etudes Psychosociologiques des Sinistres et le Leur Prevention.

Christopher, G.W. and T.J. Cieslak, J.A. Pavlin, E.M. Eitzen. 1997. "Biological Warfare: A Historical Perspective." *Journal of the American Medical Association*. 278-5:412-417.

Davis, S. and J. Botkin. 1994. *The Monster Under the Bed: How Business is Mastering the Opportunity of Knowledge for Profit*. New York: Simon and Schuster.

Demerath, Nicholas J. 1957. "Some General Propositions: An Interpretive Summary." *Human Organization* 16 (Summer) 28-29.

Drabek, Thomas E. 1968. *Disaster in Aisle 13*. College of Administrative Science. Columbus, Ohio: The Ohio State University.

Drabek, Thomas E. 1969. "Social Processes in Disaster: Family Evacuation." *Social Problems* 16 (Winter):336-349.

Drabek, Thomas E. 1986. *Human System Responses to Disaster: An Inventory of Sociological Findings*. New York: Springer-Verlag.

Drabek, Thomas E. 1996. *Sociology of Disaster*. Course Instructor Guide. Emmitsburg, Maryland: Federal Emergency Management Agency.

Drabek Thomas E., and Keith Boggs 1968. "Families in Disaster: Reactions and Relatives." *Journal of Marriage and the Family*. 30 (August):443-451.

Drabek, Thomas E., and E. L. Quarantelli 1967. "Scapegoats, Villains, and Disasters." *Transaction* 4 (March):12-17.

Drucker, P. 1993. *Post-Capitalist Society*. New York: HarperCollins.

Durham, Tom and Eileen Baumgardner. 1993. *Emergency Response and Recovery*. Monograph #4. 1993 National Earthquake Conference. Central United States Earthquake Consortium.

Dynes, Russell R. 1970. *Organized Behavior in Disaster*. Lexington, MA: Heath Lexington Books.

Dynes, Russell R., and E.L. Quarantelli. 1975. *The Role of Local Civil Defense in*

Disaster Planning. Columbus, Ohio: Disaster Research Center, The Ohio State University.

Dynes, Russell R., and E.L. Quarantelli. 1976. "The Family and Community Context of Individual Reactions to Disaster," in Parad. H., Resnick. H.L.P. and Parad, L. (Eds.), *Emergency and Disaster Management: A Mental Health Sourcebook,* The Charles Press, Bowie, MD.

Dynes, Russell R., E.L. Quarantelli, and Gary A. Kreps. 1972. *A Perspective on Disaster Planning.* Columbus, Ohio: Disaster Research Center, The Ohio State University.

Eisenberg, Debra. 2003. *Do Laypeople and Emergency Management Officials Subscribe to Disaster Mythology?* Master's Thesis. Department of Psychology, Illinois State University.

Encarta. 1995 & 1997. Seattle, Washington: MicroSoft.

Fischer, Henry W., III. 1988a. *Behavioral and Organizational Response to Disaster.* Alliance, Ohio: Social Research Center, Mount Union College.

Fischer, Henry W., III. 1988b. *Disastrous Fantasizing in the Print Media: Differences in How Natural versus Technological Disasters Are Portrayed over a Forty-year Period.* Alliance, Ohio: Social Research Center, Mount Union College.

Fischer, Henry W., III. 1989. *Hurricane Gilbert: The Media's Creation of the Storm of the Century During September 1988.* Boulder, Colorado: The Natural Research and Applications Center, The University of Colorado.

Fischer, Henry W., III. 1990. *Behavioral and Organizational Response to Disaster.* Millersville, Pennsylvania: Social Research Group, Millersville University of Pennsylvania.

Fischer, Henry W., III. 1994. *Response to Disaster: Fact Versus Fiction & Its Perpetuation.* Lanham, Maryland: University Press of America.

Fischer, Henry W., III. 1996. "What Emergency Management Officials Should Know To Enhance Mitigation and Effective Disaster Response." *Journal of Contingencies and Crisis Management.* 4-4:208-217.

Fischer, Henry W., III. 1997. *Sociology of Disaster on the Internet.* http://www.millersv.edu/~srg.

Fischer, Henry W., III. 1998a. *Behavioral Response to Chemical And Biological Terrorism: Sociological Observations Extrapolated From the Disaster Research Literature.* Final Report. Church Falls, Virginia: Research Planning, Inc.

Fischer, Henry W., III. 1998b. "The Role of the New Information Technologies in Emergency Mitigation, Planning, Response And Recovery." *The International Journal of Disaster Prevention and Management.* 7-1:28-37.

Fischer, Henry W., III. 2000. "Mitigation & Response Planning in a Bio-Terrorist Attack." *International Journal of Disaster Prevention & Management.* 9-

5. December.

Fischer, Henry W., III. 2002. "Terrorism and 11 September 2001: Does the Behavioral Response to Disaster Model Fit?" *International Journal of Disaster Prevention &Management*. 11-2:123-127. June.*Award Winning Paper: "Outstanding Paper of 2002," Emerald Literati Awards, London, 24 April 2003.

Fischer, Henry W., III. 2003. "The Sociology of Disaster: Definitions, Research Questions, & Measurements. Continuation of the Discussion in a Post-September 11 Environment." *International Journal of Mass Emergencies and Disasters*. 21-1:91-107. March.

Fischer, Henry W., III. 2004. "Behavioral and Organizational Responses to Terrorism: Research-Based Model and Evidence from September 11, 2001." *Journal of Emergency Management*. Winter 2004.

Fischer, Henry W., III. 2007. "Researcher as Disaster Historian & Practitioner as Disaster Janitor?" Editorial in *UnScheduled Events*. Vol. 26 – No. 1, January.

Fischer, Henry W., III, and Beth E. Bischoff. 1988. *Technological Disasters: As Portrayed by the National Print Media, 1945-1985*. Paper presented at the annual meetings of the North Central Sociological Association. Pittsburgh, Pennsylvania.

Fischer, Henry W., III, and Eric M. Drain. 1993. "Local Offices of Emergency Preparedness (LEMA) Belief in Disaster Mythology: What Has Changed and Why?" *The International Journal of Disaster Prevention and Management*. 2-3:58-69.

Fischer, Henry W., III, and Kathleen McCullough. 1993. "The Role of Education in Disaster Mitigation Adjustment." *The International Journal of Disaster Management*. 5-3:123-129.

Fischer, Henry W., III, and Marna L. Trowbridge. 1992. "The Limited Role of Disaster Experience in Mitigation Adjustment." *The International Journal of Disaster Management*. 4-2:131-137.

Fischer, Henry W., III, Susan Schaeffer, and Marna L. Trowbridge. 1992. *The Impact of Media Blame Assignation on the EOC Response to Disaster: A Case Study of the Response to the April 26, 1991 Andover (Kansas) Tornado*. A Quick Response Grant Final Report. Boulder, Colorado: The Natural Hazards Research & Applications Information Center, The University of Colorado.

Fischer, Henry W., III, George F. Stine, Marna L. Trowbridge, and Eric M. Drain. 1991. *Outline of Preliminary Findings of the Evacuation Behavior in Response to the May 1990 Ephrata, Pennsylvania Fire*. Millersville, Pennsylvania: Social Research Group, Millersville University of Pennsylvania.

Fischer, Henry W., III, George F. Stine, Brenda L. Stoker, Marna L. Trowbridge, and Eric M. Drain. 1995. "Evacuation Behavior: Why Do Some Evacuate, While Others Do Not? A Case Study of the Ephrata, Pennsylvania Evacuation," *International Journal of Disaster Prevention and Management*, Vol. 4, No. 4, pp. 30-36.

Fischer, Henry W., III, Kathryn Gregoire, John Scala, Lynn Letukas, Joseph Mellon, Scott Romine, & Danielle Turner. 2006. "The Emergency Management Response to Hurricane Katrina: As Told by the First Responders—A Case Study of What Went Wrong and Recommendations for the Future." A Quick Response Report, #189. Natural Hazards Center, the University of Colorado-Boulder.

Foster, Harold D. 1980. *Disaster Planning: The Preservation of Life and Property*. New York: Springer-Verlag.

Frantz, D.R. and P.B. Jahrling, A.M. Friedlander, D.J. McClain, D.L. Hoover, W.R. Bryne, J.A. Pavlin, G.W. Christopher, E.M. Eitzen. 1997. "Cinical Recognition and Management of Patients Exposed to Biological Warfare Agents." *Journal of the American Medical Association*. 278-5:399-411.

Fritz, Charles E. 1957. "Disasters Compared in Six American Communities." *Human Organization* 16 (Summer):6-9.

Fritz, Charles E. 1961. "Disasters." Pp. 651-694 in *Contemporary Social Problems*, Robert K. Merton and Robert A. Nisbet (eds.). New York: Harcourt.

Fritz Charles E., and Eli S. Marks. 1954. "The NORC Studies of Human Behavior in Disaster." *The Journal of Social Issues*. 10 (No.3):26-41.

Fritz Charles E., and J.H. Mathewson. 1957. *Convergence Behavior in Disaster*. National Research Council Disaster Study 9. Washington, D.C.: National Academy of Sciences.

Gant, D.B. 1996. *The Potential Impact of Information Technology On the Structure of Interorganizational Relationships During Crisis Response: The Pennsylvania Floods of 1996*. Boulder, Colorado: Institute of Behavioral Science.

Gates, Bill. 1995. *The Road Ahead*. New York: Viking.

Gillespie, David and Dennis Mileti. 1993. *Preparedness, Awareness, and Public Education*. Monograph #3. 1993 National Earthquake Conference. Central United States Earthquake Consortium.

Goldberg, Ron. 1996. *MultiMedia Producer's Bible*. Chicago: International Data Group Company.

Goltz, James D. 1984. "Are the News Media Responsible for the Disaster Myths? A Content Analysis of Emergency Response Imagery." *International Journal of Mass Emergencies and Disasters*. 2 (November):345-3.

Gray, Jane. 1981. "Characteristic Patterns of and Variations in Community Response to Acute Chemical Emergencies." *Journal of Hazardous*

Materials.4:357-365.

Haas, J. Eugene, Harold C. Cochrane, and Donald G. Eddy. 1976. *The Consequences of Large-Scale Evacuation Following Disaster: The Darwin Australia Cyclone Disaster of December 25, 1974*. Natural Hazards Research Working Paper No. 27. Boulder, Colorado: Institute of Behavioral Science, The University of Colorado.

Hodler, Thomas W. 1982. "Residents' Preparedness and Response to the Kalamazoo Tornado." *Disasters* 6 (No.1):44-49.

Holloway, H.C., and A.E. Norwood, C.S. Fullerton, C.C. Engel, R.J. Ursano. 1997. "The Threat of Biological Weapons: Prophylaxis and Mitigation of Psychological and Social Consequences." *Journal of the American Medical Association*. 278-5:425-427.

Hultaker, Orjan E., and Jan E. Trost. 1978. *The Family and the Shelters*. Disaster Studies No. 1. Uppsala, Sweden: Uppsala University. Interactive Multimedia Association. 1996, http://www.ima.org.

Janis, Irving L., and Leon Mann. 1977. "Emergency Decision Making: A Theoretical Analysis of Responses to Disaster Warnings." Journal of Human Stress. 3 (June):35-48.

Johnson, Norris. 1987. "Panic and the Breakdown of Social Order: Popular Myth, Social Theory, Empirical Evidence." *Sociological Focus*. 20:(August) 3.

Jones, S.G. (Ed.). 1995. *Cybersociety: Computer-Mediated Communication and Community*. Thousand Islands, California: Sage.

Kidder, G. and S. Harris. 1997. *HTML Publishing for Netscape*. 2nd Edition. Research Triangle Park, North Carolina: Ventana Communications Group.

Killian, Lewis M. 1954. "Some Accomplishments and Some Needs in Disaster Study." *The Journal of Social Issues*. 10 (No. 3):66-72.

Kreps, Gary A. 1978. "The Organization of Disaster Response: Some Fundamental Theoretical Issues." Pp. 65-85 in *Disasters: Theory and Research*, E. L. Quarantelli (ed.). Beverly Hills, California: Sage.

McComb, David. 1980. *Big Thompson: Profile of A Natural Disaster*. Boulder, Colorado: Pruett Publishing Company.

McLoughlin, David. 1985. "A Framework for Integrated Emergency Management." *Public Administration Review*. 45 (January):165-172.

McLuckie, B.F. 1977. "Italy, Japan, and the United States: Effects Of Centralization on Disaster Responses 1964-1969," *The Disaster Research Center Historical and Comparative Disasters Series, No. 1*, The Disaster Research Center, The University of Delaware, Newark, DE.

Mileti, Dennis S. 1975. *Natural Hazard Warning Systems in the United States: A Research Assessment*. Boulder, Colorado: Institute of Behavioral Science, The University of Colorado.

Mileti, Dennis S., Thomas E. Drabek, and J. Eugene Haas. 1975. *Human Systems in Extreme Environments*. Boulder, Colorado: Institute of Behavioral Science, The University of Colorado.

Moore, Harry Estill, Frederick L. Bates, Marvin V. Layman, and Vernon J. Parenton. 1963. *Before the Wind: A Study of Response to Hurricane Carla*. National Academy of Sciences/National Research Council Disaster Study #19. Washington, D.C.: National Academy of Sciences. Multimedia Development Group. 1996. http://www.mdg.org.

Myers, Mary Fran. 1993. "Bridging the Gap between Research and Practice: The Natural Hazards Research and Applications Information Center." *International Journal of Mass Emergencies and Disasters*. 11:1 (March):41-54.

Neal, David. 1993. "Integrating Disaster Research and Practice: An Overview of Issues." *International Journal of Mass Emergencies and Disasters*. 11:1 (March):5-14.

Nigg, Joanne M. 1982. "Communication Under Conditions of Uncertainty: Understanding Earthquake Forecasting." *Journal of Communication*. 32:27-36.

Nigg, Joane M. 1987. "Factors Affecting Earthquake Threat Awareness and Response." Paper presented at the Pacific Conference on Earthquake Engineering, New Zealand, August 5-8.

Nigg, Joanne M.; Alvin H. Mushkatel and Richard C. Moore. 1992. "Evaluation of the Dissemination and Utilization of the NEHRP Recommended Provisions." Washington, D.C.: Federal Emergency Management Agency.

Nimmo, Dan. 1984. "TV Network News Coverage of Three Mile Island: Reporting Disasters as Technological Fables." *International Journal of Mass Emergencies and Disasters*. 2 (March):115-145.

Oliver, John. 1975. "The Significance of Natural Hazards in a Developing Area: A Case Study from North Queensland." *Geography*. 60:99-110.

Olshansky, R.B. 1992. *Seismic Hazard Mitigation in the Central United States: The Role of the States*. Final Report submitted to the U.S. Geological Survey, Branch of Geologic Risk Assessment.

Perry, Ronald W. 1982. *The Social Psychology of Civil Defense*. Lexington, Mass.: Lexington Books.

Perry, Ronald W. 1985. *Comprehensive Emergency Management: Evacuating Threatened Populations*. Greenwich, Connecticut, and London: JAI Press, Inc.

Perry Ronald, W. 1990. "Evacuation Warning Compliance Among Elderly Citizens," *International Journal of Disaster Management*, Vol. 3, No. 2, pp. 94-96.

Perry, Ronald W., and Marjorie R. Greene. 1983. *Citizen Response to Volcanic Eruptions: The Case of Mount St. Helens*. New York: Irvington

Publishers.

Perry, Ronald W., Michael K. Lindell, and Marjorie R. Greene. 1981. *Evacuation Planning in Emergency Management.* Lexington, Massachusetts, and Toronto: Lexington Books.

Perry, Ronald W., Michael K. Lindell, and Marjorie R. Greene. 1982a. "Crisis Communications: Ethnic Differentials in Interpreting and Acting on Disaster Warnings." *Social Behavior and Personality* 10 (No. 1):97-104.

Perry, Ronald W., Michael K. Lindell, and Marjorie R. Greene. 1982b. "Threat Perception and Public Response to Volcano Hazard." *Journal of Social Psychology* 116:199-204.

Perry, Ronald W. and E.L. Quarantelli (eds.). 2005. *What is a Disaster? New Answers to Old Questions.* Xlibris.

Phillips, Brenda D. 1993. "Cultural Diversity in Disasters: Sheltering, Housing, and Long Term Recovery." *International Journal of Mass Behavior and Disasters.* 11:1 (March):99-110.

Presidential Decision Directive 39 (PDD-39). 1995. *United States Policy on Counterterrorism.* Washington, D.C.: The White House.

President's Commission on the Accident at Three Mile Island. 1979. *Report of the President's Commission on the Accident at Three Mile Island (The Need For Change: The Legacy of TMI).* Washington, D.C.: U.S. Government Printing Office.

Prince, Samuel Henry. 1920. *Catastrophe and Social Change, Based Upon a Sociological Study of the Halifax Disaster.* Ph.D. Thesis. New York: Columbia University Department Of Political Science.

Quarantelli, E.L. 2007. "The Myth and the Realities: Keeping the 'Looting' Myth in Perspective." *Natural Hazards Observer.* Boulder: University of Colorado. March.

Quarantelli, E.L. 1997. "Problematical Aspects of the Informaton/ Communication Revolution for Disaster Planning and Research: Ten Non-Technical Issues and Questions." *Disaster Prevention and Management Journal*, Vol. 6, No. 2, pp. 94-106.

Quarantelli, E.L. 1987. *Researching and Managing Human Behavior in Disasters.* Newark, Delaware: Disaster Research Center, The University of Delaware.

Quarantelli, E.L. 1984. *Organizational Behavior in Disasters and Implications for Disaster Planning.* Emmitsburg, Maryland: National Emergency Training Center, Federal Emergency Management Agency.

Quarantelli, E.L. 1981. "Panic Behavior in Fire Situations: Findings and a Model from the English Language Research Literature." Pp. 405-428 in *Proceedings of the 4th Joint Panel Meeting, The U.J.N.R. Panel on Fire Research and Safety.* Tokyo: Building Research Institute.

Quarantelli, E.L. 1980. *Evacuation Behavior and Problems: Findings and*

Implications from the Research Literature. Columbus, Ohio: Disaster Research Center, The Ohio State University.

Quarantelli, E.L. 1976. "Human Response in Stress Situations." Pp. 99-112 in *Proceedings of the First Conference and Workshop on Fire Casualties,* B.M. Halpin (ed.). Laurel, Maryland: Applied Physics Laboratory, Johns Hopkins University.

Quarantelli E.L., and Russell R. Dynes. 1972. "When Disaster Strikes (It Isn't Much Like What You're Heard and Read About)." *Psychology Today* 5 (No.9):66-70.

Quarantelli, E.L., and Russell R. Dynes. 1972. *Images of Disaster Behavior: Myths and Consequences.* Newark, Delaware: Disaster Research Center, The University of Delaware.

Quarantelli, E.L. and Kathleen Tierney. 1979. "Disaster Preparation Planning." Pp. 263-313 in *Fire Safety and Disaster Preparedness.* Washington, D.C.: Office of Public Sector Programs, American Association for the Advancement of Science.

Rubin, Claire B., and R. Palm. 1987. "National Origin and Earthquake Response: Lessons from the Whittier Narrow Earthquake." *International Journal of Mass Emergencies And Disasters.* 53:347-356.

Sandman, Peter M., and Mary Paden. 1979. "At Three Mile Island." *Columbia Journalism Review.* (July/August):43-58.

Scanlon, T. Joseph. 1977. "Post-Disaster Rumor Chains: A Case Study." *Mass Emergencies.* 2:121-126.

Scanlon, T. Joseph with Kim Dixon and Scott McClellan. 1982. *The Miramichi Earthquakes: The Media Respond to an Invisible Emergency.* Ottawa, Ontario, Canada: Emergency Communications Research Unit, School of Journalism, Carleton University.

Scanlon, T. Joseph with Rudy Luukko and Gerald Morton. 1978. "Media Coverage of Crisis: Better Than Reported, Worse Than Necessary." *Journalism Quarterly.* 55 (Spring):68-72.

Simon, J.D. 1997. "Biological Terrorism: Preparing to Meet the Threat." *Journal of the American Medical Association.* 278-5:428-430.

Singer, Timothy J. 1982. "An Introduction to Disaster : Some Considerations of a Psychological Nature." *Aviation, Space, and Environmental Medicine.* 53 (March):245-250.

Stallings, Robert A. 1984. "Evacuation Behavior at Three Mile Island." *International Journal of Mass Emergencies and Disasters.* 2 (March):11-26.

Statistical Abstract of the United States. 1997. Washington, D.C.: U.S. Department of Commerce.

Steinbruner. J.D. 1997. "Biological Weapons: A Plague Upon All Houses."

Foreign Policy. Winter, pp. 85-96.

Tucker, D. 1998. "Responding to Terrorism." *The Washington Quarterly.* Winter, pp. 103-117.

Wenger, Dennis. E. 1985. *Mass Behavior and Disaster.* Newark, Delaware: Disaster Research Center, The University of Delaware.

Wenger, Dennis E. 1980. "A Few Empirical Observations Concerning the Relationship Between the Mass Media and Disaster Knowledge: A Research Report." Pp. 241-253 in *Disasters and the Mass Media: Proceedings of the Committee on Disasters and the Mass Media Workshop.* Committee on Disasters and the Mass Media. Washington, D.C.: National Academy of Sciences.

Wenger, Dennis E. 1978. "Community Response to Disaster: Functional and Structural Alterations." Pp. 17-47 in *Disasters: Theory and Research*, E.L. Quarantelli (ed.). Beverly Hills, California: Sage.

Wenger, Dennis E., James D. Dykes, Thomas D. Sebok, and Joan L. Neff. 1975. "It's a Matter of Myths: An Empirical Examination of Individual Insight into Disaster Response." Mass Emergencies. 1:33-46.

Wenger, Dennis E., and Barbara Friedman. 1986. *Local and National Media Coverage of Disasters: A Content Analysis Of the Print Media's Treatment of Disaster Myths.* Newark, Delaware: Disaster Research Center, The University of Delaware.

Wenger, Dennis E., Thomas F. James, and Charles F. Faupel. 1980. D*isaster Beliefs and Emergency Planning.* Newark, Delaware: Disaster Research Project, University of Delaware.

White, Gilbert F., and Eugene Haas. 1975. *Assessment of Research on Natural Hazards.* Cambridge, Massachusetts, and London: The MIT Press.

Williams, Harry B. 1956. *Communications in Community Disasters.* Ph.D. Dissertation. Chapel Hill, North Carolina: University of North Carolina.

Wolensky, Robert P., and Edward J. Miller. 1981. "The Everyday Versus the Disaster Role of Local Officials--Citizen and Official Definitions." *Urban Affairs Quarterly* 16 (No.4) 483-504.

World Almanac and Book of Facts. 1998. New York: Pharos Books.

Zilinskas, R.A. 1997. "Iraq's Biological Weapons: The Past as Future?" *Journal of the American Medical Association.* 278-5:418-427

ABOUT THE AUTHOR

HENRY W. FISCHER III holds a Ph.D. in sociology which he completed at the University of Delaware in 1986. He has more than twenty years experience in conducting research into behavioral and organizational response to disasters and terrorism. His body of work includes the following: dozens of scholarly presentations at professional conferences; the publication of more than two dozen scholarly journal articles, four books, two monographs; consulting for Research Planning, Inc./Department of Defense, the Office of Emergency Management/Justice Department on TOPOFF2; completion of deliverables for the FEMA Higher Education Project, the First Responders for the Early Responders Distance Learning Center; numerous funded research projects (funding sources include the National Science Foundation, FEMA, PEMA, Natural Hazards Center/University of Colorado-Boulder); appearances on CNN and MS-NBC to discuss high consequence events issues.

Professional memberships are held in the International Sociological Association, the International Research Committee on Disasters (serving since 1998 as editor of *UnScheduled Events*, the organization's official newsletter, editor of the organization's new online journal of reviews *Contemporary Disaster Review* since 2002, and web host for the *International Journal of Mass Emergencies and Disasters* since 2004), the European Sociological Association, the American Sociological Association (served as Pennsylvania Membership Representative 1989-1993) and the International Association of Emergency Managers.

Primary expertise is in the behavioral and organizational response to high consequence events (disasters and terrorism), the role of the media in high consequence events, as well as developing educational curricula for delivery in traditional teaching environments and distance learning/internet based environments. He teaches the Sociology of Disaster, Sociology of Terrorism, and Social Dimensions of Disaster. He has worked with the FEMA Higher Education Project since 1995 and was the leading developer of the multi-disciplinary undergraduate minor in Environmental Hazards & Emergency Management (EHEM), as well as the totally online, multi-disciplinary master's degree program in Emergency Management (MSEM). He currently serves as the program chair for both. He is the founding Director of the Center for Disaster Research & Education (CDRE). In addition to the director, the CDRE includes 15 additional faculty associates from multiple disciplines from three schools across the university. It also employs a secretary and several research assistants. The CDRE is involved in consulting, contract and grant work.